PARTIES, POLITICS, AND
PUBLIC POLICY IN AMERICA

PARTIES, POLITICS, AND PUBLIC POLICY IN AMERICA

NINTH EDITION

WILLIAM J. KEEFE
University of Pittsburgh

MARC J. HETHERINGTON
Bowdoin College

CQ PRESS

A DIVISION OF CONGRESSIONAL QUARTERLY INC.
WASHINGTON, D.C.

CQ Press
1255 22nd Street, N.W., Suite 400
Washington, D.C. 20037

202-729-1900; toll free, 1-866-4CQ-PRESS (1-866-427-7737)

www.cqpress.com

♾ The paper used in this publication exceeds the minimum
requirements of the American National Standard for Information
Sciences—Permanence of Paper for Printed Library Materials, ANSI
Z39.48-1992.

Typeset by Auburn Associates Inc.

Cover design by Sims Design Co. LLC

Printed and bound in the United States of America

07 06 05 04 03 5 4 3 2 1

LIBRARY OF CONGRESS CATALOGING-IN-PUBLICATION DATA

Keefe, William J.
    Parties, politics, and public policy in America / William J. Keefe,
Marc J. Hetherington.—9th ed.
        p. cm.
    Includes bibliographical references (p.   ) and index.
    ISBN 1-56802-675-7 (paperback)
    1 Political parties—United States.   I. Hetherington, Marc J., 1968–
II. Title.
   JK2265.K44 2003
   324.273—dc21

                                                        2003004731

For Martha, Kathy, Nancy, Jodi, and John
W.J.K.

For Mom and Dad, strong partisans
M.J.H.

CONTENTS

TABLES AND FIGURES

TABLES

FIGURES

PREFACE

The American political party system is in flux. For decades, parties were eclipsed by individual candidates, interest groups, and the mass media to a degree that at times they appeared as mere bystanders to the struggles over power and policy. Recently, however, the parties have strengthened their position, challenged their competition, and produced a resurgence that most scholars and pundits did not forecast. What is more, the latest scholarship shows that party revival has occurred despite the fact that Americans still live in a candidate-centered age heavily influenced by such factors as television, personality, celebrity, mass merchandising, image making, interest groups, and the like. The conventional thesis that American parties are suffering from decay and decline is much less compelling today than it was a decade or two ago. In a word, there is new life in the parties.

In tracking the recent resurgence of parties in this ninth edition of *Parties, Politics, and Public Policy in America,* we raise and answer some important questions. In a two-party system that has traditionally rewarded moderation, why have the parties become more ideologically distinct? In a political culture that continues to hold parties in low esteem, why do ordinary Americans follow party cues more closely today than they have in generations? We keep these questions firmly in mind in our consideration of the American party system, from its core characteristics to its functions and roles in elections, nominations, campaign finance, partisanship, and the formation of public policy. This reassessment of the status of parties in the United States allows us to bring into focus the important changes that have occurred recently in the party system.

Party revitalization appears on many levels. For instance, changes in the campaign finance laws opened the soft money loophole wider than ever before, allowing parties to raise and spend hundreds of millions of dollars that were previously unavailable to them. Although such monies were recently banned by the McCain-Feingold campaign finance reform act, the proliferation of soft money in the 1990s made political parties important players again. Moreover, our treatment of the evolution of campaign finance suggests that parties will continue to play an important, if somewhat diminished, role despite the soft money ban. Even before 2002, parties had substantially increased their hard money receipts. In addition, McCain-Feingold increased the hard dollar limits for parties and, more important, indexed them for inflation.

On the governmental level, interparty conflict in Congress is more intense now than it has been in generations. Major policy differences separate the parties. Voters should have no trouble realizing that Republicans in Congress are more conservative than Democrats and that Democrats are more liberal than Republicans. Whereas seventy or more members of the House in the 1970s typically voted as if they belonged in the other party, as Keith Poole and Howard Rosenthal show, only one Democrat had a voting record that was more conservative than that of the most liberal Republican in the House at the beginning of the twenty-first century. There is now almost no ideological overlap between the parties, and mavericks have declined in number and, on the whole, in influence. The ideological polarization between the congressional parties has had important consequences, such as the election of strongly ideological leaders like the very conservative Tom Delay as House majority leader and the very liberal Nancy Pelosi as House minority leader. In decades past, when the parties in Congress were more moderate, party caucuses generally chose leaders from the political center. What more partisan Congresses will do in the future is, of course, not easy to predict. But it is reasonable to suppose that more ideological leadership, when combined with workable majorities in both houses, seems likely to lead to fundamental shifts in public policy.

With such partisan and ideological figures now leading the political debate in Washington, D.C., parties on the electoral level have become stronger in certain respects. Although it is true that many voters still see themselves as independent, a growing number do not act that way. We present new data showing that ordinary Americans have come to view politics in much more partisan and ideological terms than they once did. For example, Americans now vote straight party tickets more often, perceive more important differences between the parties, provide more reasons for liking and disliking the parties, and, finally, evaluate leaders in more partisan terms. This trend exists despite the fact that the majority of voters continue to say that they dislike and distrust parties and, moreover, favor divided over unified party government. Ironically, we show that citizens are quietly becoming what they say they dislike: partisan and ideological. We link these changes to the more partisan information environment produced by the ideological polarization between the parties in Congress.

A major explanation for this party resurgence is actually somewhat counterintuitive. We demonstrate that the recent ultracompetitive national elections and the ideological polarization between the parties in Congress result from the emergence of evenly matched regional power bases within which only moderate two-party competition occurs. Within these areas, Democrats can be very liberal and Republicans very conservative without risking defeat in the next election. The electoral map from the 2000 presidential election demonstrates the nature of the party split. George W. Bush won only three states in the more liberal Northeast, upper Midwest, and Pacific Coast, while Al Gore managed only one victory in the more conservative South, Great Plains, and Mountain West. In the 2002 elections, moreover, almost all the races that provided the Republicans with their Senate majority were predictable when viewed through this lens. Several of the critical Republican wins occurred in states like Georgia, North Carolina, Texas, Missouri, Colorado, Tennessee, and South Carolina—all of which were carried by Bush two years before, most often by very comfortable margins.

The declining number of liberal northeastern Republicans and conservative southern Democrats has eroded the center in American party politics, opening the door not only for heightened partisanship in Congress but also for the leadership of ideologues of both parties.

We also capture other important recent changes to the party system. For instance, we show that the coalitions of groups that comprise the parties have recently changed in important respects. The widening differences between men and women can hardly be exaggerated. As recently as thirty years ago, the "gender gap" between the parties was nonexistent. In the 1996 and 2000 presidential elections, however, women voted more than ten percentage points more Democratic than men did. In addition, knowing the extent of voters' religious observance now provides at least as many clues about their partisanship as about their religious affiliation. People who regularly attend church increasingly find a home in the Republican party, whereas nonregular churchgoers are disproportionately Democratic. Furthermore, racial and other minorities continue to provide much more support to Democrats than to Republicans. Since Hispanics are the fastest growing group by far in the United States, this trend will have significant future implications, especially as Hispanic voters diffuse into a larger number of states.

Although we have made significant revisions to this book, we have retained its core elements. We offer a complete treatment of what parties are in the American context, how they compete both nationally and regionally, how the nomination and campaign finance systems work, and what role partisanship plays on both the mass and the elite levels. And, as always, the treatment of these areas is designed to provide insights on the kinds of public policies that the party condition provides. In addition, we have augmented the traditional elements of the book with enhanced tables and figures, and we have updated all coverage through the 2002 election cycle whenever possible.

Acknowledgments

William J. Keefe would like to acknowledge all those good friends (colleagues, students, and family) he had thanked in the previous eight editions. They will continue to recognize their contributions. He would also like to point out that there is a lot of valuable new material in this ninth edition, due mainly to the creativity and insights of his new coauthor, Marc J. Hetherington, whom he had met when Marc was an undergraduate political science major at the University of Pittsburgh some years ago. Marc's contributions were particularly important in analyzing the new developments in the party and electoral systems and in bringing to bear the latest research that illuminates the party condition.

Marc J. Hetherington would like to thank his coauthor for letting him horn in on his book. It was a great thrill for him to complete a project with the person who had set him off on the most rewarding of career paths; working with his undergraduate mentor has been awfully gratifying. Larry Bartels and his Center for the Study of Democratic Politics at Princeton University also provided a wonderful working environment to get the revisions under way. A number of dedicated undergraduates at Bowdoin College, including David Butler, Chris Davidson, and Dave Kirkland, deserve recognition for their research assistance. Professional colleagues also were important. Bruce Larson provided extraordinary insights (and a lot more) on the campaign finance and congressional parties chapters, and Jay Mason helped guide the latter chapter's revision as well. Jonathan Weiler was willing to talk about and share his insights on party politics for long hours, and much of his thinking is reflected in these pages. Finally, as is the case with every project that he has taken on in the last decade, Hetherington would like to acknowledge that it never would have reached the finish line without Suzanne Globetti. In addition to being a wonderfully supportive wife, she is the most talented political scientist and editor around.

The authors would like to acknowledge the support of Brenda Carter, Charisse Kiino, Elise Frasier, and Talia Greenberg from CQ Press for all their help and also for coming up with a book with really small print. In their various roles, they made this project happen. Brenda coordinated the effort, Charisse brought us together, Elise kept us focused on our deadlines and the things that made our revisions significant, and Talia managed to catch all our mistakes. Their talents were indispensable.

1 POLITICAL PARTIES AND THE POLITICAL SYSTEM

THE AMERICAN POLITICAL PARTY SYSTEM is not an insoluble puzzle. But it does have more than its share of mysteries. The main one, arguably, is how it has survived for so long or, perhaps, how it survived at all, in a difficult and complicated environment. The broad explanation, arguably as well, is that the party system survives because parties are an inevitable outgrowth of civil society ("factions . . . sown in the nature of man," thought James Madison[1]); because parties perform functions important to democratic polities ("democracy is unthinkable save in terms of parties," wrote E. E. Schattschneider[2]); and because the American public has never held particularly high expectations of parties or made particularly rigorous demands on them—thus in truth their survival has not been contingent on performance.

Political party has roughly the same number of definitions as it has people who observe them. These definitions fall largely into two categories: electoral and ideological. In the electoral camp, Schattschneider defined a party as "first of all an organized attempt to get power."[3] Similarly, Leon Epstein described a party as "any group, however loosely organized, that seeks to elect governmental officeholders under a given label."[4] In this rendering, parties form, first and foremost, to win elections.

Others define parties in terms of ideology, or principles. Edmund Burke, for example, defined a party as "a body of men united, for promulgating by their joint endeavors the national interest, upon some particular principle in which they are all agreed."[5] By this definition, groups like the American Green party, which have little realistic chance of actually winning an election, are still parties because they campaign on the ideals held by their members and voiced by their leaders.

With good reason, those who study American political parties tend to rely much more on definitions that emphasize the electoral, not the ideological. Simply put, the American political system is hardwired to produce two dominant parties. Because they operate in such a large and heterogeneous political environment, American parties tend to downplay ideology. By emphasizing either strongly conservative or liberal principles, American parties run the risk of alienating voters in the political center, voters who in a two-party system invariably decide the outcome of competitive elections.[6] Compared with European democracies, which feature a multitude of sternly ideological parties, the major parties in the United States gravitate toward the political center, emphasizing elections over policies and political advantage over principle.

The Activities of Parties

A principal thesis in the scholarship on political parties is that they are indispensable to the functioning of democratic political systems. Scholars have differed sharply in their approaches to the study of parties and in their appraisals of the functions or activities of parties, but they are in striking agreement on the linkage between parties and democracy. Representative of a wide band of analysis, the following statements by V. O. Key Jr. and Schattschneider, respectively, sketch the broad outlines of the argument:

> Governments operated, of course, long before political parties in the modern sense came into existence. . . . The proclamation of the right of men to have a hand in their own governing did not create institutions by which they might exercise that right. Nor did the machinery of popular government come into existence overnight. By a tortuous process party systems came into being to implement democratic ideas. As democratic ideas corroded the old foundations of authority, members of the old governing elite reached out to legitimize their positions under the new notions by appealing for popular support. That appeal compelled deference to popular views, but it also required the development of organizations to communicate with and to manage the electorate. . . . In a sense, government, left suspended in mid-air by the erosion of the old justifications for its authority, had to build new foundations in the new environment of a democratic ideology. In short, it had to have machinery to win votes.[7]
>
> The rise of political parties is indubitably one of the principal distinguishing marks of modern government. The parties, in fact, have played a major role as *makers* of governments, more especially they have been the makers of democratic government. . . . [Political] parties created democracy and . . . modern democracy is unthinkable save in terms of the parties. . . . The parties are not . . . merely appendages of modern government; they are in the center of it and play a determinative and creative role in it.[8]

The contributions of political parties to the maintenance of democratic politics can be judged in a rough way by examining the principal activities in which they engage. Of particular importance are those activities associated with the recruitment and selection of leadership, the representation and integration of interests, and the control and direction of government.

Recruitment and Selection of Leaders

The processes by which political leaders are recruited, elected, and appointed to office form the central core of party activity.[9] The party interest, moreover, extends to the appointment of administrative and judicial officers—for example, cabinet members and judges—once the party has captured the executive branch of government.[10]

However, party organizations do not necessarily dominate the process by which candidates are recruited or nominated. Candidates are often self-starters, choosing to enter primaries without waiting for approval from party leaders. With their own personal followings and sources of campaign money, they often pay scant heed to party leaders or party politics. In addition, some candidates are recruited and groomed by political interest groups. Many candidates find interest groups a particularly lucrative source of campaign funds. The looseness of the American party system creates conditions under which party control over many of the candidates who run under its banner is thin or nonexistent.

How involved are parties in the recruitment of candidates? Sandy Maisel and his collaborators find that party influence is greater than one might guess in a supposedly candidate-centered political system, although it is also far from universal. Maisel and his group conducted a study of two hundred congressional districts throughout the country in 1997, identifying potential U.S. House candidates in each of the districts. They then asked these potential candidates whether they had been contacted by party officials and, if so, by which level of the party. Forty percent of the potential candidates reported having been contacted by at least one party committee, with local party committees by far the most active in the recruitment of candidates. Moreover, those who had been contacted by party committees in 1997 were significantly more likely to run in 1998 than potential candidates who had not been contacted by the parties.[11] Maisel's work suggests that parties can, in fact, play an important recruitment role.[12]

That said, party influence is far from complete. For example, having the blessing of the party organization does not guarantee success in seeking the party's nomination. Maisel cites the example of a Republican candidate, Linda Wilde, who had run against George Brown for a California congressional seat in 1996, losing by fewer than one thousand votes. After Brown's death in 1999, Republican leaders backed Wilde to carry the party banner in the special election to fill Brown's seat. However, the party could not get two other experienced candidates to step aside. In the end, Wilde stepped aside.

Even though their power is far from complete, the parties must play an important role in recruitment. Indeed, it is difficult to see how hundreds of thousands of elective offices could be filled in the absence of parties without turning each election into a free-for-all, conspicuous by the presence of numerous candidates holding all varieties of set, shifting, and undisclosed views. Composing a government out of an odd mélange of officials, especially at the national level, would be very difficult. Any form of collective accountability to the voters would vanish. Hence, whatever their shortcomings, by proposing alternative lists of candidates and campaigning on their behalf, the parties bring certain measures of order, routine, and predictability to the electoral process.

The constant factors in party politics are the pursuit of power, office, and advantage. Yet, in serving their own interest in winning office, parties make other contributions to the public at large and to the political system as a whole. For example, they help to educate the voters on issues and mobilize them for political action, provide a linkage between the people and the government, and simplify the choices to be made in elections. The parties do what voters cannot do by themselves: from the totality of interests and issues in politics, they choose those that will become "the agenda of formal public discourse."[13] In the process of shaping the agenda, they provide a mechanism by which voters not only can make sense out of what government does but can also relate to the government itself.

Representation and Integration of Group Interests

The United States is a complex and heterogeneous nation. An extraordinary variety of political interest groups, organized around particularistic objectives, exists within it. Conflicts between one group and another, between coalitions of groups, and between various groups and the government are inevitable. Because one of the major functions of government is to take sides in private disputes, what it decides and does is of high importance to groups. When at their creative best, parties and their leaders help to keep group conflicts within tolerable limits. Viewed from a wider perspective, the relationship between parties and private organizations is one of bargaining and accommodation—groups need the parties as much as the parties need them. No group can expect to move far toward the attainment of its objectives without coming to terms with the realities of party power, since the parties, through their public officeholders, can advance or obstruct the policy objectives of any group. At the same time, no party can expect to achieve widespread electoral success without significant group support.

Bargaining and compromise are key elements in the strategy of American parties. The doctrinal flexibility of the parties means that almost everything is up for grabs—each party can make at least some effort to satisfy virtually any group's demands. Through their public officials, the parties serve as brokers among the organized interests of American society, weighing the claims of one group against those of another, accepting some programs and modifying or rejecting others.[14] The steady bargaining that takes place between interest groups and key party leaders tends to produce settlements the participants can accept for a time, even though these compromises may not be wholly satisfactory to anyone. Of deeper significance, the legitimacy of government itself depends in part on the capacity of the parties to represent diverse interests and to integrate the claims of competing groups in a broad program of public policy. Their ability to do so is certain to bear on their electoral success.

The thesis that the major parties are unusually sensitive to the representation of group interests cannot be advanced without a caveat or two. Parties are far more solicitous toward the claims of organized interests than toward those of unorganized interests. The groups that regularly engage the attention of parties and their representatives in government are those whose support (or opposition) can make a difference at the polls. Organized labor, organized business, organized agriculture, organized medicine—all have multiple channels for gaining access to decision makers. Indeed, party politicians are about as likely to solicit the views of these interests as they are to wait to hear from them.

In the last few decades, special cause groups—those passionate and uncompromising lobbies concerned with single issues such as gun control, abortion, tax rollbacks, equal rights, nuclear power, and the environment—have also kept legislators' feet to the fire, exerting influence as they judge members on the "correctness" of their positions. The National Rifle Association, for example, has had an extraordinary effect on the election prospects of several members of Congress who have voted against its interests.

By contrast, many millions of Americans are all but shut out of the political system. The political power of such groups as agricultural workers, sharecroppers, migrants, and unorganized laborers has never been commensurate with the groups' numbers or, for that matter, with their contribution to society. With low participation in elections, weak organizations, low status, and poor access to political communications, their voices are often drowned out in the din produced by organized interests.[15] While no problem of representation in America is more important than that of finding ways to move the claims of the unorganized public onto the agenda of politics, the task is formidable: "All power is organization and all organization is power," says Harvey Fergusson. "A man who has no share in any form of organized power is not independent of organized power. He is at the mercy of it."[16]

Control and Direction of Government

A third major activity of the parties involves the control and direction of government. Parties recruit candidates and organize campaigns to win political power, gain public office, and take control of government. Given the character of the political system and the parties themselves, however, it is unrealistic to suppose that party management of government will be altogether successful.

First, the separate branches of government may not be captured by the same party. Indeed, until the Republicans won control of the Senate in 2002, the same party had controlled the presidency and both houses of Congress for fewer than three years since 1980. This fact is important because divided party control complicates the governing process by forcing the president to work not only with his own party in Congress but also with elements of the other party. For example, the legislative success of Republican presidents usually depends on gaining the support of conservative Democrats. Hence, party achievements and failures are often blurred in the mix of coalition votes. Who was to blame for the enormous budget deficits of the 1980s, the Republican president or the Democratic Congress? With divided party control, it is harder for voters to hold politicians responsible for their decisions.

Second, even though one party may control the legislative and executive branches, its margin of seats in the legislature may be too thin to permit it to govern effectively. Early in their presidencies, both Bill Clinton and George W. Bush had to expend tremendous political capital to move their programs forward despite their respective parties' control of both houses of Congress. This made it harder for them to accomplish other goals later in their presidencies. Disagreement within the majority party, moreover, may be so great on certain issues that the party finds it virtually impossible to come together to develop coherent positions.

Third, midterm (or off-year) elections invariably complicate the president's plans because his party almost always loses seats in both houses. In 1994, after the first two years of unified party government since the 1970s, the Democrats lost a whopping fifty-two seats in the House and eight in the Senate, creating the first Republican Congress in forty years. The Republicans' ability to pick up seats in both the House and Senate in 2002 is an historical anomaly almost without precedent. Indeed, since 1946 the administration party at midterm has suffered an average loss of twenty-three seats in the House and three in the Senate (see Table 1-1). Very few events are as predictable in American elections or as dispiriting for administrations as the chilly midterm verdict of the voters.

The upshot is that although the parties organize governments, they do not wholly control decision-making activities. In large measure they compete with political interest groups bent on securing public policies advantageous to their

Table 1-1   Off-Year Gains and Losses in Congress
by the President's Party: 1946–2002

Year	House		Senate	
1946	D	−55	D	−12
1950	D	−29	D	−6
1954	R	−18	R	−1
1958	R	−47	R	−13
1962	D	−4	D	+4
1966	D	−47	D	−3
1970	R	−12	R	+2
1974	R	−48	R	−5
1978	D	−15	D	−3
1982	R	−26	R	0
1986	R	−5	R	−8
1990	R	−8	R	−1
1994	D	−52	D	−8
1998	D	+5	D	0
2002	R	+6	R	+2

Source: Thomas Mann, Norman Ornstein, and Michael J. Malbin, *Vital Statistics on Congress 2001–2002* (Washington, D.C.: American Enterprise Institute, 2002).

Note: R = Republican; D = Democrat.

clienteles, and sometimes certain groups have as much influence on the behavior of legislators and bureaucrats as legislative party leaders, national and subnational party leaders, or the president. Yet, to identify the difficulties that confront the parties in seeking to manage the government is not to suggest that the parties' impact on public policy is insubstantial. Not even a casual examination of party platforms, candidates' and officeholders' speeches, or legislative voting can fail to detect the parties' contributions to shaping the direction of government or can ignore the differences that separate the parties on public policy matters.

An understanding of American parties begins with recognizing that party politicians value winning elections more than using election outcomes to achieve policy goals. Candidates have interests and commitments in policy questions, but rarely do they rule out bargaining and compromise in order to achieve half a "party loaf." Politicians tend to be intensely pragmatic and adaptable people. For the most part, they are attracted to a particular party more because of its promise as a mechanism for moving into government than as a mechanism for "governing" itself. Party is a way of organizing activists and supporters to make a bid for office.[17] This is the elemental truth of party politics. The election of one party over another has policy significance, but it is more an unanticipated dividend than a triumph for the idea of responsible party government.

Parties as a "Dependent Variable"

It is critically important to understand that parties are less what they make of themselves than what their environment makes of them.[18] In language social scientists sometimes invoke, parties typically are the dependent variable. That is, to a marked extent the party owes its character and form to the impact of four external elements: the legal-political system, the election system, the political culture, and the heterogeneous quality of American life. To the extent that these characteristics create conditions that weaken or strengthen parties, parties will be weaker or stronger. Moreover, should the character of any of these characteristics change over time, it will affect party strength in profound ways.

The Legal-Political System

The Constitution was, in part, designed to limit the reach of institutions like parties that sought to aggregate power. Hence the Founders, whose intent was to establish a government that could not easily be brought under the control of any one element, provided a system that ensures that American parties are weaker than most of their European counterparts. The underlying theory of the Founders was both simple and pervasive: power was to check power, and the ambitions of some men were to check the ambitions of others.*

---

*In addition to using terms such as "candidate," "legislator," "member," and "representative" to apply to men and women in politics, we have referred to them occasionally in the masculine gender—"he," "him," "his." This is simply a matter of style. These pronouns are employed generically.

The two main features in this design were federalism and the separation of powers—the first to distribute power among different levels of government; the second to distribute power among the legislative, executive, and judicial branches. Further division of the legislature into two houses, with their memberships elected for different terms and by differing methods, was thought to reduce further the risk that a single faction (or party) might gain ascendancy.

Federalism makes the parties' job more difficult because it decentralizes power: not only are there fifty state governmental systems, but there also are fifty state party systems. No two states are exactly alike, nor are any two state party systems. The ideology of one state party may be sharply different from that of another. Contrast, for example, the state Democratic party of Mississippi with its counterpart in New York or the state Republican party of Utah with its counterpart in Connecticut.[19] Furthermore, within each state all manner of local party organizations exist, sometimes functioning in harmony with state and national party elements and sometimes not. There are states (and localities) where the party organizations are active and well financed, and those where they are not; those where factions compete persistently within a party, and those where factional organization is nonexistent; those where ideology and issues are important, and those where they are not; those where the parties seem to consist mainly of the personal followings of individual politicians, and those where party leaders exercise significant influence.[20]

The laws that govern party activity in different states also differ, which shapes their influence. A great variety of state laws, for example, govern nominating procedures, ballot form, access to the ballot, campaign finance, and elections. On the whole, northeastern states are most likely to have statutes that foster stronger parties, whereas southern states tend to have statutes that weaken them.[21] Similarly, strong ("monopolistic") local party organizations have been more prominent and durable in the East than anywhere else.[22] The broad point is that the thrust of federalism is toward fragmentation and parochialism, permitting numerous forms of political organization to thrive and inhibiting the emergence of cohesive and disciplined national parties.

The Election System

The election system is another element that shapes American political parties. Parties and elections are so closely linked that it is difficult to understand much about one without understanding a great deal about the other. Parties are in business to win elections; election systems shape the way the parties compete for power and the success with which they do it.

The most important reason that America has exactly two major parties is the rules governing the election system. Chief among them is electing House members from single-member districts by plurality vote. Under this arrangement a single candidate is elected in each district, and he needs to receive only a plurality of the vote. Third party candidates have little inducement to run, because the prospects are poor that they could defeat the candidates of the two major parties. On the other hand, if members of Congress were elected under a proportional representation scheme, with several members chosen in each district, third party candidates would undoubtedly have a better chance of winning some seats.[23]

Third parties face the same obstacle in presidential elections that they do in congressional races: only one party can win. For the office of the presidency, the entire nation takes on the cast of a single-member district. Each state's electoral votes are awarded as a unit to the candidate receiving a plurality of the popular vote; all other popular votes are in effect wasted. In 1992, for example, Ross Perot received nearly twenty million popular votes (winning more than 27 percent of the vote in Maine, Alaska, Idaho, Utah, and Kansas), only to be skunked in the electoral college. If electoral votes were divided in proportion to popular votes in each state, third party and independent candidates would make a bigger dent in the electoral vote totals of the major parties. Electoral practices in the United States are hard on third parties—so successful in limiting competition that they force outsiders to think about running for the nomination of a major party.

In addition to ensuring the dominance of two parties, the election system was designed to keep one faction (party) from easily controlling government. For example, a state's election calendar can have a substantial impact on party fortunes. If all elections were held at once, people would tend to vote based on the governing party's performance in the years leading up to the election. Instead, states tend to separate their elections from national elections. For example, in 2000 less than one third of states held gubernatorial elections in a presidential election year. This arrangement insulates state politics from national politics. Similarly, the behavior of voters may also weaken linkages between these levels. Even in those states in which governors are elected at the same time as the president, typically more than a third of the time the party that carries the state in the presidential contest will lose at the gubernatorial level. (The outcomes in presidential-gubernatorial voting from 1964 to 2000 are indicated in Table 1-2.)

Table 1-2   Split Outcomes in Presidential–Gubernatorial Voting: States Carried by Presidential Candidate of One Major Party and by Gubernatorial Candidate of Other Major Party: 1964–2000

Year	Gubernatorial elections	Split outcomes	Percentage
1964	25	9	36
1968	21	8	38
1972	18	10	56
1976	14	5	36
1980	13	4	31
1984	13	5	38
1988	12	4	33
1992	12	4	33
1996	11	3	27
2000	11	5	45

Sources: Various issues of *Congressional Quarterly Weekly Report.*

The use of staggered terms for executive and legislative offices also diminishes the probability that one party will control both branches of government at any given time. When the governor is elected for four years and the lower house is elected for two—the common pattern—chances are that the governor's party will lose legislative seats, and sometimes its majority, in the off-year election. The same is true for the president and Congress. Whatever the virtues of staggered terms and off-year elections, they increase the likelihood of divided control of government, which weakens the influence of parties.

In addition, reformers did much to weaken party control of politics through the development of the direct primary in the early twentieth century. The primary was introduced to combat the power of party oligarchs who, insulated from popular influences, dominated the selection of nominees in state and local party conventions. In the past, if a party boss tapped a person to run for a seat, that individual received the party's nomination. Primaries challenged the power of party bosses to make such decisions. By empowering voters to choose party nominees, reformers sought to democratize the nominating process. Today, all states employ some form of primary system.

While the convention method survives for the nomination of presidential and vice-presidential candidates, the reality is that the preconvention struggle has become so decisive that it now governs the presidential selection process. The conventions simply ratify the voters' choices in caucus and primary states, and primaries have become particularly important. Today, more than forty states, including all the largest ones, select their convention delegates in presidential primaries.

The precise impact of the primary on the parties is difficult to establish. Its effects nevertheless appear to be substantial. First, by transferring the choice of nominees from party assemblies to the voters, the primary has increased the probability that candidates with different views on public policy will be brought together in the same party. Whatever their policy orientations, the victors in primary elections become the party's nominees, perhaps to the embarrassment of other party candidates. Second, observers contend that primaries have contributed to a decline in party responsibility. Candidates who win office largely on their own and who have their own distinctive followings within local electorates have less reason to defer to party leaders or to adhere to traditional party positions. Third, the primary has contributed to numerous intraparty clashes; particularly bitter primary fights sometimes render the party incapable of generating a united campaign in the general election.[24] Finally, primaries apparently contribute to the consolidation of one-party politics. In an area where one party ordinarily dominates, its primaries tend to become the arena for political battles. The growth of the second party is inhibited not only by the lack of voter interest in its primaries but also by its inability to attract strong candidates to its colors. One-party domination reveals little about the party's organizational strength—indeed, one-party political systems likely will be characterized more by factionalism and internecine warfare than by unity, harmony, and ideological agreement.

Such are the arguments developed against the primary. Of course, others can be made on its behalf. Moreover, in some jurisdictions the dominant party organization is sufficiently strong that nonendorsed candidates have little or no chance of upsetting the organization's slate. Potential challengers may abandon their campaigns once the party leaders or the organization have made their choices known. Other candidacies may not materialize because the prospects for getting the nod from party leaders appear unpromising.

Moreover, it is questionable that the direct primary actually undermines the decisions of party leaders, particularly in the case of presidential nominations. Not since 1976, when Jimmy Carter upset several better-known Democrats, has a party's solid front-runner failed to win his party's nomination. Using devices like "front loading"—that is, concentrating delegate-rich states at the beginning of the primary election calendar—the major parties almost always end up nominating the person that party leaders would have chosen in the past.[25]

In sum, election rules matter. In spite of myths to the contrary, election systems are never designed to be neutral and never are neutral. Some election laws and constitutional provisions, such as the single-member district system or the rigorous requirements that minor parties must meet to gain a place on the ballot, provide general support for the two-party system. According to the Federal Election Commission, none of the fourteen minor party candidates for the presidency in 2000 got on all fifty state ballots, although the Green, Reform, and Libertarian Parties got close.[26] Green party candidate Ralph Nader did the best of the minor party candidates, with 2.8 million votes (2.7 percent), while the other fourteen shared barely 1 million votes.

Other laws and constitutional provisions make party government difficult and sometimes impossible. These include such system features as staggered terms of office, off-year elections, and direct primaries. The major parties are not always passive witnesses to existing electoral arrangements. At times they simply endure them because it is easier to live with conventional arrangements than to try to change them or because they recognize their benefits. At other times major parties seek new schemes because the prospects for party advantage are sufficiently promising to warrant the effort. It is a good bet that no one understands or appreciates American election systems better than those party leaders responsible for defending party interests and winning elections.

The Political Culture and the Parties

A third important element in the environment of American political parties is the political culture—"the system of empirical beliefs, expressive symbols, and values which defines the situation in which political action takes place."[27] Decades of studies demonstrate that the American public is highly skeptical of the parties and their activities. Instead of choosing candidates based on party affiliation, almost all Americans believe "the best rule in voting is to pick the best candidate, regardless of party label." Indeed, an overwhelming majority of the public believes that the parties do more to confuse issues than to clarify them and that they often provoke unnecessary conflict.[28]

Support for cohesive and disciplined parties is extremely limited. Only about one out of five persons believes that a legislator "should follow his or her party leaders even if he or she doesn't want to." Moreover, in surveys of voter attitudes toward control of the presidency and Congress by the same party, a majority typically prefers divided party control.[29] Overall, little in this profile of popular attitudes suggests that the public understands or accepts the tenets of a responsible party system.[30]

Virtually all surveys that tap popular understanding and appreciation of the parties indicate that the public has little confidence in them. An ABC News–*Washington Post* survey in 1996, for example, found that two thirds of the public agreed with the proposition that "both political parties are pretty much out of touch with the American people."[31] Adding to the problem, many voters see little or no difference in the effectiveness of the parties in governing. Since 1972, the National Election Study has asked Americans "Which political party do you think would be most likely to get the government to do a better job in dealing with [the nation's most important] problem—the Republicans, the Democrats, or wouldn't there be much difference between them?" A plurality always chooses the "wouldn't be much difference" response and, more often than not, a majority does. In short, most people do not see the parties as effective problem solvers.

Despite these feelings, however, the American public has more recently exhibited party-centric behavior. Ticket-splitting (voting for candidates of more than one party in the same election) is one such example. Figure 1-1 shows the percentage of people voting for presidential and House candidates of different parties in the same year. In the 1960 Kennedy-Nixon race, occurring during a period when parties were characterized as very strong, only 14 percent of all voters split their tickets. By 1972, the percentage of ticket-splitters had more than

Figure 1-1 Percentage of Voters Casting a Split Ticket for President and House: 1952–2000

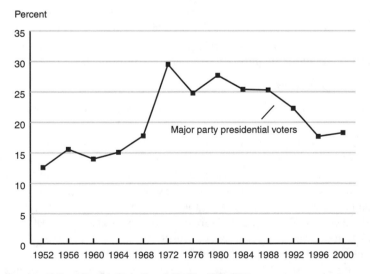

Source: American National Election Study, Cumulative File, 1948–2000.

doubled to 30 percent. Since then, however, split-ticket voting has decreased with almost every election; in fact only about 18 percent of Americans did so in 2000. Similarly, Larry Bartels demonstrates that party identification has become an increasingly important determinant of presidential and congressional voting over the last two decades. In fact, he finds that party affiliation is an even stronger predictor today than it was in the 1950s.[32]

The cause behind heightened party voting is that Americans are increasingly likely to see important differences between the parties. (See Figure 1-2.) Not without reason, many Americans viewed the parties as Tweedledum and Tweedledee in the 1970s, with only 46 percent perceiving important differences in 1972. The Democrats still had a very conservative southern wing of the party, which was significantly more conservative than many liberal northeastern Republicans. Over time, however, conservative Republicans replaced these southern Democrats, while liberal Democrats replaced many of the northeastern Republicans.[33] The public has picked up on these changes: by 2000, 64 percent of Americans perceived important differences between the parties, the highest percentage since the National Election Study started to ask this question in 1960. Moreover, the differences that people perceive are ideological in nature. Over the last two decades, Americans have gotten much better at correctly placing the Democrats to the left of the Republicans. In other words, the public is increasingly adept at attributing a conservative public policy course to Republicans and a liberal one to Democrats.[34]

While Americans are behaving in a more party-centric manner, it does not necessarily mean that they like parties. In the argot of popular appraisal, politi-

Figure 1-2   Percentage of Respondents Who See Important Differences between What the Parties Stand For: 1960–2000

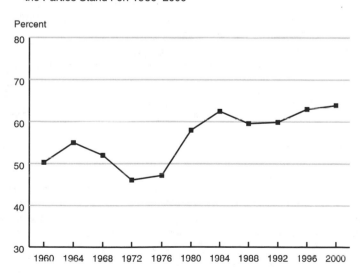

Source: American National Election Study, Cumulative File, 1948–2000.

cal organizations often turn into "machines," party workers emerge as "hacks," political leaders become "bosses," and campaign appeals degenerate into "empty promises" or "sheer demagoguery." That some politicians have contributed to this state of affairs by debasing the language of political discourse or by their behavior, as in the Watergate affair, is perhaps beside the point. The critical fact is that the American political culture contains a strong suspicion of the political process and the agencies that try to dominate it, the political parties.

A Heterogeneous Nation

To complete the analysis of the environment of American parties, it is necessary to say something about the characteristics of the nation as a whole. No array of statistics is required to make the point that the United States is a nation of extraordinary diversity. The American community is composed of a great variety of economic and social interests; class configurations; ethnic and religious groups; occupations; regional and subregional interests; and loyalties, values, and beliefs. There are citizens who are deeply attached to inherited patterns and those who are impatient advocates of change, those who care intensely about politics and those who can take it or leave it, and those who elude labeling—those who are active on one occasion and passive on another. There are citizens who think mainly in terms of farm policy, some who seek advantage for urban elements, and others whose lives and political interests revolve around business or professions. Diversity abounds. Sometimes deep, sometimes shallow, the differences that separate one group from another and one region from another make the formation of public policy that suits everyone all but impossible.

The major parties must accommodate themselves to the vast diversity of the nation. And they have done this remarkably well. Each party attracts and depends on a wide range of interests. Voting behavior in the 2000 presidential election (George W. Bush versus Al Gore) illustrates this point (see Figure 1-3). The Democratic party did particularly well among African Americans, Jews, Hispanics, Asians, women, persons with lower incomes and limited education, union members, and younger Americans.[35] For the Republicans, the most distinctive supporters were fundamentalist Christians, white Protestants, men (particularly white men), and persons with incomes of more than $100,000. An important point is that neither party excludes any group from its calculations for winning elections. On the contrary, each party expects to do reasonably well among nearly all groups.

The heterogeneity of the nation is one explanation for the enduring parochial cast of American politics. As Herbert Agar has explained:

> Most politics will be parochial, most politicians will have small horizons, seeking the good of the state or the district rather than of the Union; yet by diplomacy and compromise, never by force, the government must water down the selfish demands of regions, races, classes, business associations, into a national policy which will alienate no major groups and which will contain at least a plum for everybody. This is the price of unity in a continentwide federation.[36]

Figure 1–3   Voting Behavior of Groups in the 2000 Presidential Election

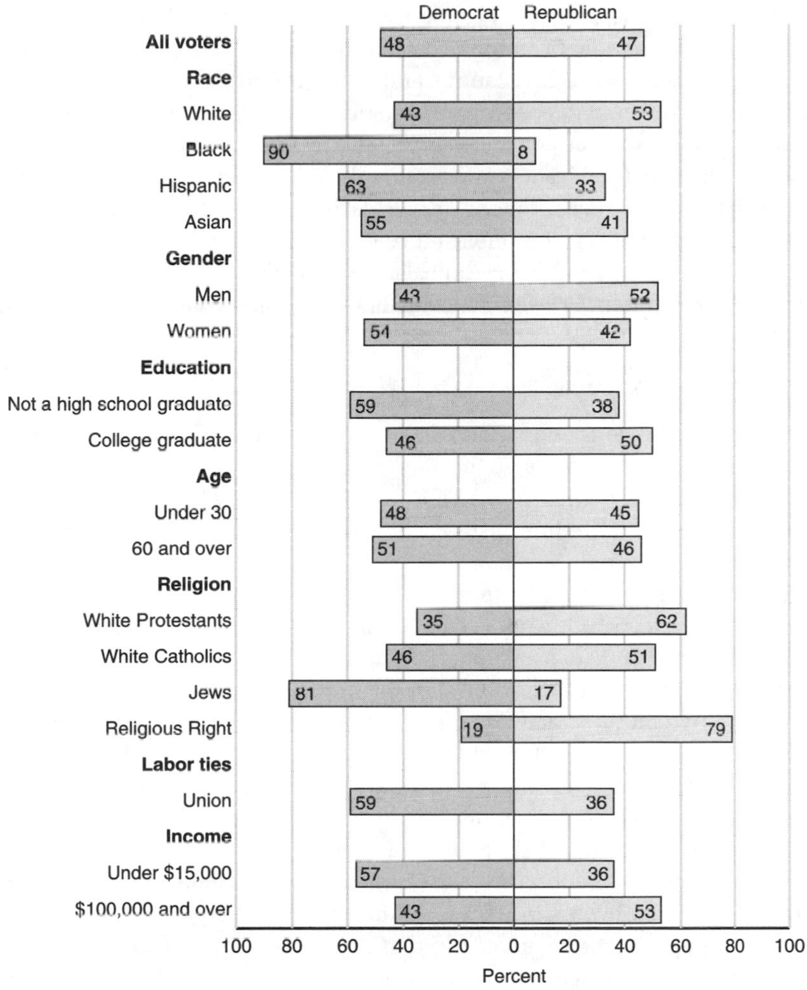

Democrat   Republican

Group	Democrat	Republican
All voters	48	47
Race		
White	43	53
Black	90	8
Hispanic	63	33
Asian	55	41
Gender		
Men	43	52
Women	54	42
Education		
Not a high school graduate	59	38
College graduate	46	50
Age		
Under 30	48	45
60 and over	51	46
Religion		
White Protestants	35	62
White Catholics	46	51
Jews	81	17
Religious Right	19	79
Labor ties		
Union	59	36
Income		
Under $15,000	57	36
$100,000 and over	43	53

100   80   60   40   20   0   20   40   60   80   100
Percent

Sources: Developed from Voter News Service exit poll data.

Party Organization

Party organization has two common features in all parts of the United States. First, parties are organized in a series of committees, reaching from the precinct level to the national committee. Second, party committee organization parallels the arrangement of electoral districts. With the exception of heavily one-party areas, party committees can be found in virtually all jurisdictions within which important government officials are elected. The presence of party committees, however, reveals little about their activities or their vitality in campaigns.

The organizational structure of American political parties is like a pyramid. At the top rests the national committee and at the bottom the precinct organizations, with various ward, city, county, and state committees lodged in between. Although it is convenient to view party organization within this pattern, it is misleading if it suggests that power flows steadily from top to bottom, from major national leaders to local leaders and local rank and file. Subnational committees actually have substantial autonomy, particularly in the crucial matters of selecting and slating candidates for public office (including federal office), raising and spending money, and conducting campaigns. (See Figure 1-4.) However, changes in the campaign finance system have made the national committees much bigger players than in the past.

The National Committee

The most prestigious and visible of all party committees is the national committee. The people who serve on the national committee of each party are prominent state politicians, chosen in a variety of ways and under a number of constraints. Their official tenure begins when they are accepted by the national convention of each party.

The selection of national committee members is not a simple matter. The Democratic party, operating under its 1974 charter, has elaborate provisions governing the composition of its national committee. Among its membership are the chair and the highest-ranking official of the opposite gender of each recognized state party; two hundred additional members allotted to the states on the same basis as delegates are apportioned to the national convention; and a number of delegates representing such organizations as the Democratic Governors' Conference, the U.S. Congress, the National Finance Council, the Conference of Democratic Mayors, the National Federation of Democratic Women, the Democratic County Officials Conference, the State Legislative Leaders Caucus, and the Young Democrats of America. As in the case of delegates to the party's national convention, the party's charter stipulates that members of the national committee must be selected "through processes which assure full, timely, and equal opportunity to participate" and with due attention to affirmative action standards.

To know what the national committee is, it is necessary to look at what it does.[37] One of its principal responsibilities is to make arrangements for the national convention every four years. In this capacity it chooses the convention site, prepares a temporary roster of convention delegates, and selects convention speakers and temporary officers who will manage the assembly in its opening phase. The committee is especially active during presidential campaigns in coordinating campaign efforts, publicizing the party and its candidates, and raising money.

In addition, the national party committee has evolved into a fund-raising machine. Loopholes in the campaign finance laws (covered in greater detail in

Figure 1-4   Party Organization in the United States: Layers of Committees and Their Chairs

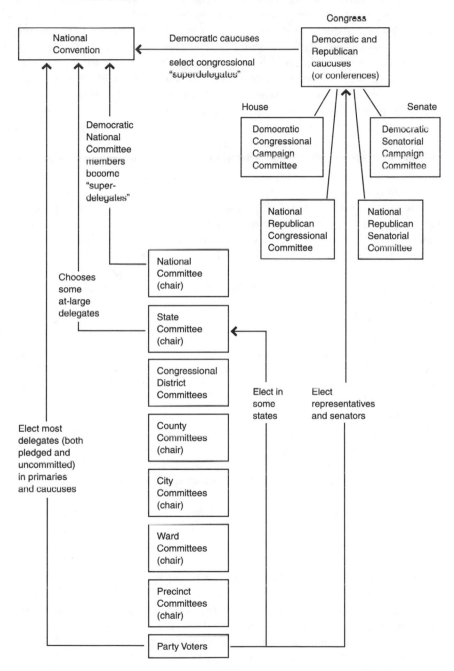

chapter 4) have allowed the national parties to raise money in unlimited sums to engage in "party building" activities. As the definition of party building was widened by the courts over the years to include even most forms of television advertising, big donors found the parties to be attractive places to contribute large sums of money. These "soft money" donations made the national party committees into clearinghouses for fund-raising, in which they directed large contributions into competitive federal races. In the 1999–2000 election cycle, both major parties raised record amounts of "soft money." Republican national party committees raised $249.9 million in soft money, up 81 percent from the previous presidential election cycle, while Democratic national party committees raised $245.2 million, a 98 percent increase over 1995–1996.[38] While recent changes in the campaign finance system may stem the tide of soft money, it is still important to note that soft money has made the national party committees important players.

The influence of the president on his party's national committee is substantial. "I don't think the Republican National Committee [RNC] can ever really be independent," a committee staff member said. "[The committee has] a responsibility to the leader. Policy is always made at the White House, not here. We accept it and support it."[39] The same is true for the Democratic National Committee (DNC). "The president likes a party that serves as a supportive tool for the president," observed a state party chair during the Carter administration. "An independent organization is looked upon as a nuisance. That is inevitable."[40]

Strains between the national committee and the White House nevertheless are not much below the surface. Tension sometimes stems from a perception that the White House is too demanding—in particular, that the administration expects the national committee to center its efforts on the president's reelection, even at the expense of other offices. Thus, for example, the former general chair of the DNC, Gov. Roy Romer (Colo.), complained that the national party had not paid sufficient attention to the election of its congressional and gubernatorial candidates in 1996. "You've got to have a very close working relationship with the president and vice president because they help you raise the money," he remarked. "But don't think that the DNC ought simply to be the campaign finance arm of the executive branch."[41]

For some time, the RNC has been more effective than its Democratic counterpart in raising campaign funds and in providing services for its party's candidates. While the Democrats narrowed the Republicans' advantage in soft money fundraising during the Clinton presidency, the money gap is substantial. During the 1999–2000 election cycle, for example, the Republican party's three national-level committees (national, senatorial, and congressional) raised $715.7 million, while the three Democratic committees raised $520.4 million.[42] Focusing on party-building activities, the RNC beat the DNC to the punch in making a variety of technical services available to party candidates at both the national and state levels; these services include fund-raising assistance, consultant advice, candidate training, public opinion surveys, and computer analyses of voting behavior.

The National Chair

The head of the national party is the national chair. Although the chair is officially selected by the members of the national committee, in practice he is chosen by the party's presidential candidate shortly after the national convention has adjourned. Very few leaders in either party have held the position for an extended period; the chair of the party winning the presidency usually receives a major appointment in the new administration, and the chair of the losing party is replaced by a new face. When the chair of the out party becomes vacant, the national committee selects the new leader. Factional conflicts may come to the surface when the committee is faced with the responsibility of finding a replacement, because the leading candidates will usually be identified with certain wings of the party.

The central problem with which the national chair must come to terms in presidential election years is the direction and coordination of the national campaign. The Republican national organization has far outstripped its Democratic rival in the task. One major reason is that such national chairs as Ray C. Bliss (1965–1969) and Bill Brock (1977–1981) concentrated their efforts on organizational reform, seeking in particular to strengthen state and local Republican organizations by providing them with all kinds of "electioneering" assistance.[43] A successful fund-raising program, based on more than two million small contributors, makes these efforts possible.[44]

An absence of adequate financial resources has been particularly burdensome for the Democratic party's national chair. Kenneth M. Curtis, who resigned in 1978 after only one year in office, described what his job was like:

> Have you ever tried to meet the payroll every two weeks of a bankrupt organization and deal with 363 bosses [national committee members] and 50 state chairs? . . . I tried it for a year and simply decided I'd like to do something else with my life. It's not the sort of job that you lay down in the street and bleed to keep.[45]

But the party's situation is changing. Under recent DNC chairs, the party has expanded its contributor base; become more competitive in raising funds; strengthened itself organizationally; and increased its support of candidates, state party organizations, and party-building activities. From an organizational standpoint, the national Democratic party is now better poised to challenge its Republican counterpart in election campaigns.

Congressional and Senatorial Campaign Committees

The other principal units of the national party organization are the congressional and senatorial campaign committees, one committee for each party in each house. These committees, composed of members of Congress, are independent of the national committees and are an outgrowth of the need of members of Congress to have organizations concerned exclusively with their political welfare. As such, they raise campaign funds for members, help to develop campaign strategies, conduct research, and otherwise provide assistance to members running for reelection.[46] A certain degree of informal cooperation occurs between the party committees of Congress and the national committees, but for the most part they go their separate ways: the former bent on securing reelection of incumbent legislators and on improving the party's prospects for winning or retaining control of Congress, the latter preoccupied with the presidential race.

The Republican campaign committees are the most active and best financed. In 2000 the National Republican Congressional Committee raised twice as much money for Republican congressional candidates as the Democratic Congressional Campaign Committee did on its candidates—$97 million to $48 million. On the Senate side, the National Republican Senatorial Committee raised $51 million to the Democrats' $48 million.[47] Although the Republicans maintain a clear advantage, it has narrowed significantly over the last twenty years.

State Committees

Midway between the national party apparatus and local party organizations are the state party committees, often called state central committees.[48] So great are the differences between these committees from state to state—in membership selection, size, and function—that it is difficult to generalize about them. In some states the membership is made up of county chairs; more commonly, state committee members are chosen in primaries or by local party conventions. Their numbers range from fewer than a hundred members to several hundred. In some states the state central committee is a genuinely powerful party unit and is customarily charged with drafting the party platform, slating statewide candidates, and waging an intensive fund-raising campaign. In other states the committee's impact on state politics is scarcely perceptible. In a fashion similar to that found at the national level, the state chair is ordinarily selected by the party's gubernatorial candidate. And like the national chair, the state leader is usually a key adviser to the governor on party affairs, particularly on matters involving the distribution of patronage.[49]

Local Party Organization

Below the state committee of the party is the county committee, ordinarily a very large organization composed of all the precinct officials within the county. At the head of this committee is the county chair, who is usually elected by the members of the county committee. Often a key figure in local party organizations, the county chair is active in the campaign planning, recruitment and slating of party candidates, supervision of campaign financing, and allocation of patronage to the party faithful. In many counties, the leader's power is enhanced by his active recruitment of candidates for precinct committee members—the very people who in turn elect him to office. Some states have congressional district party organizations, developed around the office of the U.S. representative. Where these committees exist, they function essentially as the member's personal organization, set off from the rest of the party and preoccupied with errand running for constituents and the election of the member. Although local party officials, such as the county chair, may be instrumental in controlling the original congressional nomination, their influence on the representative's policy orientations is virtually nil. Indeed, one of the dominant characteristics of congressional district organization is its autonomy. Further down the line are the city and ward committees, which vary in size and importance throughout the country. Their activities, like those of other committees, are centered on campaigns and elections.

The cornerstone of American party organization is the precinct committee, organized within the tens of thousands of election or voting districts of the nation. In metropolitan areas a precinct is likely to number one thousand or two thousand voters; in open-country areas, perhaps only a dozen. The complexity of party organization at the precinct level is mainly a function of precinct size. The precinct committee member is chosen in one of two ways: by the voters in a primary election, or by the vote of party members attending a precinct caucus.

In the lore of American politics, elections are won or lost at the precinct level. A strong precinct organization, the argument runs, is essential to party victory, and the key to a strong organization is a precinct leader bent on carrying his precinct. In attempting to advance their party's fortunes, the committee members engage in four main activities: those associated with the campaign itself; party organizational work (for example, recruitment and organization of workers); promulgation of political information; and identification and recruitment of candidates for local office. For most jurisdictions, it appears, the most important activities are those related to the campaign, such as inducing and helping people to register, contacting voters, raising money, campaigning for votes, and transporting voters to the polls. Undoubtedly differences exist in the role perceptions of party officials. A study of precinct leaders in Massachusetts and North Carolina, for example, found that about 60 percent saw their principal task as that of mobilizing voters.[50] In Connecticut and Michigan the leading activities of precinct officials are fund-raising, canvassing, and distributing literature.[51] And in Pittsburgh, about two-thirds of the committee members describe their most important task as electoral—but here they tend to be indifferent to organizational goals and more supportive of particular candidates than of the party slate as a whole.[52] One study has shown that the organizational vitality of local parties (as measured by such things as the presence of officials, allocation of time to party business, regular meetings, the existence of a budget, and participation in various kinds of campaign activities) is highest in the East (for example, New Jersey, New York, Pennsylvania, and Delaware) and the Midwest (for example, Indiana, Ohio, and Illinois), and lowest in the South (for example, Louisiana, Georgia, Florida, Kentucky, and Texas).[53]

Does the strength of local party organizations make a difference in electoral politics? A study by John P. Frendreis, James L. Gibson, and Laura L. Vertz provides a two-part answer. First, the presence of well-organized and active local party organizations does not have a significant direct effect on the persuasion of voters and thus on election results. That appears to be the domain of candidate organizations. But second, and of overlooked importance, in jurisdictions where a party organization is active, the party more likely will be involved in recruitment and therefore able to field a full slate of candidates. Party building, in other words, comes one step at a time. The structural strength of the party, this study suggests, provides a base for the eventual development of competitive party politics.[54]

The Changing Parties: "Old Style" and "New Style" Politics

In the late nineteenth and early twentieth centuries the best examples of strong party organization could be found in the large cities of the Northeast and Midwest—New York City, Boston, Philadelphia, Jersey City, Kansas City, and Chicago. Well-organized and strongly disciplined, the urban machine during this era was virtually invincible. Precinct and ward officials maintained steady contacts with their party constituencies—finding jobs for people out of work; helping those who were in trouble with the law; aiding others in securing government benefits such as welfare payments; assisting neighborhoods to secure government services; helping immigrants to cope with a new society; and helping merchants and tradespeople in their efforts to obtain contracts, licenses, and the like. The party organization was at the center of community life, an effective mediator between the people and their government. Party officials were "brokers," exchanging information, access, and influence for loyalty and support at the polls.

The picture is very different today. Numerous factors have contributed to this loss of function, including the growth of civil service systems and the corresponding decline in patronage, the relative decline in the value of patronage jobs, the arrival of the welfare state with its various benefits for low-income groups, the steady assimilation of immigrants, the growing disillusionment among better-educated voters over many features of machine politics, and the coming of age of the mass media with its potential for contacts between candidates and their publics. Where the parties have suffered a loss of function, it is reasonable to assume that they have also suffered a loss of vitality. The result has been a decline in their ability to deliver the vote on election day.

"Controlling" votes, except perhaps in a few big city wards, is a lost art. Today, the most important players are the media, and what counts in campaigns is the candidate's image. As Peter Hart, a well-known pollster, observed, "A campaign is not played out anymore so much for people or voters; it's played out for the media."[55] Assisted by their advisers, candidates plan steadily for ways to gain media attention, to establish good relationships with print and broadcast media, and to generate favorable newspaper stories or acquire a few seconds of exposure on television. An "old style" party leader of the 1930s or 1940s would be left incredulous at the scope of today's campaign activities that fall outside the purview of the party organization.

Television is central to major campaigns because "retail" politics has given way to "wholesale" politics.[56] Candidates no longer rely as much on precinct organization, and they have less time to stand at mill gates, march in parades, or visit an array of plants, businesses, farms, or halls. Another city or state (or airport) is on the day's agenda. As opportunities for personal visits with voters—including party, civic, labor, and business leaders—have diminished, emphasis has shifted to the wholesale politics of the television commercial, the fifteen- or thirty-second political spot. The mediating function of local leaders, reflected in their assessments of candidates and their interpretations of issues for rank-and-file voters, has atrophied in the face of television dominance.

In short, *candidate-centered* campaigns have replaced party-centered campaigns. Nowhere is the campaign apparatus of the parties as important as the personal organizations of individual candidates. Candidates—for minor offices and major ones, incumbents and challengers—all have their own organizations for managing the activities of campaigns. Within these units the key decisions are made on campaign strategies, issues, worker recruitment, voter mobilization, and the raising and spending of funds. Candidates often hire campaign management firms, public relations specialists, and political consultants to assist them. These professionals conduct public opinion surveys; prepare films and advertising; raise money; buy radio and television time; write speeches; provide computer analyses of voting behavior; and develop strategies, issues, and images. Less and less of campaign management is left to chance, hunch, or the party organizations.

Candidate-centered campaigns revolve around candidate-centered fundraising. Typically, House candidates obtain about half of their funds from individual contributors, whereas Senate candidates receive almost three-fifths of their funds from this source. Political action committees (PACs) rank next in importance. House incumbents in 2000 received 45 percent of all their "hard money" campaign funds from PACs, and Senate incumbents received 22 percent.[57] In addition to these regulated donations, interest groups can use independent expenditures in campaigns to assist federal candidates. Under the Federal Election Campaign Act passed in 1971 and amended several times since, limits are placed on the amount of money an individual or PAC can give to a federal candidate. But no limit exists on the amount of money that supporters of federal candidates can spend to aid their campaigns as long as the funds are spent *independently*—that is, without contact with the candidates or their campaign organizations.

As a result, groups of all kinds spend heavily, especially in media advertising, opposing as well as supporting presidential and congressional candidates. In the 2000 general election, independent expenditures by PACs exceeded $21 million, more than double that spent in 1996. About 70 percent was allocated to congressional races.[58] The intense involvement of groups in campaigns has changed the nation's political ambiance and its political structures, serving to promote the independence of candidates and officeholders from party controls while making them more reliant on interest groups and, presumably, more sensitive to their claims.

Twenty or thirty years ago, most observers felt that these changes signaled the end of parties. David Broder's 1972 book, *The Party's Over*, captured the conventional wisdom.[59] Reports of the death of party, however, turned out to be greatly exaggerated. Parties have redefined themselves in ways that increased their relevance. Instead of relying on the physical labor of party workers to turn out votes, parties now rely on capital. That is, they compete in a candidate-centered world by using their money and other resources. Nowhere is this clearer than in the raising and spending of "soft money." Just a decade ago, the major parties raised a mere $86 million for "party building activities." In the 1999–2000 election cycle, the parties raised a whopping $495 million. Although legislation enacted in 2002 may have effectively banned soft money, both parties nearly doubled hard money receipts over the last decade as well. Moreover, by indexing the limits on hard money contributions to the parties for inflation, these receipts stand to increase dramatically in the future. As a result, parties will continue to play a major role in a substantial number of races.

Along with stronger national party organizations, party responsibility in Congress is more pronounced, with a substantial increase in the percentage of party-line votes over the last two decades. The objections of Ralph Nader notwithstanding, Republicans and Democrats today stake out increasingly clear positions on issues across the political spectrum, from abortion to the environment to Social Security to tax policy to the regulation of business. As a result, ordinary citizens are more likely to think about politics in terms of the major parties. The party is far from over. It is simply being driven by a different beat.

NOTES

1. Consider the development and components of a party model based on the idea that the only standard useful in evaluating the vitality of American parties is simply the ability of the party to win office. Using this standard, Joseph Schlesinger argues that the major parties are healthier now than they were in the past. See his "On the Theory of Party Organization," *Journal of Politics* 46 (May 1984): 369–400.

2. E. E. Schattschneider, *Party Government* (New York: Holt, Rinehart and Winston, 1942), 1.

3. Ibid., 37.

4. Leon Epstein, *Political Parties in Western Democracies* (New York: Praeger, 1967), 9.

5. Edmund Burke, *Works*, vol. I (London: G. Bell and Sons, 1897), 375.

6. Anthony Downs, *An Economic Theory of Democracy* (New York: Harper, 1957).

7. V. O. Key Jr., *Politics, Parties, and Pressure Groups* (New York: Crowell, 1964), 200–201.

8. Schattschneider, *Party Government*, 1.

9. Agreement among students of political parties on the nature of party functions, their relative significance, and the consequences of functional performance for the political system is far from complete. Frank J. Sorauf points out that among the functions attributed to American parties have been simplifying political issues and alternatives, producing automatic majorities, recruiting political leadership and personnel, organizing minorities and opposition, moderating and compromising political conflict, organizing the machinery of government, promoting political consensus and legitimacy, and bridging the separation of powers. The principal difficulty with listings of this sort, according to Sorauf, is that "it involves making functional statements about party activity without necessarily relating them to functional requisites or needs of the system." He suggests that, at this stage of research on parties, emphasis

should be given to the activities performed by parties, thus avoiding the confusion arising from the lack of clarity about the meaning of function, the absence of consensus on functional categories, and the problem of measuring the performance of functions. See his instructive essay, "Political Parties and Political Analysis," in *The American Party Systems: Stages of Political Development*, ed. William Nisbet Chambers and Walter Dean Burnham (New York: Oxford, 1967), 33–53.

10. In about four-fifths of the states, judges are chosen in some form of partisan or nonpartisan election. In the remaining states they come to office through appointment. A few states employ the so-called Missouri Plan of judge selection, under which the governor makes judicial appointments from a list of names supplied by a nonpartisan judicial commission composed of judges, lawyers, and laypeople. Under this plan, designed to take judges out of politics, each judge, after a trial period, runs for reelection without opposition; voters may vote either to retain or to remove the judge from office. If a majority of voters casts affirmative ballots, the judge is continued in office for a full term; if the vote is negative, the judge loses office and the governor makes another appointment in the same manner. But even under this plan, the governor may give preference to aspirants of his own party. Irrespective of the system used to choose judges, party leaders and party interest will nearly always be involved.

11. Sandy Maisel, "American Political Parties: Still Central to a Functioning Democracy?" in *American Political Parties: Decline or Resurgence?* ed. Jeffrey E. Cohen, Richard Fleisher, and Paul Kantor (Washington, D.C.: CQ Press, 2001). Also see Cornelius P. Cotter, James L. Gibson, John F. Bibby, and Robert J. Huckshorn, *Party Organization in American Politics* (New York: Praeger, 1984); and James L. Gibson, Cornelius P. Cotter, John F. Bibby, and Robert J. Huckshorn, "Whither the Local Parties? A Cross-Sectional and Longitudinal Analysis of the Strength of Party Organizations," *American Journal of Political Science* 29 (February 1985): 139–160. For additional evidence on the vitality of local parties, see Kay Lawson, Gerald Pomper, and Maureen Moakley, "Local Party Activists and Electoral Linkage," *American Politics Quarterly* 14 (October 1986): 345–375.

12. For a similar set of findings, see Thomas A. Kazee and Mary C. Thornberry, "Where's the Party? Congressional Candidate Recruitment and American Party Organizations," *Western Political Quarterly* 43 (March 1990): 61–80. For a discussion of the role of the national parties in recruiting candidates for Congress, see Paul S. Herrnson, *Party Campaigning in the 1980s* (Cambridge, Mass.: Harvard University Press, 1988), 48–56.

13. Theodore J. Lowi, "Party, Policy, and Constitution in America," in *The American Party Systems*, ed. Chambers and Burnham, 263.

14. See a discussion of the party role in "the aggregation of interests" in Gerald M. Pomper, "The Contributions of Political Parties to American Democracy," in *Party Renewal in America: Theory and Practice*, ed. Gerald M. Pomper (New York: Praeger Special Studies, 1980), 5–7.

15. Few facts about the political participation of Americans are of greater significance than those that reveal its social class bias. A disproportionate number of the people who are highly active in politics are drawn from the upper reaches of the social order, from among those who hold higher-status occupations, are more affluent, and are better educated. Citizens from lower socioeconomic levels constitute only about 10 percent of the participants who are highly active in politics. See Sidney Verba and Norman H. Nie, *Participation in America: Political Democracy and Social Equality* (New York: Harper and Row, 1972), especially chapter 20.

16. Harvey Fergusson, *People and Power* (New York: Morrow, 1947), 101–102.

17. Consider the development and components of a party model based on the idea that the only standard useful in evaluating the vitality of American parties is simply the ability of the party to win office. Using this standard, Joseph Schlesinger argues

that the major parties are healthier now than ever in the past. See his "On the Theory of Party Organization," *Journal of Politics* 46 (May 1984): 369–400.

18. This proposition is debatable. For the counterposition—one that stresses the capacity of parties to shape themselves—see Austin Ranney, *Curing the Mischiefs of Faction: Party Reform in America* (Berkeley: University of California Press, 1975), especially chapter 1; and Jeane Jordan Kirkpatrick, *Dismantling the Parties: Reflections on Party Reform and Party Decomposition* (Washington, D.C.: American Enterprise Institute for Public Policy Research, 1978). For a wide-ranging analysis of the proposition presented in the text, see Robert Harmel and Kenneth Janda, *Parties and Their Environments* (New York: Longman, 1982).

19. For a study of ideological polarization in state party systems, see Robert D. Brown and Gerald C. Wright, "Elections and State Party Polarization," *American Politics Quarterly* 20 (October 1992): 411–426. Some states, such as Utah and California, are highly polarized (liberal Democrats versus conservative Republicans), whereas in other states, such as Louisiana and Arizona, there is little difference in the ideology of the party coalitions (both are conservative). In states in which the parties are ideologically polarized, there is less split-ticket voting, fewer party defections, less vote swing, and less volatility in election results.

20. David R. Mayhew, *Placing Parties in American Politics* (Princeton, N.J.: Princeton University Press, 1986).

21. David E. Price, *Bringing Back the Parties* (Washington, D.C.: CQ Press, 1984), particularly chapter 5.

22. Mayhew, *Placing Parties in American Politics,* particularly chapters 2 and 7.

23. Single-member districts clearly play a significant role in protecting the American major parties from the incursions of minor parties. What would happen if American states and communities were to adopt proportional representation (PR) elections, which require the use of multimember districts? For an enlightening essay on how the introduction of PR might affect the two-party system, see Douglas J. Amy, "Proportional Representation and the Future of the American Party System," *American Review of Politics* 16 (fall–winter 1995): 371–383.

24. For studies of the effects of divisive primaries on party unity and election outcomes, see Donald B. Johnson and James R. Gibson, "The Divisive Primary Revisited: Party Activists in Iowa," *American Political Science Review* 68 (March 1974): 67–77; Patrick J. Kenney and Tom W. Rice, "The Relationship between Divisive Primaries and General Election Outcomes," *American Journal of Political Science* 31 (February 1987): 31–44; Patrick J. Kenney, "Sorting Out the Effects of Primary Divisiveness in Congressional and Senatorial Elections," *Western Political Quarterly* 41 (September 1988): 765–777; James I. Lengle, Diane Owen, and Molly W. Sonner, "Divisive Nominating Mechanisms and Democratic Party Electoral Prospects," *Journal of Politics* 57 (May 1995): 370–383; and Paul S. Herrnson and James G. Gimpel, "District Conditions and Primary Divisiveness in Congressional Elections," *Political Research Quarterly* 48 (March 1995): 117–150.

25. David Dodenhoff and Kenneth Goldstein, "Resources, Racehorses, and Rules: Nominations in the 1990s," in *The Parties Respond: Changes in American Parties and Campaigns,* 3d ed., ed. Sandy Maisel (Boulder, Colo.: Westview Press, 1998).

26. Press release, Federal Election Commission, November 3, 2000.

27. Lucian W. Pye and Sidney Verba, eds., *Political Culture and Political Development* (Princeton, N.J.: Princeton University Press, 1965), 513.

28. Jack Dennis, "Support for the Party System by the Mass Public," *American Political Science Review* 60 (September 1966): 600–615. Also see Dennis, "Changing Support for the American Party System," in *Paths to Political Reform,* ed. William J. Crotty (Lexington, Mass.: Heath, 1980), 35–66; and Dennis, "Public Support for the Party

System, 1964–1984" (Paper delivered at the annual meeting of the American Political Science Association, Washington, D.C., August 28–31, 1986), 19. Also see Thomas M. Konda and Lee Sigelman, "Public Evaluations of the American Parties, 1952–1984," *Journal of Politics* 49 (August 1987): 814–829.

29. See *The American Enterprise* (January/February 1993): 107–108.

30. A system of "responsible parties" would be characterized by centralized, unified, and disciplined parties committed to the execution of programs and promises offered at elections and held accountable by the voters for their performance. For an analysis of this model, see chapter 7.

31. ABC News–*Washington Post* Poll, August 1, 1996.

32. Larry M. Bartels, "Partisanship and Voting Behavior, 1952–1996," *American Journal of Political Science* 44 (January 2000): 35–50.

33. David W. Rohde, *Parties and Leaders in the Post-Reform House* (Chicago: University of Chicago Press, 1991).

34. Marc J. Hetherington, "Resurgent Mass Partisanship: The Role of Elite Polarization," *American Political Science Review* 95 (September 2001): 619–631. Similar treatments of party resurgence in the electorate include David G. Lawrence, "On the Resurgence of Party Identification in the 1990s"; Richard Fleisher and Jon R. Bond, "Evidence of Increasing Polarization Among Ordinary Citizens," in Cohen, Fleisher, and Kantor, eds., *American Political Parties*; and Geoffrey C. Layman and Thomas M. Carsey, "Party Polarization and 'Conflict Extension' in the American Electorate," *American Journal of Political Science* 46 (October 2002): 786–802.

35. On income, see Jeffrey Stonecash, *Class and Party in American Politics* (Boulder, Colo.: Westview, 2000), for a discussion of the increase in class-based voting in the 1990s.

36. Herbert Agar, *The Price of Union* (Boston: Houghton Mifflin, 1950), xiv.

37. Two studies that trace the growing importance of the national party are Charles H. Longley, "National Party Renewal," and John F. Bibby, "Party Renewal in the National Republican Party," in Pomper, ed., *Party Renewal in America*, 69–86, 102–115.

38. Press release, Federal Election Commission, May 15, 2001.

39. *Congressional Quarterly Weekly Report*, February 16, 1974, 352.

40. *Congressional Quarterly Weekly Report*, January 14, 1978, 61.

41. *New York Times*, March 27, 1997.

42. Press release, Federal Election Commission, May 15, 2001.

43. See Cornelius P. Cotter and Bernard C. Hennessy, *Politics without Power: The National Party Committees* (New York: Atherton Press, 1964), 67–80. The authors see the roles of the national chair as "image-maker, hell-raiser, fund-raiser, campaign manager, and administrator."

44. F. Christopher Arterton, "Political Money and Party Strength," in *The Future of American Political Parties*, ed. Fleishman, 105.

45. *Congressional Quarterly Weekly Report*, January 14, 1978, 58.

46. The chair of a congressional campaign committee is a major political plum. The chair has numerous opportunities to help party candidates get elected and, more important, to help incumbents get reelected. The chair concentrates on fund-raising, "signs the checks" for the party's candidates, and inevitably gains the gratitude of winners.

47. Press release, Federal Election Commission, May 15, 2001.

48. For a study of the growing importance of state legislative campaign committees in New York, see Diana Dwyer and Jeffrey M. Stonecash, "Where's the Party? Changing State Party Organizations," *American Politics Quarterly* 20 (July 1992): 326–344.

49. For an examination of the strength of party organizations at the state level, see John F. Bibby, Cornelius P. Cotter, James L. Gibson, and Robert J. Huckshorn, "Trends in Party Organizational Strength, 1960–1980," *International Political Science Review* 4 (January 1983): 21–27; and "Assessing Party Organizational Strength," *American Journal of Political Science* 27 (May 1983): 193–222.

50. Lewis Bowman and G. R. Boynton, "Activities and Role Definitions of Grass-roots Party Officials," *Journal of Politics* 28 (February 1966): 121–143. Also see Lee S. Weinberg, "Stability and Change among Pittsburgh Precinct Politicians," *Social Science* (winter 1975): 10–16.

51. Barbara C. Burrell, "Local Political Party Committees, Task Performance and Organizational Vitality," *Western Political Quarterly* 39 (March 1986): 48–66.

52. Michael Margolis and Raymond E. Owen, "From Organization to Personalism: A Note on the Transmogrification of the Local Political Party," *Polity* 18 (winter 1985): 313–328.

53. See Sandy Maisel, "American Political Parties: Still Central to a Functioning Democracy?" in Cohen, Fleisher, and Kantor, eds., *American Political Parties*; and Gibson, Cotter, Bibby, and Huckshorn, "Whither the Local Parties?" 139–160.

54. John P. Frendreis, James L. Gibson, and Laura L. Vertz, "The Electoral Relevance of Local Party Organizations," *American Political Science Review* 84 (March 1990): 225–235. Indicators of the structural strength of a party organization include the presence of a constitution and by-laws, a complete set of officers, an active chair, bimonthly meetings, a year-round office, staff, and a budget.

55. Quoted in Albert R. Hunt, "The Media and Presidential Campaigns," in *Elections American Style*, ed. A. James Reichley (Washington, D.C.: Brookings Institution, 1987), 53.

56. See column by R. W. Apple Jr. in the *New York Times*, February 11, 1988.

57. Press release, Federal Election Commission, May 15, 2001.

58. Ibid.

59. David S. Broder, *The Party's Over: The Failure of Politics in America* (New York: Harper & Row, 1972).

2 AMERICAN PARTIES: CHARACTERISTICS AND COMPETITION

THE MAJOR PARTIES ARE FIRM LANDMARKS on the American political scene. In existence for nearly 175 years, the parties have made important contributions to the development and maintenance of a democratic political culture and to democratic institutions and practices. In essence, the parties form the principal institution for popular control of government, and this achievement is remarkable given the limitations under which they function. This chapter examines the chief characteristics and the competitiveness of the American party system.

Characteristics of Parties

Viewed at some distance, the party organizations may appear to be neatly ordered and hierarchical—committees are piled, one atop the other, from the precinct to the national level, conveying the impression that power flows from the top to the bottom. In reality, however, the American party is not nearly so hierarchical. State and local organizations have substantial independence in most party matters. The practices that state and local parties follow, the candidates they recruit or help to recruit, the campaign money they raise, the auxiliary groups they form and re-form, the innovations they introduce, the organized interests to which they respond, the campaign strategies and issues they create, and, most important, the policy orientations of the candidates who run under their labels—all bear the distinctive imprints of local and state political cultures, leaders, traditions, and interests.[1] Rather than being top-down organizations, parties reflect the bottom-up differences between members. As a result, American parties, which value winning elections over everything else, have strong incentives to be moderate and inclusive, in an attempt to knit together as large a coalition as possible.

Dispersed Power

The primary characteristic of American political parties is decentralization—that is, their power is more pronounced at the state and local levels than at the national level. This is largely a function of the legal and constitutional characteristics of the American political system. American parties must find their place within a federal system where powers and responsibilities lie with fifty states as well as with the national government. The basic responsibility for the design of the electoral system in which the parties compete is given to the states, not to the nation. Not surprisingly, party organizations have been molded by the electoral laws under which they contest for power. State and local power centers have naturally developed around the thousands of governmental units and elective offices found in the states and the localities. The typical officeholder, with his distinctive constituency (frequently a safe district), own coterie of supporters, and own channels to campaign money, has a remarkable amount of freedom in defining his relationship to his party. His and the organization's well-being are not identical; it is not too much to say that officeholders are continuously evaluating party claims and objectives in light of their own career aspirations. When the party's claims and the officeholder's aspirations diverge, the party ordinarily loses out. A federal system, with numerous elective offices, opens up an extraordinary range of political choices to subnational parties and, especially, to individual candidates.

For all of its significance for the party system and the distinctiveness of American politics, however, federalism is but one of several explanations for the fragmentation of party power. Another constitutional provision—separation of powers—also contributes to this condition. A frequent by-product of separation of powers is a truncated party majority—when one party controls one or both houses of the legislature and the other controls the executive. This arrangement has most often been the case on the federal level since the 1960s. Also, divided party control is quite common at the state level. At worst, the result is a dreary succession of narrow partisan clashes between the branches; at best, a clarification of differences between the parties occasionally may come about. At no time, however, does a truncated majority help in the development and maintenance of party responsibility for a program of public policy.

A third factor that helps to disperse party power is the method used to make nominations. It was noted earlier that nominations for national office are sorted out and settled at the local level, ordinarily without interference from national party functionaries. One of the principal supports of local control over nominations is the direct primary. Its use virtually guarantees that candidates for national office will be tailored to the measure of local specifications. Consider this analysis by Austin Ranney and Willmoore Kendall:

> A party's *national* leaders can affect the kind of representatives and senators who come to Washington bearing the party's label only by enlisting the support of the

state and local party organizations concerned; and they cannot be sure of doing so even then. Assume, for example, that the local leaders have decided to support the national leaders in an attempt to block the renomination of a maverick congressman, and are doing all they can. There is still nothing to prevent the rank and file, who may admire the incumbent's "independence," from ignoring the leaders' wishes and renominating him. The direct primary, in other words, is *par excellence* a system for maintaining *local* control of nominations; and as long as American localities continue to be so different from one another in economic interests, culture, and political attitudes, the national parties are likely to retain their present ideological heterogeneity and their tendency to show differing degrees of cohesion from issue to issue.[2]

Fourth, the distribution of power within the parties is affected by patterns of campaign finance. Few, if any, campaign resources are more important than money. A large proportion of the political money donated in any year is given directly to the campaign organizations of individual candidates instead of to the party organizations. Candidates with access to campaign money are automatically in a strong position vis-à-vis the party organization. Not having to rely heavily on the party for campaign funds, candidates can stake out their independence from it. Whether candidates can remain independent from the interest groups that pour money into their campaigns is another question.

Fifth, a pervasive spirit of localism dominates American politics and adds to the decentralization of political power. Local interests find expression in national politics in countless ways. Even the presidential nominating process may become critical for the settlement of local and state political struggles. A prominent political leader who aligns with the candidate who eventually wins the presidential nomination, particularly if his support comes early in the race, can put new life into his own career. He gains access to the nominee and increased visibility. If his party wins the presidency, he may be offered an appointment in the new administration. Or if he chooses to run for a major public office, he is likely to secure the support of the president. National conventions settle more than national matters.

Congress has always shown a remarkable hospitality to the idea that governmental power should be decentralized. A great deal of the major legislation that has been passed in recent decades, for example, has been designed to make state and local governments participants in the development and implementation of public policies—arrangements from which locally based political organizations profit. A basic explanation for Congress's defense of state and local governments lies in the backgrounds of the members themselves. Many were elected to state or local office prior to their election to Congress and are steeped in local lore, think in local terms, meet frequently with local representatives, and work for local advantage. Their steady attention to the local dimensions of national policy helps to safeguard their own careers and to promote the interests of those local politicians who look to Washington for assistance in solving community problems. The former Speaker of the House, Thomas P. ("Tip") O'Neill Jr. (D-Mass.), had it right when he said, "All politics is local."[3]

Finally, the fragmentation of party power owes much to the growing importance of outsiders in the political process. Chief among them are the media, campaign management firms, and political interest groups. Today, virtually all candidates for important offices hire expert consultants to organize their campaigns, to shape their strategies, and to mold their images. And they strain for media coverage that presents them in a favorable light. What counts, candidates know, is how the voters perceive them.

As for political interest groups, their role in campaigns, particularly in their financing, has become much more important than it was in the past. In 2000 PACs contributed about $245 million to the campaigns of candidates for Congress—$44 million more than in 1996 and nearly eight times as much as they gave in 1978. Interest group money has become a major force in American politics, particularly in congressional elections. And in all likelihood, interest group influence on officeholders has increased.[4] Indeed, many critics of the campaign finance system blame it for the string of corporate scandals that came to light in 2002, including Enron, WorldCom, Global Crossing, and Tyco. All were major political contributors who sought and received from Congress lax federal regulation of their industries' business and accounting practices.

The Power of Officeholders

Writing in the 1960s, James M. Burns sketched the organizational strength of state parties:

> At no level, except in a handful of industrial states, do state parties have the attributes of organization. They lack extensive dues-paying memberships; hence, they number many captains and sergeants but few foot soldiers. They do a poor job of raising money for themselves as organizations, or even for their candidates. They lack strong and imaginative leadership of their own. They cannot control their most vital function—the nomination of their candidates. Except in a few states, such as Ohio, Connecticut, and Michigan, our parties are essentially collections of small cliques and they are often shunted aside by the politicians who understand political power. Most of the state parties are at best mere jousting grounds for embattled politicians; at worst they simply do not exist, as in the case of Republicans in the rural South or Democrats in the rural Midwest.[5]

Is the situation different today? It is, in some respects. Recent research has shown that the parties are stronger organizationally than they were in the 1960s. At the state level, for example, most parties now maintain permanent state headquarters in the state capital with professional staffs. State party budgets have grown in size, and systematic fund-raising by leaders and staff has become a more important function. Party organizations are better equipped to provide candidates with services, including research assistance and campaign money. They are also more effective in recruiting candidates for public office in many jurisdictions. Organizational vitality is particularly evident in the Republican party. About three fourths of all Republican state parties and one fourth of all Democratic state parties can be classified as "strong" or "moderately strong" from an organizational standpoint.[6] But this still leaves a number of states in which at least one party is weak and inconspicuous.

Strong everywhere, however, are independent candidate and officeholder organizations. They dominate the campaign and election process. Candidates and officeholders—aided by hired consultants and assorted handlers—at all organizational levels develop strategies and issues, raise funds, recruit workers, interact with interest groups, assemble coalitions, cultivate the media, make news, and mobilize voters. The party organization may facilitate campaigns by providing useful services to the candidates, but that is usually the extent of its involvement. Candidates shape their own campaigns and win largely on their own efforts and on their own terms. The perspective of Barbara G. Salmore and Stephen A. Salmore is instructive.

> Technology is the development most responsible for ending party primacy in campaigns. . . . What made the advent of television and the computer unique was that they provided candidates everywhere with an effective alternative means of getting information about themselves to the voters. Newspapers, magazines, and radio paled in comparison with what television offered—a powerful combination of visual and aural messages. Candidates could enter voters' homes and give party organizations competition they had never had before. . . . Once candidates learned that they could independently compete with party organizations and that they had the direct primary as the vehicle to do it, why should they give up their independence and control of their messages to the party organizations?[7]

Coalitional in Nature

The American party is much less a collection of individuals than it is a collection of social interests and groups. In the words of Maurice Duverger, "A party is not a community but a collection of communities, a union of small groups dispersed throughout the country."[8] Functioning within a vastly heterogeneous society, the major parties have naturally assumed a coalitional form. Groups of all kinds—social, economic, religious, and ethnic—are organized to press demands on the political order. In the course of defending or advancing their interests, they contribute substantial energy to the political process—by generating innovations, posing alternative policies, recruiting and endorsing candidates, conducting campaigns, and so on. No party seriously contesting for office could ignore the constellation of groups in American political life.

Traditionally, each party has had relatively distinct followings in the electorate, a characteristic that is illustrated in Table 2-1. The urban working classes, union families, African Americans, Jewish Americans, persons at the lower end of the educational scale, and the poor have been mainstays of the Democratic party since the 1930s. Until relatively recently, southerners and Catholics also played major roles. In counterpoise, the Republican coalition has had a disproportionate number of supporters from such groups as big business, industry, farmers, small-town and rural dwellers, whites, Protestants, upper-income and better-educated persons, nonunion families, and "old stock" Americans. More

Table 2-1   The Most Loyal Groups in the Party Coalitions

Groups	Presidential election year				
	1984	1988	1992	1996	2000
Percentage points more Democratic than the nation as a whole					
African Americans	50	41	40	35	42
Jews	27	19	37	29	31
Hispanics	22	24	18	23	15
Unmarried women	10	12	10	13	15
Union households	13	12	12	10	11
Percentage points more Republican than the nation as a whole					
White fundamentalist or evangelical Christians	19	27	23	24	32
Southern whites	12	14	11	15	19
High income	10	8	10	10	6
Whites	5	6	2	5	6

Source: Developed from data in Voter News Service national exit polls, as reported in *New York Times,* November 10, 1996, and November 9, 2000.

Note: High income in 2000 is defined as $100,000 and over. Of the total vote in 2000, African Americans made up 10 percent; Hispanics, 7 percent; Jews, 4 percent; unmarried women, 21 percent; and union households, 26 percent. Whites cast 81 percent of the total vote.

recently, Christian fundamentalists have also supported the GOP in disproportionate numbers. These group inclinations make coalition politics a major feature of successful election campaigns.

Today, these coalitions are in flux, particularly on the Democratic side. For example, in the South, the Republicans have made major gains and, in many ways, dominate the region on the federal level. Whereas 1948 Republican presidential candidate Thomas Dewey failed to appear on the ballot in several southern states, George W. Bush carried every state in the former Confederacy in 2000. Similarly, Republicans went from a mere 6 percent of the House and Senate seats in this region in 1953 to nearly 60 percent after the 2000 election.[9]

Race is the primary cause of this southern realignment. Under John F. Kennedy and Lyndon Johnson, the Democratic party embraced racial integration and voting rights for African Americans. Many southern whites, uncomfortable with this policy course, bolted to Republican Barry Goldwater's presidential campaign in 1964, which promised states' rights to decide these issues. Indeed, the five Deep South states Goldwater won were the only states he carried other than his home state of Arizona. In 1968 an even greater number of southerners shunned Democratic nominee Hubert Humphrey for American Independent party candidate George Wallace, the racist governor of Alabama. In eight straight elections from 1972 to 2000, southern white voters cast a plurality of their votes for the Republican candidate. Only Jimmy Carter of Georgia, with the aid of many southern blacks, ran a stronger campaign in the region than he did nationally.

The voting behavior of certain religious groups has changed in recent years as well, again to the detriment of Democrats. With one of their own, John F. Kennedy, at the top of the Democratic ticket in 1960, Catholics voted 28 percentage points more Democratic than the electorate as a whole (78 percent to 50 percent). Protestants, in contrast, voted 12 percentage points more Republican than the national average (62 percent to 50 percent). Even in 1964, with Johnson replacing Kennedy as the Democrats' standard-bearer, Catholics voted strongly Democratic (76 percent as contrasted with Johnson's national average of 61 percent). Since then, however, Catholic support for Democratic presidential candidates has declined. In fact, white Catholics cast a solid majority (54 percent) of their ballots for George W. Bush.[10]

Two reasons help explain this change. First, Catholics are no longer as economically distinct as they were generations ago. As new immigrants for much of the early twentieth century, Catholics tended to be disproportionately poor, making the pro–welfare state Democratic party a more attractive option for them. Second, the politicization of abortion may dispose Catholics to vote Republican, since the GOP is strongly pro-life. The Republicans' recent emphasis on "family values" issues may also hold a particular attraction for certain Catholic voters as well as for Protestant fundamentalists.

Although Catholics have moved away from the Democrats, Jews have not. Indeed, the most distinctive vote of all religious groups today is the Jewish vote. In recent presidential elections, Democratic candidates have been able to count on about 80 percent support from Jewish voters.[11]

Moreover, some of the trends in the coalitions actually favor the Democrats. According to the most recent census, the fastest growing racial and ethnic groups in the United States are Latinos and Asians. Since both of these groups, along with African Americans, identify disproportionately with the Democratic party, the party has a significant opportunity to carve out a majority of supporters in the coming years—provided, of course, that Republicans fail to make inroads into these groups. Racial and ethnic groups are now dispersed much more widely throughout the United States than they were in the past, a fact that makes it difficult to predict their impact in elections.

American parties are fragile because they are coalitions. At times, they seem to be held together by nothing more than generality, personality, and promise. Perhaps what is surprising, all things considered, is that they hold together as well as they do.

Moderate and Inclusive

Because their key role is to knit together coalitions of groups that may have conflicting goals, American parties tend to be moderate and inclusive. In that sense, they are "catchall" parties in which all but the most extreme and intractable elements in society can find a place and, in the process, stake a claim to a piece of the action. All groups are invited to support the party, and in some measure all do. Almost everything about the major party at election time represents a triumph for those who press for accommodation in American politics. Platforms and candidate speeches, offering something to virtually everyone, provide the hard evidence that the parties attempt to be inclusive rather than exclusive in their appeals and to draw in a wide rather than a narrow band of voters. "No matter how devoted a party leadership may be to its bedrock elements," V. O. Key Jr. observed, "it attempts to picture itself as a gifted synthesizer of concord among the elements of society. A party must act as if it were all the people rather than some of them; it must fiercely deny that it speaks for a single interest."[12]

The inclusivity of the major American parties means that they occupy virtually all of the political space in the political system. Minor parties, then, are forced to search for distinctiveness. Some fashion narrow appeals; others press bizarre or hopeless causes; and still others maneuver only at the ideological fringes, seeking to address extreme left-wing or right-wing audiences. Their dilemma is that only a relative handful of voters are at each ideological pole and only a few will be attracted to a narrow or single-issue appeal. The net result is that most minor parties struggle to secure candidates, financing, media attention, and credibility. The major parties' inclusiveness causes minor parties to struggle just to stay in business.

The Founders established an intricate system of divided powers, checks and balances, and auxiliary precautions to reduce the government's vulnerability to factions. The "Madisonian system"—separation of powers, staggered terms of office, bicameralism, federalism, life appointments for federal judges, and fixed terms of office for the president and members of Congress, among other things— makes it difficult for any group (faction or party) to gain firm control of the political system. Today's parties qualify as James Madison's factions, but with an unexpected twist. They are in no way a factional threat. Their inclusivity and moderation represent at least as great an obstacle to factional domination of government as do formal constitutional arrangements. Because the major parties include all kinds of interests, they are not free to favor a single interest or a small cluster of interests to the exclusion of others. Standing party policies are an expression of earlier settlements among divergent interests. Virtually every new policy can be contested by interested party elements. Every affected interest expects a hearing and bargaining occurs as a matter of course, usually leading to accommodations that can at least be tolerated by most participants. The broad consequences, ordinarily, are first, that policy making is a slow process, and second, that policy changes are introduced incrementally. The parties' moderation ordinarily means that no one wins completely and no one loses completely—a consequence of which is the public often has difficulty deciding which party to single out for credit and which to blame. (See Figure 2-1.)

Ideologically Heterogeneous

To win elections and gain power is the unabashedly practical aim of the major party. Given that the United States is such a large and diverse country, parties need to build coalitions such that the policy goals of the groups and candidates

Figure 2-1   Moderate Parties and Policy Making

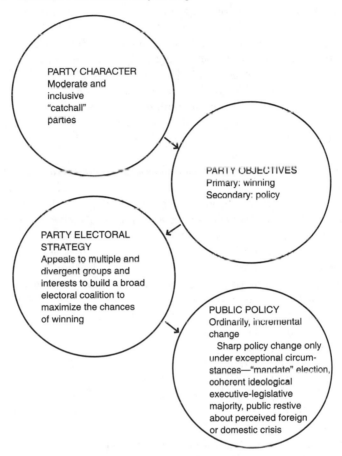

PARTY CHARACTER
Moderate and
inclusive
"catchall"
parties

PARTY OBJECTIVES
Primary: winning
Secondary: policy

PARTY ELECTORAL
STRATEGY
Appeals to multiple and
divergent groups and
interests to build a broad
electoral coalition to
maximize the chances
of winning

PUBLIC POLICY
Ordinarily, incremental
change
   Sharp policy change only
under exceptional circum-
stances—"mandate" election,
coherent ideological
executive-legislative
majority, public restive
about perceived foreign
or domestic crisis

in a given party are subordinated to their capacity to contribute to electoral victory. The natural outcome of a campaign strategy designed to attract all groups (and to repel none) is that the party's ideology is not brought into sharp focus. This means that, after elections are contested, parties are represented by people whose ideologies diverge to some degree.

One way to consider the nation's ideological heterogeneity and the challenges that it provides the parties is to examine the Americans for Democratic Action (ADA) ratings of members of the U.S. Senate. This group, well known for its identification with liberal causes, rates legislators based on how often they vote in accordance with the ADA's liberal principles. Those who support increases in government spending, closing corporate tax loopholes, protection for the environment, and raising the minimum wage, for example, receive high scores from the ADA, and those who do not receive low scores.

Figure 2-2 displays a summary of ADA scores for U.S. senators from the year leading up to the 2000 election. First, it is important to note that the parties are quite distinct ideologically. The average Democrat voted with the ADA 85 percent of the time while the average Republican voted with the ADA a mere 7 percent of the time. The parties today are certainly not Tweedledum and Tweedledee, as Ralph Nader suggested in his 2000 presidential campaign. Even for casual observers, party differences are not difficult to detect.

Nevertheless, important cleavages within the parties are quite apparent. Two of the most distinctive are regional: the Northeast (measured here as the eleven states running from Maine in the north to Maryland in the south) is known for its liberalism and the South (measured here as the eleven states of the former Confederacy plus Oklahoma and Kentucky) for its conservatism. While most Republican senators have ADA scores of either 5 or 0, northeastern Republicans score an average of 28, significantly to the left of most members of their party. Similarly, northeastern Democrats have an average ADA score of 88 compared with 75 for southern Democrats. Party leaders have to balance the wishes of these wings, especially on close votes.

Over the last two decades, however, intraparty divisions have become less confounding. Conservative southern Democrats and liberal northeastern Republicans are dying breeds. In 1986 the Democrats held fourteen of the twenty-six Senate seats in the Deep and border South. Such a large bloc of mostly conservative members had a moderating influence on the party. Their seniority, moreover, boosted their power well beyond their numbers. After the 2002 election, however, only nine southern Democrats remained in the Senate. An analysis of the Northeast turns up a similar pattern. Whereas eleven of the twenty-two were Republicans in 1986, only seven remained after the 2002 election. Thus, in Congress, ideological heterogeneity is becoming less and less of a problem for party

Figure 2-2   Democratic and Republican Support of Americans for Democratic Action (ADA) Positions, by Region, 106th Congress, First Session

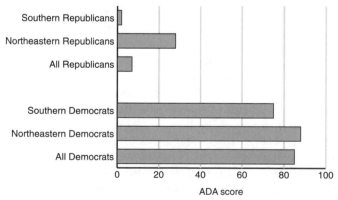

Source: www.adaction.org.

leaders, as conservatives increasingly dominate the Republican party and liberals the Democratic party.

In policy terms, this means that the parties' positions on key issues are more transparent today than they have been for generations. Democratic members of Congress and Democratic congressional candidates are much more likely to support social welfare legislation and an expanded role for the federal government, for example, than are Republican officeholders and Republican candidates. Programs to advance minority rights, make available federal funds for public education, improve the lot of low-income individuals and families, support family planning programs (including abortion counseling at federally funded clinics), provide medical care for the elderly, curtail different forms of defense spending, regulate business, and promote the interests of labor typically produce substantial disagreement between the parties, with almost all Democrats aligned on the liberal side and almost all Republicans aligned on the conservative side. The congressional parties do differ. Hence, even though some party members may seem to be marching to different drummers some of the time, most are usually playing the same tune.

An Interest Group

Although American parties are sometimes criticized for their cool detachment from important social and economic issues, the same cannot be said for their attitude toward a band of issues having high relevance for the party, *qua* party. Certain kinds of issues, or policy questions, that come before legislatures present the party with an opportunity to advance its interests as an organization—in much the same fashion as political interest groups' attempts to secure or block legislation that would improve or impair their fortunes. As E. E. Schattschneider wrote many years ago, within each party is both a "public" and a "private" personality.[13] The public dimension of the party is on display when larger questions of public policy are brought before the legislature. As often occurs on these questions, party lines fail to hold; factions ease away from the party; and biparty coalitions are born, empowered for the moment as the majority. The party's public appearance, in the judgment of many critics, leaves much to be desired. The fundamental flaw is that the party nominally in control of government, but torn by factionalism and fragmentation, cannot be held responsible by the public for its decisions. The problem is not that party unity collapses on all issues but that it collapses with sufficient frequency to make it less than a dependable agent for carrying out commitments made to the electorate. While this is less often the case today than it was twenty or thirty years ago, it is still a significant problem.

In sharp contrast is the private personality of the party. Although it would be an exaggeration to argue that the party is engaged in steady introspection, it is surely true, as Schattschneider has observed, that "the party knows its private mind better than it knows its public mind."[14] It has a sharp sense of where the best opportunities lie for partisan advantage and of the perils and pitfalls that can threaten or damage party interests. Numerous occasions arise for transmitting benefits to the party organization and its members. Patronage can be extracted from government at all levels. In some jurisdictions literally hundreds or thousands of jobs are available for distribution to party stalwarts. At the national level, "senatorial courtesy" guarantees that senators will have the dominant voice in the selection of candidates to fill various positions, such as district court judges and U.S. marshals. This custom calls on the president, before nominating a person for a position in a state, to consult with the senators of that state (if they belong to the same party as he does) to learn their preference for the position. If he should nominate someone objectionable to the senators of that state, the prospects are strong that the full Senate will reject the nominee, irrespective of his qualifications. On questions of this sort—those that touch the careers and political fortunes of members—party unity is both high and predictable.

Legislators have never won reputations for queuing up behind proposals that might limit maneuvering in the interest of their careers or their party's welfare. With only a few exceptions, for example, they have opposed plans to extend the merit system, to take judges out of politics, and to empower independent boards or commissions to assume responsibility for reapportionment and redistricting. There is a private side to such public questions—to extend the merit system is to cut back party patronage, to remove judges from the election process is to cut off a career avenue for legislators with their sights on the court, and to give a non-legislative commission control over redistricting is to run the risk of a major rearrangement of legislative districts and a resultant loss of offices. Legislators and the parties they represent take seriously their role as guardians of the welfare of the organization and the personal interests of its members. As a collectivity, the American party is most resourceful and cohesive when it is monitoring party business—and party business is about as likely to intrude on the great public questions as it is on those of narrow or parochial concern. Opportunities to advance the party cause—through debate, legislation, or investigations—are limited only by a failure of imagination.

Party Competition

Vigorous two-party competition in all political jurisdictions is clearly unattainable. Even when elections are competitive, as was the 2000 presidential contest, it does not mean that they are competitive everywhere. The American party system is in some places and at some times strongly two-party, and in other places and at other times, dominantly one-party. In some states and localities factional politics within one or both major parties is so pervasive and persistent as to suggest the presence of a multiple-party system. Competition between the parties is a condition not to be taken for granted, despite the popular tendency to bestow the two-party label on American politics.

Presidential Elections

Contests for the presidency provide the best single example of authentic two-party competition, particularly in recent decades.[15] The 2000 contest illustrates how close elections sometimes turn out; only about 500,000 votes separated the major party candidates out of more than 101 million votes cast. Indeed, with but three exceptions in all *two-party* presidential contests since 1940, the losing presidential candidate has received at least 45 percent of the popular vote; the exceptions occurred in 1964 (Barry Goldwater received 39 percent of the vote), 1972 (George McGovern, 38 percent), and 1984 (Walter F. Mondale, 41 percent). In addition to 2000, several other elections of the past several decades have been particularly close: in 1960 John F. Kennedy received 49.7 percent of the popular vote to Richard Nixon's 49.5 percent, and in 1968 Nixon obtained 43.4 percent to Hubert H. Humphrey's 42.7 percent (with George C. Wallace receiving 13.5 percent). In another extremely close race in 1976, Jimmy Carter received 50.1 percent of the vote, and Gerald R. Ford received 48.0 percent.

That present-day presidential elections tend to be close does not necessarily mean that they are competitive in all states. Indeed, in the 1992, 1996, and 2000 presidential elections, thirty-seven states cast their electoral votes for the same party all three years. Indeed, candidates routinely find certain states so uncompetitive that they do not even bother to campaign in them. This is true of even large, electorally important states. For example, many political strategists criticized George W. Bush for visiting populous California several times in the campaign's final weeks since he had little chance to win it.

The electoral map from the 2000 election, which appears as Figure 2-3, is a snapshot of the major parties' strength in presidential elections. The Democrats

Figure 2-3   2000 Electoral College Map

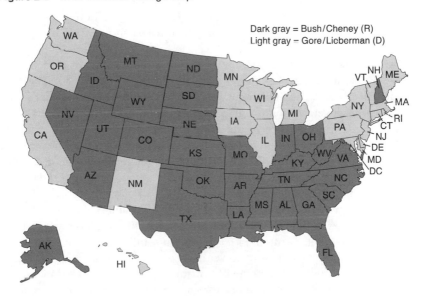

Source: Presidential Elections, 1789–2000 (Washington, D.C.: CQ Press, 2002), 227.

dominate the northeast, upper Midwest, and Pacific coast. Among these states, Al Gore lost only New Hampshire, Indiana, and Ohio. The Republicans dominate the South and the states running from the Mississippi River to the Rocky Mountains. Among these states, only New Mexico, by the thinnest of margins, escaped the Republicans' grasp in 2000.

The regions break down quite neatly, but a great deal of competitive variation exists below the surface. For example, Gore and Bill Clinton both managed to win Iowa, Maine, Wisconsin, and Oregon, but their margins in these states were often small. Similarly, Pennsylvania and Michigan are typically very competitive states. On the Republican side, the controversy surrounding Florida in the 2000 election highlighted the fierce competition for that state's electoral votes. In addition, Missouri, Louisiana, Tennessee, Arkansas, and Nevada voted for Clinton in both 1992 and 1996, which suggests that they are not necessarily Republican strongholds.

Based on the three presidential elections between 1992 and 2000, it can be argued that a handful of swing states determines who wins and loses. Arkansas, Kentucky, Louisiana, Missouri, Nevada, New Hampshire, Ohio, Tennessee, and West Virginia are the only states that voted for the winner in all three elections. If both parties hold their bases, the party that does best in these nine states wins. Since most of these states are south of the Mason-Dixon line, the Republicans' advantage is unmistakable. For both Republicans and Democrats, however, the heterogeneity of these toss-up states suggests the need to present an ideologically moderate front in presidential elections. One cannot run the risk of appearing too conservative without alienating voters in states like Nevada and West Virginia. Similarly, one cannot run the risk of appearing too liberal without alienating voters from states like Arkansas, Kentucky, and Louisiana. For the most part, presidential candidates have to perform a balancing act to win general elections.

The electoral map has undergone a stunning transformation over the last twenty-five years. Figure 2-4 shows how the states were arrayed in the 1976 presidential election, another famously close affair. In 1976, with another southerner, Georgia governor Jimmy Carter, topping the ticket, the Democrats dominated the South, winning every state of the former Confederacy except Virginia. The Democrats also did well in the East, but not in New England, where Maine, Vermont, New Hampshire, and Connecticut all voted for Gerald Ford. In addition, the upper Midwest was not the Democratic stronghold that it is today, with both Illinois and Michigan voting Republican. Perhaps most notably, the Republicans won every state west of Minnesota except Texas and Hawaii.

Of the changes in regional voting behavior, that of the South is starkest. From shortly after the Civil War to the mid-twentieth century, the Democratic party maintained a virtual monopoly of power in the states of the former Confederacy. The cohesion of the South stemmed from the experience of secession and the collective bitterness over the loss of the war, from the durable economic interests of an agricultural society, and most important, from a widespread desire to

Figure 2-4   1976 Electoral College Map

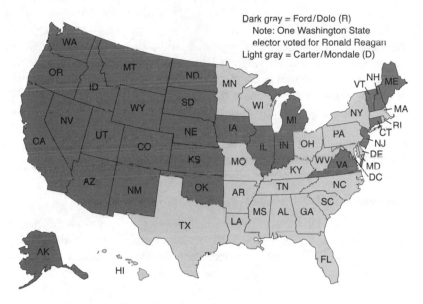

maintain segregation and white supremacy by excluding African Americans from the political system.

Southern support for Republicans in presidential elections grew significantly in 1952 when Dwight D. Eisenhower carried four southern states (Florida, Tennessee, Texas, and Virginia), narrowly missing victories in several others. The Republican party reached its high point of appeal in 1972, when Nixon received 70 percent of the southern vote in his landslide defeat of the very liberal George McGovern. Since Carter's near sweep in 1976, Republicans have dominated the region. In 1980 Ronald Reagan received 53.6 percent of the southern major party vote, winning all of the region's states except Georgia. In 1984 his percentage jumped to 62.6, a level well above his national average of 58.8. In 1988 George H. W. Bush also substantially exceeded his national showing in winning 58.8 percent of the southern vote. In 1992 and 1996, even with Clinton, a former governor of Arkansas at the top of the ticket, Republicans carried more than half of the former Confederate states in each election. And, of course, in 2000, they swept the region.

At the other end of the scale, some Republican strongholds have become either more competitive or now fall regularly in the Democratic camp. At one time immoderately Republican, Maine and Vermont almost always support Democrats today. In 2000 New Hampshire was the only Republican holdout north of the Mason-Dixon line. Most notably, California, a state that voted for Republican presidential candidates in every election between 1968 and 1988, is largely beyond their reach today. In addition, Washington and Oregon are now regular supporters of the Democrats.

The decrease in ideological heterogeneity within the parties is at the root of a trend toward regional party strongholds. As conservative southerners have come to dominate the Republican party, the GOP has become increasingly unattractive to northern and western moderates. An economic conservative from New York who is pro-choice, for example, will be uncomfortable with the highly conservative southern Republicans who strongly influence the party. Similarly, as the Democrats appeal to their increasingly homogenous liberal constituency, moderates from the South and Great Plains states will find little in common with the national Democratic party.

Congressional Elections

Whereas presidential elections are usually rather close, U.S. House elections are not. Many congressional districts have a long history of one-party or incumbent domination. The diversion of House and Senate elections from the mainstream of competitive politics is obvious (see Table 2-2). In the typical election during the 1990s, about 20 percent to 25 percent of the House elections were marginal—that is, elections in which the winning candidate received less than 55 percent of the vote. In 2000 only about 13 percent were marginal. Incumbency is the key factor in limiting turnover of congressional seats. As would be expected, party control is most likely to shift when a seat is open—when no incumbent is running. Both parties thrive on safe-district politics, and in most elections fewer than a dozen House seats switch party hands.

As Table 2-3 shows, the incumbency advantage is enormous in the House. In the usual election, well over 90 percent of House incumbents on the ballot are returned to Washington. With few exceptions, these percentages have been in the very high nineties recently, particularly in the last years of a redistricting cycle when incumbents are toughest to beat.[16] Even in "bad" years for incumbents, like 1992 and 1994, 93 percent and 90 percent, respectively, were

Table 2-2 Marginal, Safe, and Uncontested Seats in House and Senate Elections: Presidential Years 1992–2000 (by percentage of total seats)

	House			Senate		
	1992	1996	2000	1992	1996	2000
Marginal	25.4	22.5	13.2	54.3	58.8	32.4
Safe	67.7	69.8	82.7	42.9	41.2	67.6
Uncontested	6.9	3.9	4.1	2.8	0	0

Sources: Congressional Quarterly Weekly Report, April 17, 1993, 973–980; February 15, 1997, 447–455; and November 11, 2000, 2694–2703.

Table 2-3 The Advantage of Incumbency in House and Senate Elections: 1974–2000

Year		Defeated in primary	Total number of incumbents			Percentage of incumbents running in general election elected
		Defeated in primary	Running in general election	Elected in general election	Defeated in general election	
1974	House	8	383	343	40	89.56
	Senate	2	25	23	2	92.00
1976	House	3	381	368	13	96.59
	Senato	0	25	16	9	64.00
1978	House	5	377	358	19	94.96
	Senate	3	22	15	7	68.18
1980	House	6	392	361	31	92.09
	Senate	4	25	16	9	64.00
1982	House	4	383	354	29	92.42
	Senate	0	30	28	2	93.33
1984	House	3	408	392	16	96.07
	Senate	0	29	26	3	89.65
1986	House	2	391	385	6	98.46
	Senate	0	28	21	7	75.00
1988	House	1	408	402	6	98.53
	Senate	0	27	23	4	85.18
1990	House	1	406	391	15	96.31
	Senate	0	32	31	1	96.88
1992	House	19	351	327	24	93.16
	Senate	1	27	23	4	85.18
1994	House	4	382	345	37	90.31
	Senate	0	26	24	2	92.31
1996	House	2	381	360	21	94.49
	Senate	1	19	18	1	94.74
1998	House	1	401	395	6	98.50
	Senate	0	29	26	3	89.66
2000	House	3	400	394	6	98.50
	Senate	0	29	23	6	79.31

Sources: Various issues of *Congressional Quarterly Weekly Report.*

returned to Washington, although some by closer than usual margins. The blunt truth is that the House is an arena for two-party politics not because its members are produced by competitive environments but because both parties have managed to develop and protect large blocs of noncompetitive seats. Incumbency is a major factor in each party's success in reducing competition.[17]

Since House members are not often threatened electorally, they typically do not need to appeal to the political center the way that presidential candidates do. Although House members often overestimate their vulnerability,[18] their recent behavior suggests that they understand their freedom. A conservative like House Majority Leader Tom Delay (R-Tex.) can be as conservative as he wants without much fear of losing his seat in an extremely conservative district. Similarly, a liberal like Barney Frank (D-Mass.) has little need to appeal to the middle in his liberal Democratic district. This lack of competition, then, has actually helped to make the party's positions on policy issues more distinct.

The Senate features much stronger party competition.[19] Indeed, after the 2002 election fully thirteen states had one Republican and one Democratic senator. Moreover, of the thirty-seven states with two members of the same party, eight (Arkansas, Florida, Louisiana, Maine, North Dakota, Pennsylvania, South Dakota, and West Virginia) voted for the presidential candidate of the party opposite their senators in the 2000 election. This suggests an extraordinary degree of party competition. Even in states with two senators of the same party that voted for that party's presidential candidate in 2000, Senate elections can be very close. For example, Jon Corzine (D-N.J.) won his race in 2000 with a mere 52 percent of the two-party vote, and Maria Cantwell (D-Wash.) prevailed in a race so close it required a recount. Viewed more systematically, Table 2-2 reveals that more than 30 percent of Senate races were decided by less than 10 percentage points in 2000, compared with only 13 percent of House races.

Although Senate incumbents face stiffer opposition than do House members, they still win more often than they lose. Some years, like 1996, are particularly incumbent friendly, with only one incumbent losing in the general election. However, other years can create substantial turnover, as was the case in 1980 and 1986, when a quarter or more of incumbents lost. Indeed, the 2000 election produced a similarly large number of incumbent defeats, with 21 percent of challengers ousting incumbents.

Congressional elections also produce interesting regional variation. Table 2-4 shows the party shares in each region in 1953, 1981, and 2001. Several findings are noteworthy. In 1953 Republicans in the South held no seats in the Senate and only 6 percent of the 106 House seats. In 2001 they held nearly 60 percent of these seats. Of further consequence, population shifts favoring the South have increased the number of House seats in this region to 125. Outside the South and border states the trends, though less stark, favor the Democrats. For example, in 1953 the Republicans held 75 percent of Senate seats and 65 percent of House seats in eastern states. By 2001 eastern Democrats controlled the majority, with 60 percent of seats both in the Senate and House. The number of House seats in the East over this time period has declined, however, from 116 in 1953 to 89 in 2001, making Democratic gains in this region less impressive than Republican gains in the South. A Republican stronghold in the 1950s, western states— driven by partisan changes in Washington, Oregon, and California—now elect a majority of Democrats to the House.

State-Level Competition

A great deal of party competition also exists for state offices. Indeed, as one study notes, "Party competition in the states is stronger today than at any time in recent history."[20] One indication of this is the number of divided state governments. As Table 2-5 demonstrates, governors in a majority of states regularly face at least one house of the legislature controlled by the other party. After the 2000 election, twenty-two states had divided governments, which suggests not

Table 2-4   Party Shares of Regional Delegations in the House and Senate: 1953, 1981, and 2001

Region	1953 Demo-crats (%)	1953 Repub-licans (%)	1953 (N)	1981 Demo-crats (%)	1981 Repub-licans (%)	1981 (N)	2001 Demo-crats (%)	2001 Repub-licans (%)	2001 (N)
House									
East	35	65	(116)	56	44	(105)	61	39	(89)
Midwest	23	76	(118)[a]	47	53	(111)	46	54	(96)
West	33	67	(57)	51	49	(76)	54	46	(93)
South	94	6	(106)	64	36	(108)	42	58	(125)
Border	68	32	(58)	69	31	(35)	38	62	(32)
Total	49	51	(435)	56	44	(435)	49	51	(435)
Senate									
East	25	75	(20)	50	50	(20)	60	40	(20)
Midwest	14	86	(22)	41	59	(22)	64	36	(22)
West	45	55	(22)	35	65	(26)	39	61	(26)
South	100	0	(22)	55	45	(22)	41	59	(22)
Border	70	30	(10)	70	30	(10)	50	50	(10)
Total	49	51	(96)	47	53	(100)	50	50	(100)

Source: Paul R. Abramson, John H. Aldrich, and David Rohde, *Change and Continuity in the 2000 Elections* (Washington, D.C.: CQ Press, 2002).

[a]Includes one independent.

only that both parties are viable players in these states but that the public may well prefer not to consolidate power in one party.[21]

The data in Figure 2-5 more systematically examine party competition in the states. The degree of interparty competition was calculated for each state by blending four separate state scores: the average percentage of the popular vote received by Democratic gubernatorial candidates; the average percentage of Democratic seats in the state senate; the average percentage of Democratic seats in the state house of representatives; and the percentage of all terms for governor, state senate, and state house in which the Democrats were in control. Taken together, these percentages constitute an "index of competitiveness" for each state.

Table 2-5   Incidence of Party Division (Governor versus Legislature) Following 1992, 1996, and 2000 Elections

Relation between governor and legislature	Following 1992 Election Number	Following 1992 Election Percentage	Following 1996 Election Number	Following 1996 Election Percentage	Following 2000 Election Number	Following 2000 Election Percentage
Governor opposed[a]	29	59	31	63	22	45
Governor unopposed	20	41	18	37	27	55

Source: Various issues of the *Congressional Quarterly Weekly Report.*

[a]At least one house controlled by a majority of the other party.

Figure 2-5 The Fifty States Classified According to Degree of Interparty Competition: 1989–1994

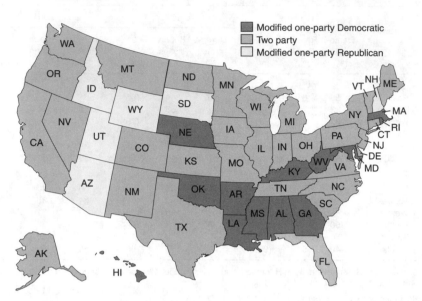

Source: Based on the classification of John F. Bibby and Thomas M. Holbrook, "Parties in State Politics," in *Politics in the American States: A Comparative Analysis*, ed. Virginia Gray and Herbert Jacob (Washington, D.C.: CQ Press, 1996), 105. The classification scheme was originally developed by Austin Ranney.

In about 40 percent of the states, party competition for state offices lacks an authentic ring. Over the period of this study—1989 to 1994—thirteen states were classified as modified one-party Democratic and six states as modified one-party Republican. Thirty-one states met the test of two-party competition—a larger number than at any time in the past several decades.[22] No state emerges as a one-party state, though these states were commonly found in the past, particularly in the once solidly Democratic South.

The results of this analysis are somewhat surprising. In direct contrast to the national level, the Democratic party on the state level is strongest in the Deep South and in certain border states, in addition to New England. Thus, while states like Alabama and Mississippi have cast their electoral votes for Republican presidential candidates in each election since 1980, they generally choose Democrats for state offices. Other regions are more consistent with their national profile. As the competitiveness of federal elections foreshadowed, the Republican party dominates many of the states that lie between the Mississippi River and the Rocky Mountains, such as Utah, Idaho, and Wyoming. Two-party states are found throughout the country and include such southern states as Texas, Florida, South Carolina, and North Carolina. Virtually all of the most populous and industrialized states are competitive in elections for state offices, though many of them, like California and Illinois, regularly vote for Democratic presidential candidates. All this suggests that party competition must be explored along several dimensions.

That party strength differs between the state and federal levels points both to the power of the parties and to their ideological weakness. It is an extraordinary measure of vitality that states such as Alabama and South Carolina elected Democratic governors in 1998, despite the fact that a Democratic presidential candidate has not won or come close to winning either state since 1976. Indeed, after the 2000 elections all of the Deep South states (Georgia, Alabama, Mississippi, Arkansas, and Louisiana) except South Carolina boasted Democratic majorities in both houses of their state legislatures, most often by very wide margins.[23] But it is also important to note that state level Democrats who win in the South today are ideologically more like national Republicans than national Democrats. For the most part, state political figures bear a stronger ideological resemblance to their state or region than to their national party.

Party Competition and Issue Positions

Critics of the two major parties, such as George Wallace in the 1960s and Ralph Nader today, have argued that "there's not a dime's worth of difference between them." Although true to some extent when Wallace contended for the presidency, the observation is simply not true today. The strategies of the presidential candidates, nevertheless, can make it appear that way.

In a political system with only two political parties, Anthony Downs argues, each party has a strong incentive to appeal to the center in order to minimize the differences that exist between the parties and the median voter.[24] The reason is that, with only two candidates in the contest, one party needs to get only one more vote than the other to win the election. In an ideologically heterogeneous jurisdiction, the median voter will tend to settle in the political center. Hence, in presidential campaigns, for example, both parties make distinct and continuing appeals to moderates as they seek to form a winning coalition. Thus, it made sound strategic sense for George W. Bush to characterize himself as a "compassionate conservative" in order to declare his conservatism to his party's faithful and his moderation to the centrist voters who would ultimately determine the election outcome.

For the most part, congressional candidates are not constrained to move toward the center and need not camouflage their ideological colors. Republicans from the Deep South can espouse their conservatism, and liberals from New England can advertise their liberalism, with neither group much concerned about its electoral future. They know what counts in their districts: conservatism on the one hand and liberalism on the other hand. The median voter, of course, is on one side or the other.

The disconnect between the presidential and congressional levels affects not only policymaking but also political fortunes. Not uncommonly, congressional leaders can pull the president from the center toward the periphery, or ideological pole. Consider Clinton. In 1992 he campaigned as a New Democrat who was socially liberal and fiscally conservative. During the first two years of his administration, however, he followed the more liberal Democratic congressional leadership in implementing the most liberal public policy course of any president since the mid-1960s. For this and other reasons, he paid a price. Dissatisfied voters in 1994 took away the Democrats' congressional majority for the first time in forty years. The rule is that every administration party faces a balancing act in representing its multiple interests and in shaping public policy; how well any one succeeds in this balancing effort determines whether the party can keep its coalition intact or not.

The Persistent Two-Party System in America

Political competition in the United States generally comes down to competition between the two major parties, Democratic and Republican. The reason American politics has been receptive to a two-party rather than a multiple-party system, as in many European democracies, is the result of a number of factors involving the election system, public law, and party behavior.

The election system is a major support for the two-party system. Most important, the single member district, first-past-the-post election system offers no rewards for coming in second or third place. Minor parties would benefit from a proportional representation system, as used in much of Europe, because it would reward a relatively good showing with an opportunity to gain influence in the government. Since third parties cannot hope to win elections outright in the United States, there is less incentive for them to challenge the major parties.

Given that members of the two major parties write the election laws, it is not surprising that the laws treat minor parties badly. Only the most well-organized and well-financed third parties can even hope to gain a place on the ballot. Whereas the major parties almost always receive a place on the ballot automatically, minor parties have to go through an arduous petition process, gathering enough signatures to secure a line on the ballot. The petition rules vary by state, with some states requiring few signatures and others a great many. Moreover, their rules differ as to when the signatures can be gathered and who is eligible to sign a petition. The crux of the problem for a minor party presidential effort is that it has to coordinate signature campaigns in numerous states, taking into account a cornucopia of different rules.[25] This effort requires a well-schooled, well-funded, and disciplined organization in fifty states—requirements that are foreign to most minor parties. Independent candidate John Anderson in 1980, for example, spent more than half of the money he raised in an attempt to get his name on all fifty state ballots.[26] The campaign finance laws do not treat third parties well either. The Federal Election Campaign Act of 1974 provides block grants to the major party candidates to run their general election campaigns after they receive their party's nomination. This money is paid out to major party candidates in the late summer *before* the general election. The law treats third parties differently. Unless a minor party has received more than 5 percent of the vote in a previous presidential election—which is, historically speaking, an unlikely occurrence—its candidate receives federal money *after* the election, and only if he receives 5 percent of the popular vote. This money is helpful for retiring a campaign debt but not in competing on equal footing with the major parties. (A more detailed account of this system appears in chapter 4.)

In addition to the rules, the diversity and flexibility that characterize the two major parties contribute to the preservation of the two-party system. The policy orientations of the parties are rarely so firmly fixed as to preclude a shift in emphasis or direction to attract emerging interests within the electorate. Moreover, each party is made up of officeholders with different views. Almost any political group, as a result, can discover some officials who share its values and predilections and who are willing to represent its point of view. The adaptability of the parties and the officeholders not only permits them to siphon off support that otherwise might contribute to the development of third parties but also creates a great deal of slack in the political system. Groups pressing for change know that there is always some chance that they can win acceptance for their positions within the existing party framework.

In addition, strange as it may seem, one-partyism enhances the two-party system. Each party has a number of areas (states or districts) that vote consistently and heavily for its candidates, irrespective of the intensity of forces that play on voters there and elsewhere. Even when one of the major parties has a particularly bad election year, it is never threatened with extinction. Republicans may clean up in outstate and downstate Illinois, but Chicago will remain safely Democratic. Most of the rural, less-populous counties of Pennsylvania will vote Republican " 'til the cows come home," but Pittsburgh, Philadelphia, and other industrial areas will vote to elect Democratic candidates. Year in and year out, for most offices, Maryland and Rhode Island turn to the Democrats, while Utah and Kansas faithfully vote Republican. One-party areas remove some of the mystery that surrounds American elections. Each major party owes something to them, counts on them, and is not often disappointed.

A final central explanation for the durability of the two-party system in America is found in a tradition of dualism.[27] Early political conflict occurred between those who favored adoption of the Constitution and those who opposed it. Subsequently, dualism was reflected in struggles between Federalists and Antifederalists and, later still, between Democrats and Whigs. Since the Civil War, the main party battle has been fought between Democrats and Republicans. In sum, the main elements of conflict within the American political system have ordinarily found expression in competition between two dominant groups of politicians and their followings.

Although the deck is stacked against them, minor parties have been around as long as have the major parties. The Jacksonian Era, which ran roughly from 1828 through 1860, was the first period of true party competition in the United States, and it was also the period when third parties had the most success. (Table

2-6 shows the third party presidential candidates that won more than 5 percent of the popular vote.) Indeed, internal divisions within the Whig party, at the time the alternative to the Democrats, led to its being replaced by the Republican party as the second major party in the late 1850s. This is the only time that such a change has occurred. There are, however, identifiable periods when minor parties do better than others.

Steven Rosenstone, Roy Behr, and Edward Lazarus identify a number of factors that help determine the success of challengers to the major parties.[28] Chief among them is fielding an experienced, well-financed candidate. National reputation is critical. Candidates like Theodore Roosevelt, a former president who ran as a Bull Moose in 1912, was by far the most successful. Similarly, George Wallace of Alabama did quite well in 1968, especially in the South, because of his national reputation as an opponent of racial integration. Given the major parties' near monopoly of power, however, few well-known politicians are willing to risk their careers by becoming the candidate of a third party. John Anderson, a Republican presidential candidate in 1980, formed his own third party after losing the nomination to Ronald Reagan. Although he would have to be considered a relatively successful third party candidate, having won 6.6 percent of the popular vote, Anderson was never again a significant force in Republican politics. In fact, his third party maneuvering doomed his political career.

Access to money is critically important to all parties. Since established interest groups are inclined to give their money to candidates who they think can win, they favor those of the major parties. Hence, it helps to be independently wealthy to launch a third party candidacy. That is the major reason that Ross

Table 2-6   Third Party and Independent Presidential Candidates Receiving 5 Percent or More of Popular Vote

Candidate (party)	Year	Percentage of popular vote	Electoral votes
Theodore Roosevelt (Progressive)	1912	27.4	88
Millard Fillmore (Whig-American)	1856	21.5	8
Ross Perot (Independent)	1992	18.9	0
John C. Breckinridge (Southern Democrat)	1860	18.1	72
Robert M. LaFollette (Progressive)	1924	16.6	13
George C. Wallace (American Independent)	1968	13.5	46
John Bell (Constitutional Union)	1860	12.6	39
Martin Van Buren (Free Soil)	1848	10.1	0
James B. Weaver (Populist)	1892	8.5	22
Ross Perot (Reform)	1996	8.4	0
William Wirt (Anti-Masonic)	1832	7.8	7
John B. Anderson (Independent)	1980	6.6	0
Eugene V. Debs (Socialist)	1912	6.0	0

Source: Congressional Quarterly Weekly Report, October 18, 1980, 3147 (as adapted and updated).

Perot did so well in 1992. In spending nearly $100 million of his own fortune, he spent roughly the same amount of money as Clinton and George H. W. Bush spent. It is not surprising that he won nearly 20 percent of the popular vote, a percentage that likely would have been much higher had he not dropped out of the race for several months in the summer. Even so, Perot's showing was the best third party vote since Roosevelt's Bull Moose candidacy in 1912.

Third parties also do better when people hold the major parties in particularly low esteem, as was the case in 1992. The nation was mired in recession, Congress had been wracked by the House banking scandal, and Washington was beset by gridlock. People had little confidence in the major parties, making Perot a more viable option. The importance of partisanship also bears on the chances of third parties. For instance, no third party candidate received as much as 5 percent of the vote between 1928 and 1968, which political scientists consider the twentieth century's golden age of strong partisanship. With parties becoming more salient to voters in the early twenty-first century, it is easy to understand why Nader received only about 3 percent of the vote in 2000.[29]

In sum, two major parties have dominated American politics for nearly two hundred years. Because of the election system and election laws adopted by representatives of the major parties, this situation is likely to persist. Conditions affect the success of third parties: when they can field good candidates, when partisanship is weak, and when political dissatisfaction is high, minor party candidates do relatively well. Yet, they do not often win; most, in fact, do not stay on the political stage very long.

Minor parties are nevertheless not unimportant. In isolated cases, they can affect an election's outcome. In 2000 Nader attacked corporate power and entrenched special interests, a line of argument that was much more attractive to liberals than to conservatives or moderates. Had Nader not been in the race, those who supported him would have voted disproportionately for Gore. Even though Nader received only about 3 percent of the national vote, he robbed Gore of more than enough votes to win the election. Just an additional handful of votes for Gore in either New Hampshire or Florida would have elected him president. Nader's candidacy cost Gore the election. Similarly, Roosevelt's Bull Moose candidacy almost certainly cost Republican Howard Taft the 1912 election. With Republicans splitting their votes between Taft and Roosevelt, Woodrow Wilson led the Democrats to victory.[30]

In addition, third parties can place issues on the political agenda that the major parties might otherwise ignore. Ross Perot's candidacy in 1992 provides another good example. He made the growing federal budget deficit a central feature of his campaign. The deficit had ballooned during the 1980s under Reagan and George H. W. Bush, both Republican presidents, who confronted consistent Democratic majorities in the House of Representatives. As a result, neither Republicans nor Democrats were disposed to talk much about this issue—which, in turn, meant the public was not inclined to care much about it. By raising the issue over the course of his campaign, however, Perot moved public concern

about the deficit to the top of the political agenda, which almost certainly provided the impetus for the balanced budgets that were achieved in the late 1990s.
Absent Perot's candidacy, such swift attention to this problem would likely have
not occurred.

The Party Condition

The party in America is the center of the political process. Nonetheless, its grip
on political power is far from secure. To be sure, the people who are recruited for
party and public offices, the issues that they bring before the electorate, the campaigns in which they participate, and the government that they help to organize
and direct—all are influenced by party. The basic problem remains, however,
that the party is unable to control all the routes to political power. In some jurisdictions, nonpartisan election systems have been developed to try to remove
parties from politics, and to a degree they have succeeded. Moreover, so thoroughly are some states and localities dominated by one party that party itself has
come to have little relevance for the kinds of people recruited for office or for the
voters in need of cues for casting their votes. Devices such as the direct primary
have also cut into the power of the party organization, serving in particular to
discourage national party agencies from attempting to influence nominations,
including those for national office, and to open up the nominating process to all
kinds of candidates. In addition, divided party control of government has
become a chronic problem of both state and national governments. Typically,
one party winds up controlling the executive branch and the other one or both
houses of the legislative branch. Determining which is the majority party has
become increasingly difficult.

On the whole, the nation's political culture is a hostile environment for parties. From the perspective of party leaders, the Constitution is a vast wasteland,
scarcely capable of supporting vigorous parties; federalism, separation of powers,
checks and balances, and staggered elections have all proved inimical to the
organization of strong parties. The party itself is an uneasy coalition of individuals and groups fused together for limited purposes. Within government, power
is about as likely to be lodged in nooks and crannies as it is in central party agencies. Conflict within the parties is sometimes as intense as it is between the parties. Parties compete vigorously in some states and scarcely at all in others. As for
the individual party member, he has a great many rights but virtually no responsibilities for the well-being of the parties. Public skepticism concerning the parties is pervasive.

Still, party competition has rarely been more vigorous in the nation's history.
Fewer than one million votes separated the 2000 presidential candidates. Partisan control of Congress is so close that it could change in almost any election
year. At the state level, formerly one-party areas such as the South now exhibit
real two-party competition. And increases in party competition may well be
good for American democracy. Charles Barrilleaux shows that, in places where

party majorities receive stiff competition from the other major party, it produces public policy more in keeping with the preferences of the electorate.[31] In other words, a competitive party system is likely to give the people what they want in terms of public policy.

While most Americans do not think highly of parties, the parties still structure their political world. Compared with European democracies, American parties will never be particularly strong. However, American parties have been strengthened over the last two decades, and there is little to suggest a return to the weak-party 1970s any time soon.

NOTES

1. *The People, the Press, and Politics, 1990* (Washington, D.C.: Times Mirror Center for the People and the Press, 1990), 2, 32.

2. Austin Ranney and Willmoore Kendall, *Democracy and the American Party System* (New York: Harcourt, 1956), 497.

3. Thomas P. O'Neill with William Novak, *Man of the House: The Life and Political Memoirs of Speaker Tip O'Neill* (New York: Random House, 1987), 26.

4. See the interesting evidence of the influence of moneyed interests on congressional decision making marshaled by Richard L. Hall and Frank M. Wayman, "Buying Time: Moneyed Interests and the Mobilization of Bias in Congressional Committees," *American Political Science Review* 84 (September 1990): 797–820.

5. James M. Burns, *The Deadlock of Democracy: Four Party Politics in America* (Englewood Cliffs, N.J.: Prentice Hall, 1963), 236–237. For an instructive study of state party organizations and leaders, see Robert J. Huckshorn, *Party Leadership in the States* (Amherst: University of Massachusetts Press, 1976).

6. See Cornelius P. Cotter, James L. Gibson, John F. Bibby, and Robert J. Huckshorn, *Party Organizations in American Politics* (New York: Praeger, 1984); and John F. Bibby, Cornelius P. Cotter, James L. Gibson, and Robert J. Huckshorn, "Parties in State Politics," in *Politics in the American States: A Comparative Analysis*, ed. Virginia Gray, Herbert Jacob, and Kenneth Vines (Boston: Little, Brown, 1983).

7. Barbara G. Salmore and Stephen A. Salmore, *Candidates, Parties, and Campaigns: Electoral Politics in America*, 2d ed. (Washington, D.C.: CQ Press, 1989), 255–256.

8. Maurice Duverger, *Political Parties* (New York: Wiley, 1965), 17.

9. Paul R. Abramson, John H. Aldrich, and David W. Rohde, *Change and Continuity in the 2000 Elections* (Washington, D.C.: CQ Press, 2002), 203.

10. Ibid., 98.

11. See, for instance, the Voter News Service exit poll from the 2000 presidential election. Eighty percent of Jews reported having voted for Al Gore, while only 17 percent reported having voted for George W. Bush.

12. V. O. Key Jr., *Politics, Parties, and Pressure Groups* (New York: Crowell, 1964), 221.

13. E. E. Schattschneider, *Party Government* (New York: Holt, Rinehart and Winston, 1942), 133–137.

14. Ibid., 134.

15. The competitiveness of presidential elections also can be examined from the perspective of the electoral college. Of the forty-six presidential elections held up to 1968, twenty-one can be classified as "hairbreadth elections"—those in which a slight shift in popular votes in a few states would have changed the outcome in the electoral college. See Lawrence D. Longley and Alan G. Braun, *The Politics of Electoral College Reform* (New Haven: Yale University Press, 1972), especially 37–41.

16. Marc J. Hetherington, Bruce A. Larson, and Suzanne Globetti, "The Redistricting Cycle and Strategic Candidate Decisions in U.S. House Races," *Journal of Politics*, forthcoming.

17. The literature on legislative-constituency relations, which includes examination of the incumbency factor in elections, is impressive. Anyone who takes the time to read the following studies on the subject will know vastly more than any normal person should know: David R. Mayhew, "Congressional Elections: The Case of the Vanishing Marginals," *Polity* 6 (spring 1974): 295–317; Gary C. Jacobson, "The Effects of Campaign Spending in Congressional Elections," *American Political Science Review* 72 (June 1978): 469–491; Jon R. Bond, Gary Covington, and Richard Fleisher, "Explaining Challenger Quality in Congressional Elections," *Journal of Politics* 47 (May 1985): 510–529; Donald A. Gross and James C. Garrand, "The Vanishing Marginals, 1824–1980," *Journal of Politics* 46 (February 1984): 224–237; Robert S. Erikson and Gerald C. Wright, "Voters, Candidates, and Issues in Congressional Elections," in *Congress Reconsidered*, 3d ed., ed. Lawrence C. Dodd and Bruce I. Oppenheimer (Washington, D.C.: CQ Press, 1985), 87–108; John C. McAdams and John R. Johannes, "Constituency Attentiveness in the House: 1977–1982," *Journal of Politics* 47 (November 1985): 1108–1139; Glenn R. Parker and Suzanne L. Parker, "Correlates and Effects of Attention to District by U.S. House Members," *Legislative Studies Quarterly* 10 (May 1985): 223–242; Melissa P. Collie, "Incumbency, Electoral Safety, and Turnover in the House of Representatives, 1952–1976," *American Political Science Review* 75 (March 1981): 119–131; John R. Alford and John R. Hibbing, "Increased Incumbency Advantage in the House," *Journal of Politics* 43 (November 1981): 1042–1061; James E. Campbell, "The Return of the Incumbents: The Nature of the Incumbency Advantage," *Western Political Quarterly* 36 (September 1983): 434–444; Diana Evans Yiannakis, "The Grateful Electorate: Casework and Congressional Elections," *American Journal of Political Science* 25 (August 1981): 568–580; Richard Born, "Generational Replacement and the Growth of Incumbent Reelection Margins in the U.S. House," *American Political Science Review* 73 (September 1979): 811–817; Candice J. Nelson, "The Effect of Incumbency on Voting in Congressional Elections, 1964–1974," *Political Science Quarterly* 93 (winter 1978–1979): 665–678; John R. Johannes and John C. McAdams, "The Congressional Incumbency Effect: Is It Casework, Policy Compatibility, or Something Else?" *American Journal of Political Science* 25 (August 1981): 512–542; Warren Lee Kostroski, "Party and Constituency in Postwar Senate Elections," *American Political Science Review* 67 (December 1973): 1213–1234; and Lyn Ragsdale, "Incumbent Popularity, Challenger Invisibility, and Congressional Voters," *Legislative Studies Quarterly* 6 (May 1981): 201–218. Also see these books: David R. Mayhew, *Congress: The Electoral Connection* (New Haven: Yale University Press, 1974); Richard F. Fenno, *Home Style: House Members in Their Districts* (Boston: Little, Brown, 1978); Gary C. Jacobson and Samuel Kernell, *Strategy and Choice in Congressional Elections* (New Haven: Yale University Press, 1981); and Gary C. Jacobson, *The Politics of Congressional Elections* (Boston: Little, Brown, 1987), especially chapter 3.

18. See Fenno, *Home Style: House Members in Their Districts*, especially chapter 1.

19. Although Senate elections are more competitive than those of the House, the trend since 1970 has been toward less competitive nonsouthern Senate races. See Donald Gross and David Breaux, "Historical Trends in U.S. Senate Elections, 1912–1988," *American Politics Quarterly* 19 (July 1991): 284–309; and *Congressional Quarterly Weekly Report*, May 6, 1989, 1060–1065.

20. Thomas R. Dye, *Politics in States and Communities*, 10th ed. (Upper Saddle River, N.J.: Prentice Hall, 2000).

21. See Morris P. Fiorina, *Divided Government*, 2d ed. (Boston: Allyn Bacon, 1996). For a different view, see Barry C. Burden and David C. Kimball, "A New Approach to

the Study of Ticket Splitting," *American Political Science Review* 59 (September 1998): 533–544.

22. See John F. Bibby and Thomas M. Holbrook, "Parties in State Politics," in *Politics in the American States: A Comparative Analysis*, ed. Virginia Gray and Herbert Jacob (Washington, D.C.: CQ Press, 1996), 103–109. Also see the early study by Austin Ranney, "Parties in State Politics," in *Politics in the American States: A Comparative Analysis*, ed. Herbert Jacob and Kenneth Vines (Boston: Little, Brown, 1976), 63–65.

23. Dye, *Politics in States and Communities*.

24. Anthony Downs, *An Economic Theory of Democracy* (New York: Harper, 1957).

25. Major party nominees are automatically given access to the general election ballot. Minor, new party, and independent candidates have to qualify for the ballot by establishing a certain level of support, which is set by state law. For an analysis of ballot access laws, see Bruce W. Robeck and James A. Dyer, "Ballot Access Requirements in Congressional Elections," *American Politics Quarterly* 10 (January 1982): 31–45. Also see Richard Winger, "How Ballot Access Laws Affect the U.S. Party System," *American Review of Politics* 16 (winter 1995): 321–350.

26. Steven J. Rosenstone, Roy L. Behr, and Edward H. Lazarus, *Third Parties in America*, 2d ed. (Princeton, N.J.: Princeton University Press, 1996).

27. For analysis of the dualism theme, see Key, *Politics, Parties, and Pressure Groups*, 207–208.

28. Rosenstone, Behr, and Lazarus, *Third Parties in America*.

29. A similar line of argument is true for increasing trust in government throughout the 1990s. See Marc J. Hetherington, "The Effect of Political Trust on the Presidential Vote, 1968–1996," *American Political Science Review* 93 (June 1999), 311–326. For an opposing point of view, see Morris P. Fiorina, "Parties and Partisanship: A 40-Year Retrospective," *Political Behavior* 24 (June 2002): 93–115.

30. Although many commentators have suggested that Ross Perot may have cost George H. W. Bush the 1992 election, political scientists have turned up little evidence to support this assertion. See R. Michael Alvarez and Jonathan Nagler, "Economics, Issues and the Perot Candidacy: Voter Choice in the 1992 Presidential Election," *American Journal of Political Science* 39 (August 1995): 714–744; and Dean Lacy and Barry C. Burden, "The Vote-Stealing and Turnout Effects of Ross Perot in the 1992 U.S. Presidential Election," *American Journal of Political Science* 43 (January 1999): 233–255.

31. Charles Barrilleaux, "Party Strength, Party Change and Policy Making in the American States," *Party Politics* 6, no. 1 (2000): 61–73.

3 POLITICAL PARTIES AND THE ELECTORAL PROCESS: NOMINATIONS

IT IS PROBABLE THAT NO NATION has ever experimented as fully or as fitfully with mechanisms for making nominations as has the United States. The principal sponsor of this experimentation is the federal system itself. Under it, responsibility for the development of election law lies with the states. Their ingenuity, given free rein, has often been remarkable. A wide variety of caucuses, conventions, and primaries—the three principal methods of making nominations—has been tried out in the states. The devices that lasted owe their survival not so much to widespread agreement on their merits as to the inability of opponents to settle on alternative arrangements and to the public at large's general indifference to major institutional change.

Nominating Methods

Caucus

The oldest device for making nominations in the United States is the caucus. In use prior to the adoption of the Constitution, the caucus is an informal meeting of political leaders held to decide questions concerning candidates, strategies, and policies. The essence of the caucus idea, when applied to nominations, is that by sifting, sorting, and weeding out candidates before the election, leaders can assemble substantial support behind a single candidate, thus decreasing the prospect that the votes of like-minded citizens would be split among several candidates. Historically, the most important form of caucus was the legislative caucus, which, until 1824, was used successfully for the nomination of candidates for state and national offices, including the presidency. The major drawback to

59

the legislative caucus was that membership was limited to the party members in the legislature, thereby exposing the caucus to the charge that it was unrepresentative and undemocratic. A modest reform in the legislative caucus occurred when provisions were made for seating delegates from districts held by the opposition party. Nevertheless, when the (Jeffersonian) Republican caucus failed to nominate Andrew Jackson for the presidency in 1824, it came under severe criticism from many quarters and shortly thereafter was abandoned for the selection of presidential nominees.

It is important to note that another form of caucus survives in the presidential nominating process: the caucus-convention system for choosing delegates to the parties' national nominating conventions. It should not be confused, however, with the original caucus system.

Party Conventions

Advocates of reform in the nominating process turned to the party convention, already in use in some localities, as a substitute for the legislative caucus. The great merit of the convention system, they argued, was that it could provide for representation, on a geographical basis, of all elements within the party. The secrecy of the caucus was displaced in favor of a more public arena, with nominations made by conventions composed of delegates drawn from various levels of the party organizations. As the convention method gained in prominence, so did the party organizations; state and local party leaders came to play dominant roles in the selection of candidates.

The convention system, however, failed to live up to its early promise. Although used for the nomination of presidential candidates since the 1830s, it has given way to the direct primary for most other offices. Critics found that it suffered from essentially the same disabling properties as the caucus. In their view, it was sheer pretense to contend that the conventions were representative of the parties as a whole; instead, party bosses ran the conventions without regard either for the views of the delegates or for the rules of fair play. A great many charges involving corruption in voting practices and procedures were made, and there was a lot of truth in them. Growing regulation of conventions by the legislatures failed to assuage the public's doubts. The direct primary came into favor as reformers came to understand its potential as a device for dismantling the structure of "boss and machine" influence and for introducing popular control over nominations.

Direct Primary

Popular control of the political process has always been an important issue in the dogma of reformers. The direct primary, with its emphasis on voters instead of on party organization, was hard to resist. Once Wisconsin adopted it for nomination of candidates for state elective offices in 1903, its use spread steadily throughout the country. Indiana became the last state to adopt it for nominating statewide candidates in 1975.[1]

Part of the attractiveness of the primary is its apparent simplicity. From one perspective, it is a device for transferring control of nominations from the party leadership to the rank-and-file voters; from another, it shifts this control from the party organization to the state. The primary rests on state law: it is an official election held at public expense on a date set by the legislature and is supervised by public officials. It has often been interpreted as an attempt to institutionalize intraparty democracy.

It is not surprising that the direct primary has had a better reception in reformist circles than anywhere else. For the party organization, it poses problems, not opportunities. If the organization becomes involved in a contested primary for a major office, it probably will have to raise large sums of money for the campaign of its candidate. If it remains neutral, it may wind up with a candidate who is either hostile to the organization or unsympathetic toward its programs and policies. Even if it abandons its neutrality, there is no guarantee that its candidate will win; indeed, a good many political careers have been launched in primaries in which the unendorsed candidate has convinced the voters that a vote for him is a vote to crush the "machine." Finally, the primary often works at cross-purposes with the basic party objective of harmonizing its diverse elements by creating a balanced ticket for the general election. The voters are much less likely to nominate a representative slate of candidates, one that recognizes all major groups within the party, than is the party leadership. Moreover, if the primary battle turns out to be bitter, the winner may enter the general election campaign with a sharply divided party behind him.[2] It is no wonder that some political leaders have viewed the primary as a systematically conceived effort to bring down the party itself.

Types of Primaries

Five basic types of state primaries are in use: closed, open, blanket, nonpartisan, and runoff. Recently the federal courts have called into question the constitutionality of blanket primaries. Presidential primaries are distinct in many ways and hence are analyzed in a separate section on the presidential nomination process below.

Closed Primary

Twenty-seven states use a closed primary of one sort or another to make nominations, meaning that those registered with another party may not participate. In thirteen of these states, registration with the party in which a voter wants to participate is required, although a voter may change his party affiliation before primary election day. Sometimes the amount of time to make such a change is quite short, such as in Connecticut, where it is a single day, and in South Dakota, where it is fifteen. In other states like New York and Kentucky, the deadline to declare an affiliation is eleven months before the election. The mean requirement is roughly two months. In fourteen other closed primary states, independents can vote in a party primary or voters can register with a party on election day. Hence states like Iowa, which allows people to declare an affiliation at the polls, are palpably open. Some closed primary states prohibit voters from switching parties once the candidates have filed declarations of candidacies, and other less restrictive states encourage "voter floating" by permitting changes in party registration after candidates have declared themselves.

Other differences in closed primary systems may result from the 1986 Supreme Court ruling in *Tashjian v. Republican Party of Connecticut.* The case arose from the efforts of the Connecticut state Republican party to attract independents by permitting them to vote in its primary elections. Unable to change the state's closed primary law in the legislature, the party successfully challenged it in court. By a 5–4 vote, the Supreme Court ruled that states may not require political parties to hold closed primaries that permit only voters previously enrolled in a party to vote. This ruling leaves the choice of primary system to the parties instead of to state legislatures. Hence a state party may choose to open its primary to unaffiliated (or independent) voters, or it may choose to bar their participation. Within a year of the Court's decision, seven other states enacted legislation under which a party could permit unaffiliated voters to vote in its primary. The trend is clearly toward openness. In 2000, for example, more than two thirds of the Republican *presidential* primaries and caucuses were open at least to registered independents. The *Tashjian* decision does not outlaw closed primaries, and presumably many state parties will continue to permit only registered party members to vote in their primaries.[3]

Open Primary

From the point of view of the party organization, the open primary is less desirable than the closed primary. Twenty states (not counting those that use blanket or nonpartisan primaries) have some form of open primary—defined as one in which voters can be registered with any party or as independents and still participate in a party primary of their choice. Provisions for open primaries differ from state to state. In nine states the voter is given the ballots of all parties, with instructions to vote for the candidates of only one party and to discard the other ballots.[4] In eleven other states, voters can cast ballots in any primary, but they have to publicly declare their choice of a party ballot at the polling place. In either case, nothing can prevent Democrats from voting to nominate Republican candidates or Republicans from voting to nominate Democratic candidates.

Party leaders suffer from a special anxiety in open primary states: the possibility that voters of the competing party will raid their primary, hoping to nominate a weak candidate who would be easy to defeat in the general election. Moreover, a study by Lynn Vavreck suggests that many candidates in open primary states produce campaign advertisements that make no mention of party but highlight issues that tend to be of interest to partisans of the other party, thus undermining the role of the party faithful.[5] Although a study of Arkansas voters by Gary D. Wekkin finds that most crossover voters are not mischievous,[6] in some states large numbers of voters do cross over to vote in the other party's primary when an exciting contest is present. Indeed, one of the central arguments used by the state of Connecticut in *Tashjian* was the party's need to protect itself from raiding by members of the other party.

While the Supreme Court found this defense of the closed primary "insubstantial" in 1986, a recent federal court ruling suggests that jurists are now taking this position more seriously. In August 2002 a federal judge struck down the 1998 law proposed by the Arizona legislature and approved by voters, which implemented an open primary system. In the suit brought by the Arizona Libertarian party, the judge ruled that the fact that non-Libertarians, who greatly outnumber Libertarians in Arizona, might determine the party's nominee violated party members' right of free association. At this writing, the decision is pending appeal.[7]

The use of open, or "crossover," primaries in the presidential nominating process has been a continuing source of aggravation for some party leaders, because these primaries permit nonparty members to influence the choice of a party's nominee. In Wisconsin, one study has shown, roughly 8 to 11 percent of all voters in presidential primaries are partisan crossovers—that is, Democrats voting in the Republican primary or Republicans voting in the Democratic primary. And a surprising one third of each party's primary participants are self-styled independents.

In a close race, the presence of outsiders can make a difference in the outcome, as John McCain demonstrated in the 2000 presidential primaries.[8] According to Philip Paolino and Daron R. Shaw, McCain's early success in states like New Hampshire, South Carolina, and Michigan had much less to do with his campaign tactics than with the fact that each of these states had open or only semi-closed primaries. In fact, Voter News Service exit polls showed that Republican partisans favored George W. Bush over McCain, often by wide margins, in every state holding a primary before mid-March, with the exception of McCain's home state of Arizona. By contrast, independents and Democrats favored McCain over Bush in all of these states except Georgia. Open primaries allowed reform-minded independents and meddlesome Democrats to vote in Republican primaries, thus favoring McCain, a reform-minded candidate.[9]

Blanket Primary

The states of Alaska, Washington, and California have traditionally used a "blanket" or "jungle" primary system. No other primary is as open, nor does any other type offer voters a greater range of choice. Under its provisions the voter is given a ballot listing all candidates of all parties under each office. Voters may vote for a Democrat for one office and a Republican for another office; or they may vote for a candidate of a third party. They cannot vote for more than one candidate per office. Independents, of course, can participate. The blanket primary is an invitation to ticket-splitting. This system, which is consistent with the emergence and consolidation of candidate-centered politics, is anathema to anyone who believes parties stand for something and that they should be held accountable for the performance of government.

Providing some good news for parties, the federal courts have recently cast a disapproving eye on blanket primaries. In 2000 the California "jungle" primary, which was adopted in 1996, was ruled unconstitutional by the U.S. Supreme Court in *California Democratic Party v. Jones*. Providing the precedent for the recent Arizona open primary case, the Court argued that "the burden (California's voting system) places on (the political parties') rights of political association is both severe and unnecessary."[10] In 2002, however, a federal district court judge upheld Washington's blanket primary, which was adopted in 1935. Both major parties in the state along with the Libertarian party have appealed the decision on "free association" grounds.[11] The only difference between the Washington and California laws is that California law requires voters to register to vote by party while Washington's does not. Whether this distinction will be relevant to the federal courts in ultimately deciding the fate of Washington's law remains to be seen.

Nonpartisan Primary

In a number of states, judges, school board members, and other local government officials are selected in nonpartisan primaries. State legislators in Nebraska are also selected on this basis. The scheme itself is simple: the two candidates receiving the greatest number of votes are nominated; in turn, they oppose each other in the general election. No party labels appear on the ballot in either election. The nonpartisan primary is defended on the ground that partisanship should not be permitted to intrude on the selection of certain officials, such as judges. By eliminating the party label, runs the assumption, the issues and divisiveness that dominate national and state party politics can be kept out of local elections and offices. Although nonpartisan primaries muffle the sounds of party, they do not eliminate them. It is not uncommon for the party organizations to slip quietly into the political process and to recruit and support candidates in these primaries; in such cases, about all that is missing is the party label on the ballot.

Runoff Primary

The runoff, or second primary, is a by-product of a one-party political environment. As used in many southern states, this primary provides that if no candidate obtains a majority of the votes cast for an office, a runoff is held between the two leading candidates. The runoff primary is an attempt to come to terms with a chronic problem of a one-party system—essentially all competition is jammed into the primary of the dominant party.

With numerous candidates seeking the nomination for the same office, the vote is likely to be sharply split, with no candidate receiving a majority. A runoff between the top two candidates in the first primary provides a guarantee, if only statistical, that one candidate will emerge as the choice of a majority of voters. This is no small consideration in those southern states where the Democratic primary was traditionally the real election and where factionalism within the party grew so intense that no candidate would stand much of a chance of consolidating his party position without two primaries—the first to weed out the losers and the second to endow the winner with the legitimacy a majority can offer.

Probably the best-known runoff primary belongs to Louisiana, which combines the runoff with a nonpartisan primary. Under this system, all candidates for an office are grouped together in a primary election. A candidate who receives a majority of the primary vote is elected, thus eliminating the need for a general election. If no candidate obtains a majority of the votes cast, the top two, irrespective of party affiliation, face each other in a runoff general election. Although the Supreme Court has recently questioned blanket primaries, it has stated explicitly that runoff primaries are, in fact, constitutional, and that blanket primary states ought to consider the Louisiana approach.[12]

Runoff primaries have a number of negative effects: Incumbents enjoy a pronounced advantage; voter turnout often drops substantially from the first primary to the second; a growing number of candidates face the voters with no party affiliation; campaigns tend to cost significantly more; and, perhaps most important, institutionalized multifactionalism develops, marked by intensified campaigning at the primary stage with numerous candidates competing for the same office. Party obviously counts for little in the Louisiana setting. Even the ballot has been modified, changing from party column to office block as a means of inhibiting straight party voting.[13] A wholesale move to this type of primary would certainly be bad news for parties.

An Assessment of the Direct Primary

The great virtue of the direct primary, from the perspective of its early Progressive sponsors, was its democratic component, its promise for changing the accent and scope of popular participation in the political system. Its immediate effect, they hoped, would be to diminish the influence of political organization on political life. What is the evidence that the primary has accomplished its mission? What impact has it had on political party organization?

On the positive side, an important outcome of having the primary system is that party leaders have been sensitized to the interests and feelings of the most active rank-and-file members. Fewer nominations are cut and dried, and even though candidates who secure the organization's endorsement win more frequently than they lose, their prospects often are uncertain.[14] The possibility of a revolt against the organization, carried out in the primary, forces party leaders to take account of the elements that make up the party and to pay attention to the claims of potential candidates. There is always a chance—in some jurisdictions, a strong possibility—that an aspirant overlooked by the leadership will decide to challenge the party's choice in the primary. The primary thus induces caution among party leaders. A hands-off policy—one in which the party makes no endorsement—is sometimes its only response. If the party has no candidate, it cannot lose; some party leaders have been able to stay in business by avoiding the embarrassment that comes from primary defeats. In some jurisdictions, party intervention in the primary is never even considered, so accustomed is the electorate to party-free contests. For the public at large, the main contribution of the primary is that it opens up the political process.[15]

For the most part, the direct primary has had a decidedly negative impact on party leaders. Malcolm E. Jewell and Sarah Morehouse show that the percentage of contested primaries has increased moderately over the last twenty years, and, worse, the proportion of party-endorsed candidates winning contested races has dropped precipitously, at least in gubernatorial elections. Whereas 79 percent of endorsed candidates for governor in contested primaries won the party nomination from 1960 to 1978, only 53 percent did so from 1980 to 1994.[16] Endorsements are most effective when the party organizations provide their endorsees with organizational assistance, financing, and personnel—resources not all state and local parties have in large supply.[17]

While the primary has not immobilized party organizations completely, it has caused a number of problems for them. The party leaders' lack of enthusiasm for primaries is not hard to understand knowing that, among other things, the primary:

1. greatly increases party campaign costs (if the party backs a candidate in a contested primary);
2. diminishes the capacity of the organization to reward its supporters through nominations;
3. makes it difficult for the party to influence nominees who establish their own power bases in the primary electorate;
4. creates opportunities for people hostile to party leadership and party policies to capture nominations;
5. permits anyone to wear the party label and opens the possibility that the party will have to repudiate a candidate who has been thrust upon it; and
6. increases intraparty strife and factionalism.[18]

It seems no institution is better designed than the primary to stultify party organization and processes.

On the whole, the primary has not fulfilled the expectations of its sponsors. Most notably, primaries have not made politics significantly more competitive. For example, only three Senate incumbents have been defeated in primaries since 1982, and, over the same period, only once (in 1992) did more than ten House incumbents lose. Most incumbents face token opposition for the nomination, if they face any at all.[19]

The surprising number of nominations won by default has several causes. First, uncontested primaries may be evidence of party strength—that is, potential candidates stop short of entering the primary because their prospects appear slim for defeating the organization's choice. Second, the deserted primary simply may demonstrate the pragmatism of politicians: they do not struggle to win nominations that are unlikely to lead anywhere. As V. O. Key Jr. and others have shown, primaries are most likely to be contested when the chances are strong that the winner will be elected to office in the general election and will be least likely to be contested when the nomination appears to have little value.[20] Thus, the tendency is for electoral battles to occur in competitive districts or in the primary of the dominant party. Third, the presence of an incumbent reduces competition for a nomination. In fact, over the last twenty years, less than two percent of incumbent members of Congress have actually lost their party's nomination. Overall, the prospects for a primary contest are greatest in districts where the party has a chance to win in November and where no incumbent is in the race.

Experience with the primary has also shown that it is one thing to shape an institution so as to induce popular participation and quite another to realize such participation. No fact about primaries is more familiar than that large numbers of voters assiduously ignore them. A majority of voters usually stays away from the polls on primary day, even when major statewide races are to be settled. Even in years when both parties have contested gubernatorial primaries, an average of only about 30 percent of the voting age population turns out. For all states holding primaries in 1998, the turnout rate was a paltry 17 percent.[21] The promise of the primary is thus only partially fulfilled. The reality is that the public is not keenly interested in the nominating process.

Presidential Selection

The presidential nominating process is unusually complicated, and it is doubtful that average citizens understand it very well. If they do, they know that it is an awkward mix of conventions, primaries, and caucuses regulated by both pubic law and party rules and that, additionally, the parties differ in the methods they use to select their nominees.

The National Convention

The American national convention is surely one of the most remarkable institutions in the world for making nominations. In use since the Jacksonian Era, it is the official agency for the selection of each party's candidates for president and vice president and for the ratification of each party's platform. At the same time, it is the party's supreme policy-making authority, empowered to make the rules that govern party affairs.

The national convention historically has served another function of prime importance to the parties. It has been a meeting ground for the party itself, one in which leaders could tap rank-and-file sentiments and in which the divergent interests that make up each party could, at least in some fashion, be accommodated. In its classic role, the national convention presents an opportunity for the national party—the fifty state parties assembled—to come to terms with itself, permitting leading politicians to strike the necessary balances and to settle temporarily the continuing questions of leadership and policy. Under the pressure of other changes in the presidential nominating process, however, the party role in conventions has recently been diminished.

Until the 1970s, national convention decisions could best be explained by examining the central role of national, state, and local party leaders, and the behavior of state delegations. These were the "power points" in the classic model of convention politics, aptly described by the authors of *Explorations in Convention Decision Making:*

> Historically, state delegations have been thought to be the key units for bargaining in conventions; operating under the unit rule, they bargain with each other and with candidate organizations. The rank-and-file delegates are manipulated by hierarchical leaders holding important positions in national, state, and local party organizations. In order to enhance their bargaining position, these leaders often try to stay uncommitted to any candidate until the moment that their endorsement is crucial to victory for the ultimate nominee. After the presidential balloting is over, the vice-presidential nomination is awarded to a person whose selection will mollify those elements of the party who did not support the presidential choice. At the end of the convention, all groups rally around the ticket and the party receives a boost in starting the fall campaign.[22]

The classic model of convention decision making bears only modest resemblance to the patterns of influence at play in the most recent party conventions. In broad terms, decentralization of power is now the chief characteristic of the struggle for the presidential nomination. State delegations have given way to candidate blocs in importance, and party leaders have been displaced by the leaders of candidate organizations. Party leaders have few resources with which to bargain in those state delegations that are split among candidates. Indeed, candidates and their organizations dominate today's party conventions. Accordingly, the influence that party and elected officials wield in conventions is largely a product of their affiliation with one of the candidate organizations.

The decline of party presence in national conventions results from a confluence of forces: the delegate selection rules that opened up the parties to amateur activists and contributed to the spread of presidential primaries; the capacity of candidates to dominate campaign fund-raising (using government subsidies under a matching system since 1976); and the general weakness of state and local party organizations.[23] What matters to the candidate is winning the immediate primary or placing well (as judged by the mass media) to attract new funds and to build momentum for the next contest. In the modern scheme of campaigning, expert consultants, an active personal organization spread out around the state, and the mass media play much more significant roles to the candidates than do party structures and party leaders.

Selection of Delegates

National convention delegates are chosen by two methods: presidential primaries and caucus-conventions. Each state chooses its own system, and it is not unusual for a state to switch from one method to another between elections in response to criticisms by the press, the public, and politicians unhappy about recent outcomes.

Loosely managed by the parties, the caucus-convention system provides for the election of delegates by rank-and-file members (mixed with candidate enthusiasts) from one level of the party to the next—ordinarily from precinct caucuses to county conventions to the state convention, and from there to the national convention. The first-tier caucuses (mass meetings at the precinct level) are crucial because they establish the delegate strength of each candidate in the subsequent conventions, including the national convention. Candidates and their organizations must turn out their supporters for these initial party meetings; a loss at this stage cannot be reversed.

At one time, the chief criticism of the caucus-convention system was that it was essentially closed, dominated by a few party leaders who selected themselves, key public officials, "fat cats" (major financial contributors), and lesser party officials as delegates. The democratizing reforms of the 1970s changed all this, opening up the caucuses to participation by average party members and short-term activists willing to spend an afternoon or evening discussing and voting. Today, competing candidate organizations and their enthusiasts dominate the delegate-selection caucuses, and prominent party officials may or may not be found in their ranks. Preoccupied with the struggle for delegates, the media pay scant attention to the caucus as a party event.

Delegate selection systems vary from state to state and from party to party. On the Democratic side, national party rules mandate that primaries used for delegate selection must be closed (that is, only Democrats or Democrats and registered independents may participate), with the exception of a few states like Wisconsin that have open primary traditions. About one fifth of states use caucuses instead of primaries. Some use both primaries and caucuses; typically, in this arrangement, the caucus selects the delegates to reflect the primary results.

For the Republicans, the most common method for selecting delegates is the open primary; it is used in over half of the states, including populous California, Illinois, Ohio, and Texas. Just under a quarter of the states use closed primaries, including Florida, New York, and Pennsylvania. And less than one fifth of the states use caucuses, all but a few of which are open. As in the case of the Democrats, Republican caucus states tend to be rural, less populous, and midwestern (e.g., Iowa, Minnesota) or western (e.g., Alaska, Nevada, North Dakota, and Wyoming).

Popular participation is much lower in caucus states than it is in primary states. In 2000, for example, fewer than 100,000 voters (about 16 percent) took part in the key Iowa Republican caucuses, whereas 238,000 voted (54 percent) in the Republican primary in New Hampshire.[24] Generally speaking, New Hampshire's first-in-the-nation primary produces twice as many participants as Iowa's first-in-the-nation caucus, despite the fact that New Hampshire is half the size of Iowa.

The caucus-convention system poses major problems for party leaders.[25] In most caucus states party regulars have been reduced to bystanders as candidate organizations, bolstered by amateur enthusiasts, vie with one another for votes and delegates. Intraparty conflict also appears to occur more frequently in caucus states than it does in primary states. Finally, party leaders have become sensitive to the charge that caucus results may not be representative of general voter sentiment. For these reasons, particularly the latter, states that change their nominating systems in the future are more likely to switch to primaries than to caucuses.[26]

Used by all of the most populous states, presidential primaries are easier for the public to understand. A large majority of each state's delegates is chosen on primary day by the direct vote of the people; the remaining delegates are chosen through party processes following the primary. Like the direct primary used to nominate national, state, and local officials, the presidential primary was designed to wrest control of nominations from the "bosses" (the party professionals) and to place it in the hands of the people by permitting them to choose the delegates to the nominating conventions in a public election. In 1904 Florida became the first state to adopt a presidential primary law. In little more than a decade, about half of the states had adopted some version of it. Following the Progressive Era, its use dropped, with only fourteen states and the District of Columbia holding presidential primaries in 1968. The popularity of presidential primaries, however, exploded in the 1970s and 1980s. By 2000, presidential primaries were held in one or both parties in forty-one states, with Republicans using this method somewhat more than Democrats. Altogether, Democrats chose over 85 percent of their delegates in primaries; Republicans, nearly 90 percent.[27]

The broad objective of presidential primaries is to encourage popular participation in the selection of presidents, but many voters do not attach importance to the nominating process, even when the presidency is at stake.[28] In 2000, for example, 20.7 million people voted in the Republican primaries and 14.7 million in the Democratic primaries—only about 15 percent of the voting-age population.[29] (See Table 3-1.) Several hundred thousand voters took part in caucuses. Perhaps thirty-six million voters participated in choosing the nominees in 2000, as contrasted with 105.4 million who voted in the general election. This level of primary and caucus participation, however, is actually on the high end, historically. Only in 1988 did a higher percentage of eligible voters participate in the nominating process than in 2000.

Rules of Delegate Selection

Prior to the 1970s, the manner in which national convention delegates were selected was left to the states. Today, the Democratic party in particular tightly regulates the methods of delegate selection. In the selection of delegates, the

Table 3-1 Presidential Primary Turnout: 1968–2000

Year	Number of states holding primaries	Democratic vote	Republican vote	Total major party vote
1968	14 and D.C.	7,535,069	4,473,551	12,008,620
1972	20 and D.C.	15,993,965	6,188,281	22,182,246
1976	26 and D.C.	16,052,652	10,374,125	26,426,777
1980	35 and D.C.	18,747,825	12,690,451	31,438,276
1984	29 and D.C.	18,009,192	6,575,651	24,584,843
1988	36 and D.C.	22,961,936	12,165,115	35,127,051
1992	38 and D.C.	20,239,385	12,696,547	32,395,932
1996	41 and D.C.	10,947,364	13,991,649	24,939,013
2000	41 and D.C.	14,665,119	20,717,198	35,382,317

Source: Rhodes Cook, *Race for the Presidency: Winning the 2000 Nomination* (Washington, D.C.: CQ Press, 2000), 4, as updated.

rules make clear, not much is left to chance or to the discretion of individual state parties.

An amalgam of recommendations by five party study commissions, stretching from 1969 to 1985, the rules were designed to serve several major objectives:

1. to stimulate the participation of rank-and-file Democratic voters in the presidential nominating process;
2. to increase the representation of certain demographic groups (particularly women, African Americans, and young people) in the convention through the use of guidelines on delegate selection;
3. to eliminate procedures held to be undemocratic (such as the unit rule, under which a majority of a state delegation could cast the state's total vote for a single candidate);
4. to enhance the local character of delegate elections (by requiring 75 percent of the delegates in each state to be elected at the congressional district level or lower); and
5. to provide through proportional representation that elected delegates fairly reflect the presidential candidate preferences of Democratic voters in primary states and Democratic participants in caucus-convention states. (The proportional representation rule was relaxed in the 1980s but is mandatory today.)

For many members of the first commission, the McGovern-Fraser Commission, the underlying objective was to diminish the power of party professionals in the convention while at the same time increasing that of party members and activists at the local level. They succeeded to an extraordinary degree. A new type of participant, to whom candidates and issues were central, came to predominate in the Democratic convention. Party leaders and public officials, thoroughly overshadowed in the 1972 and 1976 conventions, gradually have been readmitted since then. Following a recommendation of the Winograd Commission, the Democratic National Committee (DNC) adopted a provision to expand each 1980 state delegation by 10 percent to include prominent party and elected officials. Since then, the number of these officials, who gain their seats automatically (that is, without facing the voters) has grown. "Superdelegates," as they are called, made up nearly 20 percent of the 2000 Democratic convention, composed of Democratic members of Congress, the party's governors, members of the DNC, and various prominent state party officials.

Superdelegates were introduced to the delegate-selection process to provide for peer review of candidates by professional politicians and, at the same time, to diminish the influence of amateur activists and interest groups. They were to be the new power brokers of the convention. But it has not worked out that way. Because the candidates campaign for superdelegates' votes in the same way that they campaign for popular support, the vast majority of the superdelegates arrive at the convention not as free agents but as delegates fully committed to individual candidates. Like other politicians in search of influence, superdelegates want to endorse the ultimate winner and to do so as early as possible, when endorsements count the most.

The way in which delegates are allocated to candidates has been a persistent problem for the Democrats. Tinkering and temporizing, the party has vacillated between winner-take-all and proportional representation since the 1970s. In 1988, for example, the national Democratic rules permitted state parties to choose from among three broad plans. First, states could select the *proportional representation* method, under which any Democratic candidate who reached the 15 percent threshold of the primary or caucus vote was entitled to a proportionate share of the delegates; candidates who failed to reach the threshold did not qualify for any delegates. Second, states could adopt what amounts to a *winner-take-all* system. In this direct-election form, voters cast ballots for individual delegates who were pledged to candidates or uncommitted. The candidate who came in first in a district could win all or most of the delegates instead of sharing them with the trailing candidates. Third, states could choose a *winner-take-more* plan. Here, the winning candidate in each district was given a bonus delegate before the rest were divided proportionally. For the last three conventions, Democratic party rules required all states to allocate their publicly elected delegates on a proportionate basis, giving each candidate who reached the 15 percent threshold the appropriate share of delegates.

Proportional representation has several side effects, not all of them positive. A party's first objective must be to minimize divisiveness, and contested primaries cause divisiveness. Enmities and resentment among party elites and voters generated in the nominating process can have a significant influence on their behavior in general elections. An analysis of Democratic presidential primaries, caucuses, and general election outcomes over a sixty-year period by James I. Lengle, Diane Owen, and Molly W. Sonner found that divisiveness at the nominating stage hurts the party's prospects for winning the general election. From 1932 to 1992, Democratic presidential candidates lost more than three fourths of the states that experienced divisive primaries but only half of those with nondivisive primaries or those with caucuses. "Political loyalties, attitudes, and perceptions of voters in nominating campaigns," the authors wrote, "are influenced enormously by the structure and intensity of the competition fostered by nominating mechanisms."[30]

The Democrats' reliance on proportional representation in delegate selection certainly does not help in this regard. While proportional representation does permit the front-runner to pile up delegates even in states won by another candidate, it still takes a long time for him to assemble a majority of delegates. Winner-take-all systems allow front-runners to land knockout blows at any point, thus ending ugly intraparty struggles. As Priscilla L. Southwell notes, proportional representation can be advantageous for some lesser-known, outsider candidates because their second- and third-place finishes in the early caucuses and primaries will entitle them to delegates and perhaps keep their candidacies alive.[31] In the end, proportional representation leads to longer nomination struggles, more contested primaries, and more negative feelings within the party in the general election campaign.

The Republican party was considerably less active than the Democratic party in the 1970s and 1980s in restructuring its delegate selection rules, but it did make a few changes. Its current rules require open meetings for delegate selection; ban automatic (ex officio) delegates; and provide for the election, not the selection, of congressional district and at-large delegates (unless otherwise provided by state law). State Republican parties are urged to develop plans for increasing the participation of women, young people, minorities, and other groups in the presidential nominating process, but they are not required to do so. The push to nationalize party rules, pronounced among Democratic reformers for the last several decades, finds only limited support among Republicans. Rather, Republicans continue to stress the federal character of their party. The basic authority to reshape delegate selection rules remains with state parties.[32]

Republican delegate selection practices differ in several major respects from those of the Democrats. First, Republicans have resisted the allure of proportionality in delegate allocation, placing much more emphasis on some version of winner-take-all. In 2000, for example, well over one half of the Republican state parties used winner-take-all or direct election and only about one fourth used proportional representation. A few Republican state parties use winner-take-all but provide for proportional representation if no candidate receives a majority of the vote. Second, the Republican party has no provision for the automatic selection of party or public officials—superdelegates, in Democratic nomenclature. Third, the party has no requirement that state delegations be evenly divided between men and women, a rule imposed on state Democratic parties beginning in 1980. (The numbers of women delegates has increased nonetheless in Republican conventions—35 percent of the total in 2000.) Fourth, each state Republican party is free to schedule its primary or caucus as it sees fit. On the Democratic side, the primary-caucus calendar is tightly regulated by national party rules. Party differences in delegate selection reflect basic party differences in philosophy and organization that can be summed up in the appellations "federal" Republicans and "national" Democrats.

Evaluating Presidential Primary and Caucus-Convention Systems

Sometimes it appears as though the only persons who are satisfied with the presidential nominating process are the winners—the nominees and their supporters. Everyone else, it seems, can find reasons to be unhappy or frustrated with the process.

To the initiated and uninitiated voter alike, the primaries and caucuses are a mass of oppositions and paradoxes. Unpredictability reigns, victory in a single state can be the key to the nomination, and victories in the early primaries and caucuses are usually crucial. Consider recent outcomes. In the judgment of many observers, on the day that John F. Kennedy defeated Hubert H. Humphrey in the West Virginia primary in 1960—a Catholic winning in an overwhelmingly Protestant state—he sewed up the nomination. Jimmy Carter's string of early primary victories in 1976, beginning with his narrow win in New Hampshire, gave him a commanding lead. His weakness in late primaries, marked by several losses to California governor Jerry Brown, had no effect on the nomination. In 1988 George H. W. Bush's victory over Kansas senator Bob Dole in New Hampshire and his sweep of the South on "Super Tuesday" three weeks later settled the nomination for all intents and purposes.

Bill Clinton's sweep of the southern primaries in the second week of March 1992, followed by major victories in Illinois and Michigan the next week, all but sewed up the nomination. In 1996 Bob Dole survived a rocky start, narrowly defeating Pat Buchanan in Iowa (26 percent to 23 percent) and losing to him in unpredictable New Hampshire (26 to 27 percent). But when Dole swept the South on Super Tuesday a week later, his nomination was all but inevitable. Similarly, in 2000 both Al Gore and George W. Bush had effectively sewn up their parties' nominations within two months of the start of the primary and caucus season. While Bush lost a few early contests to John McCain, notably in New Hampshire, Massachusetts, Arizona, and Michigan, Bush's superior national organization forced McCain out of the race in early March.

The location of state victories makes a difference. Early contests in Iowa and New Hampshire give these states disproportionate influence. George McGovern in 1972 and Jimmy Carter in 1976, both long shots to win the nomination, owed their success to their strong showings in these states. And Gary Hart, another outsider, almost parlayed a better-than-anticipated vote in the Iowa caucuses in 1984 (15 percent to Walter Mondale's 45 percent) and a victory in New Hampshire into the nomination. For George H. W. Bush and Michael Dukakis in 1988, New Hampshire's results obliterated their poor showings in Iowa and, most important, made them the clear-cut front-runners. Clinton's impressive second-place finish in New Hampshire in 1992 (after neighboring-state candidate Paul Tsongas) put him in a strong position for the approaching southern primaries, which he won decisively.[33]

The most important result of an early victory or unanticipated good showing is the free media time it produces. Even though the race between Carter and Morris Udall was very close in New Hampshire in 1976 (Carter received 28 percent of the vote to Udall's 23 percent), the press hailed Carter as the clear-cut winner. As a result, he received 2,600 lines of the coverage in *Time* and *Newsweek* in the week following New Hampshire to Udall's ninety-six, a proportion mirrored on both television news and in major newspapers.[34]

For anyone except their residents, it is simply mind-boggling to learn that Iowa and New Hampshire, which comprise only about 3 percent of the nation's population, receive nearly 30 percent of the media coverage given the entire campaign for the presidential nomination.[35] Many find this focus on Iowa and New Hampshire problematic since these states are not representative of the country as a whole. Neither state has a major metropolitan area, a large urban (unionized) workforce, or a sizable minority population—characteristics of special importance for the Democrats. In short, the voters in these states are patently not a cross section of the nation as a whole.[36]

Regional variation in candidate strength also can be decisive. Recent evidence suggests that the South is becoming increasingly important in choosing party nominees. In 1980 both Carter and Ronald Reagan gained critical momentum by winning a string of early southern primaries. Southern primaries and caucuses were also crucial for George H. W. Bush in 1988, Clinton in 1992, Dole in 1996, and George W. Bush in 2000. It is hardly surprising, then, that between 1988—when most southern states started to hold their primaries on the same day, Super Tuesday—and 2000, six of the eight major party nominees have had some kind of connection to the South. Sequence and region obviously affect the choice of nominees.

Front Loading

The opening weeks of the nominating process are absolutely critical; more and more states have shifted their primaries and caucuses to the early part of the season—"front loading," in the argot of analysts and political junkies. Since 1992 California has moved its presidential primary date from June to the fourth Tuesday in March (1996) to the first Tuesday in March (2000), ostensibly to increase its influence in the process. With other populous states following suit, March is now the key month in securing the presidential nomination. Nearly one half the delegates to both the Republican and Democratic conventions in 2000 were chosen by the first Tuesday in March (Titanic Tuesday), which features races in several large states such as California and New York, while fully two thirds were decided by the second Tuesday in March (Super Tuesday).

Front loading has several critical effects. Potential candidates must begin raising money, building campaign organizations, and securing endorsements at least a year or more before the primary season officially begins. This period is often referred to as the *invisible primary*—an interval in which no official contests occur but candidacies are made or broken. For example, for all intents and purposes George W. Bush had all but secured his party's nomination even before 2000. His campaign had raised over $36 million by July of 1999, much more than any of his competitors. As a result, he was able to lock up important endorsements from many governors, members of Congress, and other party leaders. In fact, the candidate running in second place during most of the invisible primary season, Elizabeth Dole, had great difficulty finding a national finance chairman because of Bush's domination of fund-raising and endorsements.

Money separates the serious candidate from the dilettante or the rank outsider. Of course, there is never enough of it, and the law does not make it easy to raise. Under the McCain-Feingold revisions to the Federal Election Campaign Act of 1971, no individual can contribute more than $2,000 to any campaign.[37] Moreover, candidates can qualify for matching federal funds only after they have raised $100,000 in small sums ($250 or less, $5,000 per state) in each of twenty states. Political action committees may contribute up to $5,000 to a candidate, but their gifts are not eligible for matching public money. Candidates are thus compelled to develop a large network of small contributors, spread around the country—making fund-raising a chore for all candidates and a major obstacle for some. Plans and activities to raise money must be launched long in advance of the election year. It is thus easy to mark the opening of a new campaign; it begins with the creation of fund-raising committees and the scramble for money.

Next, candidates must get out of the blocks fast. Slow starters usually find themselves out of the race in a matter of weeks. Clinton had the 1992 Democratic nomination nailed down before half of the states, including many big ones, had even voted. In contrast, despite his raising huge amounts of money in the 1996 invisible primary period, the poor showing in several early primary and caucus states by Sen. Phil Gramm (R-Tex.) quickly sent him to the sidelines. For most candidates who do poorly in early contests, their financial coffers run dry, they find it impossible to raise more money, and their end of the race comes early. For example, in 2000 both McCain and Bill Bradley were forced to exit the race by mid-March. Without doubt, front loading gives an advantage to well-known candidates with campaign organizations in place, to those with large amounts of money on hand, and to those with significant national followings.[38]

In addition, front loading has virtually eliminated the ability of dark-horse candidates to translate momentum, built on stronger than expected showings in states like Iowa and New Hampshire, into strong showings elsewhere. After Carter won his surprising victory in New Hampshire in late February 1976, he only had to prepare for seven primaries in the next two months. Most primaries were then held in May. In contrast, McCain's surprise win in New Hampshire was quickly followed by five more primaries in February, not to mention twenty in March. (See Table 3-2.) Even after McCain won another surprising victory in Michigan in late February, he had only two weeks to mount comprehensive

Table 3-2 Number and Timing of Presidential Primaries: 1968–2000

Month	1968	1972	1976	1980	1984	1988	1992	1996	2000
February	0	0	1	1	1	2	2	5	6
March	1	3	5	9	8	20	15	24	20
April	3	3	2	4	3	3	5	1	2
May	7	11	13	13	11	7	10	8	9
June	4	4	6	9	7	5	7	4	5
Total	15	21	27	36	30	37	39	42	42

Source: Rhodes Cook, *Race for the Presidency: Winning the 2000 Nomination* (Washington, D.C.: CQ Press, 2000), 8, as updated.

campaigns in the thirteen states that ultimately determine the nomination on Titanic Tuesday. Before the primary season was front loaded, a momentum candidate like Carter had time on his side. With the primaries front loaded in 2000, a lack of time was McCain's undoing.

In short, protracted struggle for the nomination is now more likely to be the exception than the rule. Front loading has led to a more compact process and to a strengthened opportunity for a quick knockout. In 2000 more than seventy percent of Republican and Democratic delegates had been decided by the end of March. (See Table 3-3.) As a result, early money and standing organization are more important than ever. Once the campaign begins, in this tighter schedule of events, scant time is available to raise money, solicit endorsements, shape issues, or put an organization in place. In the 2000 Republican struggle, following Michigan only Bush was sufficiently well positioned, financially and organizationally, to compete effectively in all states. For serious contenders, the nominating campaign must begin two or more years in advance of the presidential year. No one can wait around for lightning to strike.

Table 3-3 Percentage of Delegates Allocated: 2000

	Republican		Democratic	
Month	Percentage of delegates allocated	Cumulative percentage allocated to date	Percentage of delegates allocated	Cumulative percentage allocated to date
January	2	2	1	1
February	15	17	1	2
March 7 (Titanic Tuesday)	29	46	39	41
Rest of March	25	71	32	73
April	7	78	10	83
May	14	92	11	94
June	8	100	6	100
Total	100		100	

Source: Rhodes Cook, *Race for the Presidency: Winning the 2000 Nomination* (Washington, D.C.: CQ Press, 2000), viii–ix, as adapted.

The Democratic party has sought to diminish the significance of the early phase of the presidential nominating process by adopting rules to restrict the nominating season (the caucus-primary "window"). These efforts have actually *increased* the significance of the early contests. In the early 1990s the Democrats mandated that all their primaries had to occur between early March and early June, with a few exceptions, such as Iowa and New Hampshire. This step provided the impetus for Titanic Tuesday (March 7), as many states scrambled to move their primaries to the start of the window to increase their importance. In 2001 the Democrats adopted a plan to widen the window to include February. In response, no fewer than eleven states are considering a move to a February primary date for 2004. It is almost certain that a clear-cut front-runner will emerge by mid-March, making the last three months of the primary season nothing more than the mop-up stage. The Republican party has also become sensitive to the scheduling of nominating events. In an effort to combat front loading and to stretch out the nominating process, the 1996 Republican convention approved changes in party rules that gave states a bonus in delegates if they moved their caucus or primary to a later date in 2000; any state that voted after May 15, for example, would receive 10 percent more delegates, whereas those that voted in the last half of April or the first half of May received only a 7.5 percent increase. The convention also restricted the nominating season by barring delegate-selection events in January of 2000.[39] In the end, however, there was no rush to move primaries backward in the calendar, and only sixteen states held their contests in April, May, or June of 2000, only three more than in 1996.

In sum, the electoral results in the early caucus-convention and primary system are peculiar to the presidential nominating process. And overemphasis of the results by the media is the norm. Often speaking with greater finality than the voters themselves, the media create winners and losers, front-runners and also-rans, candidates who should "bail out," and candidates who have earned "another shot." Voters learn who did better than expected and who did worse, and indeed they even start to evaluate the candidates on these terms rather than on policy.[40] Winning or placing well is translated into a major political resource, with the psychological impact greater than the number of delegates won. The rewards for capturing the media's attention are heightened visibility, an expanded and more attentive journalistic corps, television news time, interest group cynosure, endorsements, campaign funds,[41] and a leg up on the next contest. The truth is that in the nominating process the media have become the new parties.[42]

Primaries and the End of Party-Boss Influence

The system of caucus-conventions and presidential primaries is a crazy quilt of activity. Candidates fly from one end of the country to the other and back again, emphasizing certain states, de-emphasizing others, and doing their best to impose their interpretations on the most recent results. Candidates are never wholly confident about how or where they should spend their time or money, and voters are not quite sure of what is going on. Yet there is more to the system than its awkwardness, complexity, and unpredictability.

Popular participation in the presidential nominating process generally was not of much consequence prior to the reforms of the 1970s. Candidates, following their instincts and the advice of assorted national and state politicians, chose to enter primaries, to avoid them, or to participate in certain ones while skipping others. As recently as 1968, only fourteen states even held primaries. And Hubert Humphrey captured the Democratic nomination that year even though he did not contest any primaries, which were dominated by Eugene McCarthy and Robert F. Kennedy. In states using the caucus-convention system, the chief method of nomination, one or a few leaders typically controlled the selection of delegates and thus the outcome. To win the nomination, candidates spent much of their time cultivating key state party leaders. Only a few candidates at any time, moreover, were thought to be "available" for the office—that is, possessing attributes that would prompt party leaders around the country and the media to take them seriously. Presidential nominees were chosen in a relatively closed system from among a very select group.

That ambiance and the rules and practices that fostered it have disappeared. Today, the system is remarkably open. The impact of party leaders and organizations is minimal in the process. No leader can "deliver" a state. Candidates rarely write off a primary or caucus, though they often downplay the significance of certain ones. And, most important, the rank-and-file voters now play a central role in the presidential nominating process.[43] Whether the new system produces better presidential candidates (or better presidents) than those previously chosen in smoke-filled rooms is another matter.

Presidential primaries, because they tap voters' preferences in a more direct fashion than caucuses and involve a much larger sector of the electorate, present a particularly good opportunity for testing candidates, policies, and issues in a variety of states.[44] Consider the evidence of recent decades. The Vietnam War was the pivotal issue in both the 1968 and 1972 Democratic primaries. It contributed to President Lyndon Johnson's decision not to seek reelection in 1968 and, four years later, was central to George McGovern's nomination. When an outsider, Jimmy Carter, won a large majority of the Democratic primaries in 1976, the intensity of voters' resentment toward the "Washington establishment" was revealed. Voter attitudes toward conservatism were brought to light in 1980. Ronald Reagan easily won the first primary in New Hampshire (following a narrow loss to George H. W. Bush in Iowa, the first caucus-convention state), lost narrowly to Bush in Massachusetts, and then won twenty-seven of the next thirty primaries he entered. In 1992 Clinton demonstrated his personal resiliency and the appeal of his centrist message in an often-bruising beginning to the primary season; he won more primaries—thirty-two—than any previous Democratic candidate. And, in 2000, George W. Bush demonstrated the appeal of his message of "compassionate conservatism" in winning thirty-five of the forty-two Republican primaries.

What has been the overall impact of the preconvention struggle on the choice of nominees? The primary and convention-caucus process has become decisive, all but eliminating the significance of the national conventions in the selection of presidential nominees. The last truly open convention was the Democratic convention of 1968, which selected Hubert Humphrey as the nominee despite the fact that he did not participate in any primaries. Since the adoption of the McGovern-Fraser reforms, one of the few convention uncertainties to be settled is which state will cast the votes (of already committed delegates) that will push the winning candidate over the top. Everyone has known the winner for months.

The Convention Delegates

The ramifications of political reforms are often much larger than anticipated. The new emphasis on popular participation in the delegate selection process, coupled with the requirements for affirmative action plans to promote the representation of disadvantaged groups, has sharply changed the composition of Democratic national conventions. Prior to the 1970s, Democratic delegates were preponderantly male, middle-aged, and white. And they were usually party regulars—officials of the party, important contributors, and reliable rank-and-file members. Public officeholders were prominent in all state delegations. The selection process itself was dominated by state and local party leaders.

The reforms produced a new breed of delegate. As a result of the guidelines adopted by the McGovern-Fraser Commission, the representation of women, African Americans, and the young in the national convention increased dramatically. For example, the proportion of women delegates grew from 13 percent in 1968 to 40 percent in 1972, and that of African Americans from 5.5 to 15 percent. Under current rules, each Democratic state party is required to develop outreach programs to increase the number of delegates from groups that have been significantly underrepresented in the past, such as individuals who are over sixty-five years old, physically handicapped, or with low or moderate incomes. Another affirmative action rule specifies that in the selection of at-large delegates, preference should be given to African, Hispanic, Native, and Asian/Pacific Americans, and to women. Moreover, all state delegation selection plans must provide for an equal division of delegates between men and women. These mandated changes have had a profound impact on the composition of state delegations.

The chief losers in the reordering of the 1970s were Democratic party professionals and public officeholders, as delegates animated by particular issues or candidates ("amateurs," in broad terms) replaced them in state after state. Changes in party rules—marked by adding superdelegates—have altered the composition of the convention. A survey of Democratic delegates in 1988 found that 43 percent held some party office and 26 percent held an elective (or public) office. Seventy-four percent of the delegates reported that they were engaged in party activities on a year-round basis. Twenty-two percent of the delegates, by contrast, said that they engaged in party work only when the issues or candidates were important to them.[45] Clearly, professional politicians have reemerged after being sidelined by various party reform commissions. Whether their presence will make much difference remains to be seen. Recent conventions have been cut and dried, the presidential nominees having been chosen earlier by primary voters and caucus participants.

Changes in the composition of Republican convention delegations have come more gradually. Even so, a larger proportion of women, African Americans, and young people are being elected as Republican delegates than ever before. Amateur activists are also more numerous in Republican conventions, but not on the scale found on the Democratic side. Party leaders, long-time party members, and public officials have steadily played key roles in Republican conventions.

Convention delegates reflect neither a cross section of the population nor of the party membership. Two particular characteristics differentiate delegates from the wider public and rank-and-file party members: high income and substantial education. In 2000 three quarters of both Republican and Democratic delegates had completed four years of college, compared with about one quarter of the population as a whole. Fifty-seven percent of the delegates in each party reported incomes in excess of $75,000 annually, which is more than twice the nation's median income. Moreover, 23 percent of Republican delegates and 12 percent of Democratic delegates reported being millionaires.[46]

The racial, gender, and union differences in the parties are reflected in their delegates. African Americans made up both 19 percent of the Democratic delegates and 19 percent of the party's membership, while they represented only 2 percent of both the Republican delegates and party membership. Despite the Republicans' efforts to highlight African Americans at their convention in 2000, the percentage of African American delegates represented a low point this century.[47] The percentage of Hispanic Democratic delegates was 12 percent compared with 6 percent among Republican delegates. Similarly, 48 percent of the Democratic delegates were women, compared with 35 percent of the Republican delegates. And just under one third of the Democratic delegates were labor union members, as contrasted with 1 percent for the Republicans.[48]

Liberals are regularly overrepresented in the Democratic convention, conservatives in the Republican convention. In 2000, 14 percent of the Democratic delegates described themselves as "very liberal" as contrasted with 6 percent for the Democratic membership as a whole. And whereas 49 percent of rank-and-file Republicans saw themselves as "very conservative" or "somewhat conservative," 57 percent of the Republican delegates described themselves in that fashion. Fully 30 percent of all Republican delegates, in fact, identified themselves as very conservative—a proportion much greater than found among Republican voters. Only 1 percent of Republican delegates identified themselves as liberals, as contrasted with 11 percent for GOP registered voters. Four percent of the Democratic delegates were somewhat or very conservative, as contrasted with 16 percent for rank-and-file party members.[49] Ideologically, these two party elites are quite different. What is more, ideological distinctiveness is much more characteristic of delegates than of average party voters.

The Politics of the Convention

Three practical aims dominate the proceedings of the national convention: to nominate presidential and vice-presidential candidates, to draft the party platform, and to lay the groundwork for party unity in the campaign. The way in which the party addresses itself to the tasks of nominating the candidates and drafting the platform is likely to determine how well it achieves its third objective: to heal party rifts and forge a cohesive party. To put together a presidential ticket and a platform that satisfies the principal elements of the party is difficult. The task of reconciling divergent interests within the party occupies the convention from its earliest moments until the final gavel—at least in most conventions. By and large, convention leaders have been successful in shaping the compromises necessary to keep the national party, such as it is, from flying apart.

The Convention Committees

The initial business of the convention is handled mainly by four committees. The *committee on credentials* is given the responsibility for determining the permanent roll (official membership) of the convention. Its specific function is to ascertain the members' legal right to seats in the convention. In the absence of challenges to the right of certain delegates to be seated, or of contests between two delegations from the same state trying to be seated, the review is handled routinely and with dispatch. Most state delegations are seated without difficulty. When disputes arise, the committee holds hearings and takes testimony; its recommendations for seating delegates are then reported to the convention, which ordinarily (but not invariably) sustains them. The *committee on permanent organization* is charged with selecting the permanent officers of the convention, including the permanent chair, the clerks, and the sergeant at arms. The *committee on rules* devises the rules under which the convention will operate and establishes the order of business.

Ordinarily the most important convention committee is the *committee on resolutions*, which is in charge of drafting the party platform. The actual work of this committee begins many weeks in advance of the convention, so that usually a draft of the document exists by the time the convention opens and the formal committee hearings begin. When a president seeks reelection, the platform is likely to be prepared under his direction and accepted by the committees (and later by the floor) without major changes.

A fight over the nomination may influence the drafting of the platform, because the leading candidates have an interest in securing planks that are compatible with their views. Indeed, the outcomes of clashes over planks may provide a good indication of which candidate will capture the nomination. In the 1968 Democratic convention, for example, it was all but certain that Humphrey would win the nomination when the convention, after a lengthy and emotional floor debate, adopted by a comfortable margin a plank that reflected the Johnson administration's position on the Vietnam War. Humphrey's two principal opponents, Sens. Eugene McCarthy and George McGovern, were the most prominent supporters of the losing minority plank, which called for an unconditional halt to the bombing of North Vietnam.

The 1980 Republican and Democratic platforms were fashioned in sharply different ways. Harmony prevailed at the Republican convention, and the members quickly approved a platform with planks that meshed comfortably with the views of its nominee, Ronald Reagan. The document of the platform committee was adopted without change. Debate over the Democratic platform, by contrast, was acrimonious and protracted. Numerous minority reports were adopted on the floor. In the end, the delegates adopted a platform that in major respects, particularly in its economic and human needs planks, was more in line with the liberal views of Sen. Edward Kennedy and his partisans than with those of President Carter. The high level of conflict over the platform was surprising given that an incumbent president, the certain nominee, was seeking reelection. No one expects the president's forces to lose on key convention votes.[50]

In 1988 Jesse Jackson, who ran second in the fight for the nomination, won numerous platform concessions from Michael Dukakis as party leaders worked hard to unify the party for the campaign. On the few planks that were controversial, however, Dukakis's forces prevailed. Adopted with a minimum of controversy, the 1988 Republican platform followed the conservative doctrines set down in the Reagan platforms of 1980 and 1984.

Winning a decisive majority of the Democratic delegates in 1992, Arkansas governor Bill Clinton thoroughly controlled the platform-writing process and the convention. The delegates of former California governor Jerry Brown, the last candidate standing against Clinton, were largely ignored by the Clinton majority, which was bent on fashioning a centrist platform. Several weeks later, the Republican convention adopted, without debate, a strongly conservative platform. Abortion-rights activists were unable to get six state delegations to support a motion for a floor debate on the subject. Many delegates who favored abortion rights attached higher priority to party harmony.[51]

The most remarkable feature of the 1996 Republican convention, arguably, was its preoccupation with conformity and unity. The discussion of contentious issues, such as abortion and affirmative action, was suppressed; platform fights never materialized; and speakers who might rock the boat, such as Pat Buchanan and several pro-choice governors, were kept away from the podium. Although party moderates, such as Colin Powell, were the featured speakers at the convention, the platform that was adopted was ultraconservative. The party's presidential nominee, Bob Dole, said that he had not read it and, moreover, did not feel bound by it.

In 2000 the Republicans, concerned about their reputation as anti-minority and anti-gay, made an effort to highlight their diversity. Although fewer than five percent of their delegates were actually black, a number of noteworthy African Americans from Powell, who spoke favorably about affirmative action, to the Rock, a professional wrestler, addressed the convention. Arizona representative Jim Kolbe, who is gay, was allowed to speak as well. Although the Texas delegation threatened to boycott Kolbe's speech, they instead waged a silent protest by removing their cowboy hats and mouthing prayers. On the Democratic side, the best-remembered moment was likely Al Gore's long kiss of his wife, Tipper, before his acceptance speech. The speech itself had a strong populist character, pitting "the people versus the powerful." After Gore lost the election despite an extraordinarily strong economy, Democratic leaders came to question the efficacy of such a populist approach.

Selecting the Presidential Ticket

To some party leaders, the best convention is the one that opens with significant uncertainties and imponderables—a good, though not surefire, prescription for generating public interest in the convention, the party, and its nominees.[52] In the usual convention, however, uncertainties are far from numerous. Doubts are much more likely to surround the choice of the vice-presidential nominee than the presidential nominee. Indeed, with the proliferation of primaries after 1968 and the increase in front loading since 1988, the presidential nominee is almost sure to be known months before the convention.

Recent experience tells us that the front-runner going into the election year nearly always wins the nomination. Although the first two post–McGovern-Fraser elections produced two surprises with the nominations of George McGovern in 1972 and Jimmy Carter in 1976, there have been no real surprises in the last six elections. Some early front-runners may wobble for several weeks, as Bob Dole did in 1996, but their superiority in organizing and fund-raising generally leads to their nomination. Open conventions have all but disappeared. In fact, first-ballot nominations have occurred at both conventions every year from 1956 through 2000.

In only a few conventions in the past five decades has there been substantial doubt about the ultimate winner: both conventions in 1952 (Dwight D. Eisenhower versus Robert A. Taft in the Republican convention and a wide-open contest in the Democratic convention); the Democratic convention in 1960 (John F. Kennedy, who won the presidential primaries, versus the field); and the 1976 Republican convention (Gerald R. Ford versus Ronald Reagan). Now that so many delegates are chosen in primaries, it is almost certain that the front-runner will have won enough delegates prior to the convention to lock up the nomination.

The final major item of convention business is the selection of the party's vice-presidential nominee. Here the task of the party is to come up with the right political formula—the candidate who can add the most to the ticket and detract the least. The presidential nominee most often makes the choice, following rounds of consultation with various party and candidate organization leaders.[53] Although a great deal of suspense is usually created over the vice-presidential nomination, convention ratification comes easily once the presidential nominee has decided and cleared the selection with key leaders.

Unless the presidential nominee is inclined to take a major risk to serve the interest of his own faction or ideology (as Barry Goldwater did in choosing Republican national chair William E. Miller in 1964), he has traditionally selected a candidate who can help to balance the ticket and unify the party.[54] Jimmy Carter's choice of Walter Mondale in 1976 fits neatly into this category (a southern moderate and a midwestern liberal), as does Ronald Reagan's choice of George Bush in 1980 (a western conservative and an eastern moderate), and Michael Dukakis's choice of Sen. Lloyd Bentsen (a northeastern "liberal" and a southern conservative). As Dukakis's experience suggests, however, such regional and ideological balancing does not ensure success.

Other vice-presidential choices do not follow this pattern. For example, Mondale's selection of Geraldine A. Ferraro in 1984 broke with major party tradition in more ways than one: Representative Ferraro was the first woman to be nominated for the vice presidency, the first Italian American to be nominated for national office, and the first nominee to be anointed prior to the opening of the convention. Similarly, George H. W. Bush's surprising selection of a younger, telegenic U.S. senator, Dan Quayle of Indiana, in 1988, reflected his desire to merge conservative and generational appeals. He hoped to satisfy the party's powerful conservative wing, win the attention of the postwar "baby boomers," improve the party's lagging position with women voters, and strengthen its prospects in the Midwest. In the end, Quayle, a political neophyte, probably cost Bush more votes than he won. And, in 2000, Al Gore chose a fellow moderate in Sen. Joseph Lieberman (D-Conn.), although Lieberman was perceived as somewhat more conservative than Gore on so-called "morality" issues. The selection of Lieberman, the first Jewish vice-presidential nominee, energized Democrats, providing the ticket with a double-digit bounce in the polls the week following the convention.

Arguably, regional and ideological balancing have become less important in recent years. Seeking to give the Democratic party a moderate and youthful image in 1992, Clinton chose Senator Gore of Tennessee as his running mate, creating the party's first all-southern ticket since 1852.[55] The strategy proved successful: stressing change, the "new Democrats" carried five southern states and received strong support from younger (and also older) voters throughout the country. In 2000 George W. Bush from Texas won the White House after choosing a fellow westerner, Dick Cheney of Wyoming (who had been living in Texas for nearly a decade). Both Bush and Cheney brought strong conservative credentials to the race.

Furthermore, recent experience suggests certain pitfalls in choosing a running mate who is not in ideological agreement with the president. For almost everyone, including the pundits, Bob Dole's choice of Jack Kemp as his running mate in 1996 was a surprising choice, in part because of their strained personal relationship but also because of their incompatibility on certain issues. In the press, Dole's choice of Kemp was framed as hypocritical; he hoped to get a lift in the polls, to reenergize his campaign, to unify his party (bringing together the tax-cutting and deficit-reducing wings), and to make his economic plan (to cut taxes while also balancing the budget) the centerpiece of his campaign. Many interpreted the choice of Kemp, the party's most prominent advocate of deep tax cuts, as Dole's conversion to supply-side economics—an economic model he had often ridiculed.

The main point is that the presidential candidate has a great deal of leeway in choosing the vice-presidential nominee. The need to reward or placate a certain party element may of course reduce the list of possible choices. Except for the most doctrinaire presidential candidate, the prime consideration is to choose a running mate who strengthens the ticket in terms of the party's strategy for winning the election.

The Media, the Presidential Nominating Process, and the Parties

It would be hard to exaggerate the importance of the print and broadcast media in shaping the presidential nominating process. Not surprisingly, media influence is as controversial as it is pivotal.

Critics charge that the media are preoccupied with the competitive, or "horse race," aspects of the presidential campaign and give too little attention to the candidates' records and issue positions. Complicated policy questions tend to be ignored by television and even by much of the print media. By contrast, horse race stories are easy for journalists to write, for television reporters to portray, and for the public to understand. These stories have a standard format: where the candidates have been and where they are going; how their strategies have emerged; how crowds and organized groups are responding to them; how politicians evaluate them and their campaigns; how they have dealt with events and mistakes; who has endorsed them; and, most important, who is winning and who is losing. What the campaign is all about is ordinarily lost in horse race accounts.

Numerous studies have shown that more than half of all stories on presidential campaigns have a horse race theme.[56] During the crucial first half of the 1988 presidential nominating season, 80 percent of the network news airtime was devoted to horse race stories and 20 percent to substantive issues, and, in 1992, the split was closer to 90–10.[57] One of the campaign's early casualties in 1988, Dole, had these observations on campaign reporting:

> What I witnessed generally on my own campaign plane was an aircraft filled with reporters who became each other's best audience. It was an ultra-insider's game of gossip and nit-picking that turned presidential campaign coverage into trivial pursuits. It was a daily spin from the experts on the state of the campaign, whether it came from a reporter who had been on board for one month, or one stop. . . . Preconceived notions, prewritten stories and premeditated clichés were all confirmed regardless of the facts. And if there was a nice soap opera campaign story out there, it would be kept on the spin cycle for a good week or so. All the while, reporters' necks were craned in the rear of the plane scanning the campaign staff up front for smiles or frowns, or seating arrangements that would somehow reveal the inside story. Meanwhile, the issues disappeared somewhere over Iowa airspace. . . . I just wish I was hounded on the federal deficit as I was on my staff. I just wish I was interrogated about American agriculture as I was about fund-raising. I just wish my voting record was as thoroughly scrutinized as were my wife's personal finances.[58]

Another feature of media coverage of nominating campaigns singled out by critics is the practice of focusing on front-runners at the expense of providing information on other candidates' campaigns. The early public opinion polls provide the initial impetus to prepare press and television stories on the front-runners. Thin on evidence, these early and speculative stories nevertheless generate additional coverage of the leaders, even before the first caucus or primary is held. In natural progression, the candidates who win or place well in the Iowa precinct caucuses, the New Hampshire primary, or both become media darlings and gain even more coverage. The interpretation of the election by candidates, handlers, and the media—so-called "spin control"—is what really counts. A narrow win can sometimes be translated into a striking victory in the next day's news or treated as a virtual loss, because the winner's vote failed to meet expectations set by the media.[59] For example, Edmund Muskie "lost" the 1972 Democratic primary in New Hampshire to George McGovern despite receiving 46 percent of the vote to McGovern's 37. The *Washington Post's* well-known reporter David Broder had declared that Muskie could only "win" if he garnered more than 50 percent of the vote, an interpretation adopted by the rest of the news media. Muskie's candidacy soon collapsed.

The media's role is particularly important in the early phase of the presidential nominating process. Television and press journalists sort out the candidates (ranking them as "the hopeless, the plausible, and the likely, with substantial differences between the three in the amount and quality of coverage"[60]), establish performance expectations, boost some campaigns while writing off others, and launch the bandwagons. Their evaluations create winners and losers. Candidates who capture the media's attention are rewarded out of proportion to the significance of the contests and perhaps to their shares of the vote as well. Early winners and surprise candidates gain momentum in this system of "lotteries driven by media expectations and candidate name recognition."[61]

The media also play a critical role in publicizing the factional appeals of candidates in primaries and caucuses. Increasingly, presidential candidates have eschewed coalition building while seeking to mobilize narrow ideological, religious, ethnic, or sectional followings. The more crowded the field, the greater the probability that an active, passionate, well-organized faction can keep the candidate in contention from one Tuesday to the next in the crucial early weeks of the season. Through extensive coverage of the campaign, the media help the candidates to attract, instruct, and mobilize their distinctive factional followings.[62]

Campaign schedules, speeches, and statements all revolve around the media. Candidates fly from one airport tarmac or television market to the next in their quest for press attention and free media time on local television stations. Nothing may be more important than free media time. Brief stops are the order of the day. It is not uncommon in the days leading up to Super Tuesday—when most of the action is concentrated in the South—for some candidates to visit five or six states (or, more accurately, assorted airports in these states) in a single day, not to see crowds of voters but to secure a few seconds of exposure on the local evening news—and, with luck, a snippet on the network news.

The influence of the media on the presidential nominating process is obviously pervasive. But two broad effects stand out. The first is that the media have undercut the position of party elites. As almost every candidate could testify, free media time and paid advertising are a much more effective means for influencing mass electorates than working through party leaders and party organizations. The media also provide an excellent opportunity for candidates, tutored by media consultants, to raise campaign money by gaining public attention. Impressive televised speeches sometimes produce a flood of campaign contributions. It is not far from the truth to suggest that the media are now used to "deliver" votes and money in a way that state and local politicians did a generation ago. What is more, political consultants and handlers are at least as important as any party professional in shaping campaign decisions.

Second, the media have played a key role in the transformation of the national party convention. They did so by becoming the vehicle by which candidates and candidate organizations distanced themselves from the party organization. Today's conventions are run by candidates and their organizations; the influence that party and elected officials wield is a function of their affiliation with candidate organizations. The vast majority of the delegates arrive at the convention committed to a candidate, and the convention meets to ratify the voters' choice, expressed in primaries and caucuses, as the presidential nominee. Typically, the nominee is known long in advance of the convention. The old "deliberative" convention, marked by high-stakes bargaining among party leaders, with the nomination in suspense, is all but extinct.

In virtually every phase, the new party convention is a media event. Activities are scheduled at times that will produce maximum television audiences. Deals are struck to avoid controversy. Politics is sanitized. Celebrities are properly honored. Speeches are kept brief. Trivial events and "news" are magnified by television reporters scurrying around for interviews. Orchestration and entertainment pervade the convention agenda as leaders strive to showcase their candidates, enhance the party's image, and hold an audience notorious for its short attention span. Elaborate efforts are made to avoid boring the viewers.

In this new environment, the convention takes on the appearance of a prepackaged television show or tightly scripted infomercial. The absence of genuine news and spontaneity—in the midst of patriotic bunting, stagecraft, films, tributes, inspirationalism, and the celebration of average citizens, their lives, and even their dogs—had led the major networks to cut back convention coverage to a minimum, often to only a single prime-time hour per day. Even over the last decade, the amount of coverage has dropped from fifteen hours in 1992 to eight and one half in 2000. As for television viewers of the convention, their numbers have declined precipitously as well. During the 1950s and 1960s, about 25 percent of potential viewers tuned in, increasing perhaps to 50 percent at the time of important speeches. Now, most Americans report seeing none of the convention, and the majority of those who report seeing some of it are "inadvertent" viewers who caught a few minutes of coverage while channel surfing.[63]

National party conventions have turned into spectacles, or made-for-TV shows, because they no longer actually choose the candidate; because they are trying to stay in business in a mass-oriented political system; because they are driven by the entertainment imperative; because party leaders prefer choreography to controversy; and because the media control the interpretation, and thus shape the politics, of the preconvention season. Not a great deal—maybe nothing—is left for the convention to decide. That at least has been the experience of the past several decades.

NOTES

1. In 1955 Connecticut, another longtime direct primary holdout, only adopted the primary after much tampering with the idea. The Connecticut model (the challenge primary) combines convention and primary under an arrangement in which the party convention continues to make nominations, but with this proviso: if the party nominee at the convention is challenged by another candidate who receives as much as 20 percent of the convention votes, a primary must be held later; otherwise, no primary is required, and the name of the convention nominee is automatically certified for the general election.

2. Does a hard-fought, divisive primary hurt the party's chances in the general election? Politicians and political observers tend to believe that it does—that supporters of the candidate or candidates who lost in the primary will switch their allegiance or decline to vote in the general election. Although the question is not settled, the preponderance of evidence suggests that conflictual (or competitive) primaries do have an adverse impact on the parties' chances for victory in the general election. The candidate who survives a primary battle is not as likely to win in November as one who had little or no primary opposition. Support for this interpretation appears in Patrick J. Kenney and Tom W. Rice, "The Effect of Primary Divisiveness in Gubernatorial and Senatorial Elections," *Journal of Politics* 46 (August 1984): 904–915; and Robert A. Bernstein, "Divisive Primaries Do Hurt: U.S. Senate Races, 1956–1972," *American Political Science Review* 71 (June 1977): 540–545. But for a study that finds the relationship weak, see Richard Born, "The Influence of House Primary Divisiveness on General Election Margins, 1962–76," *Journal of Politics* 43 (August 1981): 640–661. The "carryover effect" has also been studied in presidential elections by Walter J. Stone. He finds a strong carryover effect among partisan and committed activists: that is, activists who supported candidates who lost the nomination were less active in the general election. See his article, "The Carryover Effect in Presidential Elections," *American Political Science Review* 80 (March 1986): 271–279. For additional evidence on the importance of the carryover effect, see Patrick J. Kenney and Tom W. Rice, "Presidential Prenomination Preferences and Candidate Evaluations," *American Political Science Review* 82 (December 1988): 1309–1319. For the most recent studies of the effects of divisive primaries, see Kenney and Rice, "The Relationship between Divisive Primaries and General Election Outcomes," *American Journal of Political Science* 31 (February 1987): 31–44; and Patrick J. Kenney, "Sorting Out the Effects of Primary Divisiveness in Congressional and Senatorial Elections," *Western Political Quarterly* 41 (September 1988): 765–777. Preoccupation with the effects of divisive primaries may lead researchers to ignore the positive, *mobilizing* effects of participation in nominating campaigns. See a new study by Walter J. Stone, Lonnie Rae

Atkeson, and Ronald B. Rapoport, "Turning On or Turning Off? Mobilization and Demobilization Effects of Participation in Presidential Nominating Campaigns," *American Journal of Political Science* 36 (August 1992): 665–691.

3. *Tashjian v. Republican Party of Connecticut*, 479 U.S. 208 (1986). See a comprehensive analysis of the *Tashjian* decision by Leon D. Epstein, "Will American Political Parties Be Privatized?" *Journal of Law and Politics* 5 (winter 1989): 239–274.

4. The states with the purest form of open primary are Hawaii, Idaho, Michigan, Minnesota, North Dakota, Utah, Vermont, and Wisconsin. See a comprehensive classification scheme for state primary systems in Malcolm E. Jewell and David M. Olson, *Political Parties and Elections in American States* (Chicago: Dorsey Press, 1988), 89–94.

5. Lynn Vavreck, "The Reasoning Voter Meets the Strategic Candidate: Signals and Specificity in Campaign Advertising, 1998," *American Politics Research* 29 (September 2001): 507–529.

6. See Gary D. Wekkin's article, "Why Crossover Voters Are Not 'Mischievous Voters': The Segmented Partisanship Hypothesis," *American Politics Quarterly* 19 (April 1991): 229–257.

7. See "Federal Judge Strikes Down Arizona's Open Primary," *CongressDaily,* August 6, 2002, 12.

8. The "crossover" voting data are drawn from Ronald D. Hedlund and Meredith W. Watts, "The Wisconsin Open Primary, 1968 to 1984," *American Politics Quarterly* 14 (January–April 1986): 55–73. Also see Ronald D. Hedlund, Meredith W. Watts, and David M. Hedge, "Voting in an Open Primary," *American Politics Quarterly* 10 (April 1982): 197–218; David Adamany, "Communication: Cross-over Voting and the Democratic Party's Reform Rules," *American Political Science Review* 70 (June 1976): 536–541; and James I. Lengle and Byron E. Shafer, "Primary Rules, Political Power, and Social Change," *American Political Science Review* 70 (March 1976): 25–40.

9. Philip Paolino and Daron R. Shaw, "Lifting the Hood on the Straight-Talk Express: Examining the McCain Phenomenon," *American Politics Research* 29 (September 2001): 483–506.

10. See *California Democratic Party v. Jones,* 530 U.S. 567 (2000). Also see "The Supreme Court: Freedom of Association; Court Strikes Down California Primary Placing All Parties on a Single Ballot," *New York Times,* June 27, 2000.

11. For more details see "Parties Appeal Ruling on Blanket Primary," *Seattle Times,* April 26, 2002, B3.

12. See "The Supreme Court: Freedom of Association; Court Strikes Down California Primary Placing All Parties on a Single Ballot," *New York Times,* June 27, 2000.

13. The observations made in this paragraph are based mainly on an analysis by Charles D. Hadley, "The Impact of the Louisiana Open Elections System Reform," *State Government* 58, no. 4 (1986): 152–157. Also see Thomas A. Kazee, "The Impact of Electoral Reform: 'Open Elections' and the Louisiana Party System," *Publius* 13 (winter 1983): 132–139; and for a general analysis of factionalism, see Earl Black, "A Theory of Southern Factionalism," *Journal of Politics* 45 (August 1983): 594–614.

14. Laws in a few states make provisions for the parties to hold preprimary conventions for the purpose of choosing the organization slate. The candidates selected by these conventions will usually appear on the ballot bearing the party endorsement. In the great majority of states, however, slating is an informal party process; the party depends on its organizational network and the communications media to inform the voters which candidates carry party support.

15. For an unorthodox argument that the intraparty competition afforded by primaries encourages the parties to be responsive to voters, see John G. Geer and Mark E. Shere, "Party Competition and the Prisoner's Dilemma: An Argument for the Direct Primary," *Journal of Politics* 54 (August 1992): 741–761.

16. See Malcolm E. Jewell and Sarah A. Morehouse, "What Are Party Endorsements Worth? A Study of Preprimary Gubernatorial Endorsements," *American Politics Quarterly* 24 (July 1996): 338–362.

17. Jewell and Olson, *Political Parties and Elections in American States,* 94–104. Also see a study of the various factors that influence the value of a political party's preprimary endorsement to the candidate who received it.

18. These themes appear in Frank J. Sorauf, *Party Politics in America* (Boston: Little, Brown, 1980), 220–224.

19. Thomas Mann and Norman Ornstein, *Vital Statistics on Congress* (Washington, D.C.: American Enterprise Institute, 2001).

20. V. O. Key Jr., *American State Politics: An Introduction* (New York: Knopf, 1956); William H. Standing and James A. Robinson, "Inter-Party Competition and Primary Contesting: The Case of Indiana," *American Political Science Review* 52 (December 1958): 1066–1077; and Malcolm E. Jewell, "Party and Primary Competition in Kentucky State Legislative Races," *Kentucky Law Journal* 48 (summer 1960): 517–535.

21. John F. Bibby, *Politics, Parties, and Elections in America,* 5th ed. (New York: Thomson-Wadsworth, 2003).

22. Denis G. Sullivan, Jeffrey L. Pressman, and F. Christopher Arterton, *Explorations in Convention Decision Making* (San Francisco: Freeman, 1976), 17.

23. Ibid., 20–21.

24. These data were taken from the Federal Election Commission's Web site, www.fec.gov.

25. Ideologically extreme candidates tend to run better in caucus states than in primary states. See Barbara Norrander, "Nomination Choices: Caucus and Primary Outcomes, 1976–88," *American Journal of Political Science* 37 (May 1993): 343–364.

26. Changing from one system to another has unanticipated consequences. Richard W. Boyd has shown, for example, that frequent elections depress turnout. Thus, states that switch from caucus-convention systems to direct primaries to select candidates and convention delegates will have a lower general election turnout. See his article, "The Effects of Primaries and Statewide Races on Voter Turnout," *Journal of Politics* 51 (August 1989): 730–739.

27. Stephen J. Wayne, *The Road to the White House 2000* (Boston: Bedford/St. Martins, 2001), 340–343.

28. Turnout in presidential primaries tends to be highest in those states distinguished by high levels of education, facilitative legal provisions on voting, and competitive two-party elections. Interestingly, high turnout is not associated with high levels of campaign spending. See Patrick J. Kenney and Tom W. Rice, "Voter Turnout in Presidential Primaries: A Cross-Sectional Examination," *Political Behavior* 7, no. 1 (1985): 101–112. In terms of participation in presidential primaries, there is little or no difference between Democrats and Republicans. See Jack Moran and Mark Fenster, "Voting Turnout in Presidential Primaries," *American Politics Quarterly* 10 (October 1982): 453–476. Candidate strategy does influence turnout. For a study of how the number of candidates in the opposition party and the intensity of campaigning in the presidential party influence aggregate turnout levels, see Barbara Norrander and Gregg W. Smith, "Type of Contest, Candidate Strategy, and Turnout in Presidential Primaries," *American Politics Quarterly* 13 (January 1985): 28–50. Turnout for first-tier caucuses is heightened by the presence of significant ideological choice among candidates, though no relationship exists between ideological range and turnout in primary states. See Steven E. Schier, "Turnout Choice in Presidential Nominations," *American Politics Quarterly* 10 (April 1982): 231–245. For a model of how individual voters decide which candidate they prefer during the presidential nomination campaign, see Patrick J. Kenney and Tom W. Rice, "A Model of Nomination Preferences," *American Politics Quarterly* 20 (July 1992): 267–286.

29. Wayne, *The Road to the White House 2000.*

30. James I. Lengle, Diane Owen, and Molly W. Sonner, "Divisive Nominating Mechanisms and Democratic Party Electoral Prospects," *Journal of Politics* 57 (May 1995): 370–383. Quotation on page 381.

31. Priscilla L. Southwell, "Rules as 'Unseen Participants': The Democratic Presidential Nominating Process," *American Politics Quarterly* 20 (January 1992): 64.

32. William J. Crotty, *Political Reform and the American Experiment* (New York: Crowell, 1977), 255–260.

33. Bill Clinton was the first presidential candidate of either party since 1952 to be elected who did not win the New Hampshire primary. Perhaps an indication of New Hampshire's declining importance, George W. Bush was the second.

34. Thomas Patterson, *Out of Order* (New York: Knopf, 1993).

35. See William C. Adams, "As New Hampshire Goes. . . ," in *Media and Momentum: The New Hampshire Primary and Nomination Politics,* ed. Gary R. Orren and Nelson W. Polsby (Chatham, N.J.: Chatham House Publishers, Inc., 1987), 42–49.

36. Are the voters who take part in presidential primaries ideologically unrepresentative? Evidence offered by Barbara Norrander indicates that they are not. See her article "Ideological Representativeness of Presidential Primary Voters," *American Journal of Political Science* 33 (August 1989): 570–587. Also see John G. Geer, "Assessing the Representativeness of Electorates in Presidential Primaries," *American Journal of Political Science* 32 (November 1988): 929–945.

37. Until 2002, the maximum donation was $1,000 for individuals. The $2,000 donation limit is indexed for inflation.

38. For a study of how state party leaders seek to enhance media coverage of their state's primary or caucus, see David S. Castle, "Media Coverage of Presidential Primaries," *American Politics Quarterly* 19 (January 1991): 33–42. Front loading has been a particularly effective device for drawing attention to the state's delegate selection process.

39. *Congressional Quarterly Weekly Report,* August 17, 1996, 2299.

40. Larry M. Bartels, *Presidential Primaries* (Princeton: Princeton University Press, 1988).

41. For evidence that heavy candidate spending influences the outcome of the presidential nominating process, see Audrey A. Haynes, Paul-Henri Gurian, and Stephen M. Nichols, "The Role of Candidate Spending in Presidential Nomination Campaigns, *Journal of Politics* 59 (February 1997): 213–225.

42. No one articulates this thesis better than Patterson, *Out of Order.*

43. Voters in primary and caucus states do not respond to exactly the same forces. A study of the 1984 Democratic party primaries and caucuses found that sociodemographic groups (particularly African Americans and labor) and general economic circumstances (levels of unemployment and income) were the major factors in influencing candidates' vote shares. Their vote shares in caucus states were heavily influenced by the sociodemographic makeup of the population and by levels of campaign spending. Candidates have very little control over the dominant factors in primary states, but they have considerable control over the major factor of campaign spending in caucus states. See T. Wayne Parent, Calvin C. Jillson, and Ronald E. Weber, "Voting Outcomes in the 1984 Democratic Party Primaries and Caucuses," *American Political Science Review* 81 (March 1987): 67–84.

44. But see a study of the 1980 presidential primaries that finds that voters made little use of candidates' issue positions in deciding how to vote. The most frequent correlates of vote choice are the qualities of the candidates. Barbara Norrander, "Correlates of Vote Choice in the 1980 Presidential Primaries," *Journal of Politics* 48 (February 1986): 156–166. Additionally, for a study of the characteristics of voters who participate in presidential primaries, see Barbara Norrander, "Explaining Individual Participation in Presidential Primaries," *Western Political Quarterly* 44 (September 1991): 640–655.

45. *New York Times*, July 17, 1988.

46. *New York Times*, August 14, 2000.

47. Frank Rich, "Bonfire of the Vanities," *New York Times*, December 21, 2002.

48. *New York Times*, August 14, 2000.

49. Ibid.

50. Few contributions of the major parties are more likely to be criticized or ridiculed than the party platforms. Commentators have found them meaningless, irrelevant, and nearly useless in charting the direction of the government by the winning candidate and party. The truth is something else. Platform pledges tend to be adopted by the parties once they take control of government. Recently, about two thirds of all platform promises have been fulfilled in some measure. See Gerald M. Pomper and Susan S. Lederman, *Elections in America* (New York: Longman, 1980), especially 161–167; and Alan D. Monroe, "American Party Platforms and Public Opinion," *American Journal of Political Science* 27 (February 1983): 27–42. Also see the persuasive evidence of Ian Budge and Richard I. Hofferbert that the policy positions and platforms of the parties have a significant impact on policy adopted by the party that wins the presidency. They conclude that party government in the United States largely reflects mandate theory. "Mandates and Policy Outputs: U.S. Party Platforms and Federal Expenditures," *American Political Science Review* 84 (March 1990): 111–131.

51. *Congressional Quarterly Weekly Report*, August 22, 1992, 2519–2520.

52. One of the most important functions of the convention is the "rally function"—bringing the party together and creating enthusiasm for the ticket. One manifestation of this is that candidates usually benefit from a "bump" of five to seven percentage points in public opinion surveys. See James E. Campbell, Lynna L. Cherry, and Kenneth A. Wink, "The Convention Bump," *American Politics Quarterly* 20 (July 1992): 287–307.

53. An exception to this rule occurred in 1956 when Adlai Stevenson, the Democratic presidential nominee, created a stir by declining to express a preference for his vice-presidential running mate. Left to its own devices, the convention quickly settled on a choice between Sens. Estes Kefauver and John F. Kennedy. Kefauver, who had been an active candidate for the presidency, won a narrow victory. Kennedy came off even better; he launched his candidacy for the presidential nomination in 1960.

54. The preference of party professionals for a balanced ticket grows out of their instinct for the conservation of the party and their understanding of the electorate. In the view of party professionals, the ticket should be broadly appealing instead of narrowly ideological or sectional. The factors that ordinarily come under review in the consideration of balance are geography, political philosophy, religion, and factional recognition.

55. Does balancing a ticket geographically make a difference? Specifically, does it increase the vote for the ticket in the vice president's home state? The answer is that it makes some positive difference if the candidate is from a small state, but "it is the presidential candidates who dominate the nation's politics." See Robert L. Dudley and Ronald B. Rapoport, "Vice Presidential Candidates and the Home State Advantage: Playing Second Banana at Home and on the Road," *American Journal of Political Science* 33 (May 1989): 537–540. Also see an earlier study by Michael S. Lewis-Beck and Tom W. Rice, "Localism in Presidential Elections: The Home State Advantage," *American Journal of Political Science* 27 (May 1983): 548–556.

56. Doris A. Graber, *Mass Media and American Politics*, 4th ed. (Washington, D.C.: CQ Press, 1993), 273–275. The tendency to treat elections as horse races did not begin with television, but horse race coverage increased dramatically in the television era. Although coverage of policy issues has declined somewhat in recent years, Lee Sigel-

man and David Bullock report, it is still greater than it was during the newspaper era. See their article, "Candidates, Issues, Horse Races, and Hoopla: Presidential Campaign Coverage, 1888–1988," *American Politics Quarterly* 19 (January 1991): 5–32.

57. Patterson, *Out of Order.*

58. U.S. Congress, Senate, *Congressional Record,* daily ed., 100th Cong., 2d sess., April 26, 1988, S4734–4735. The data on horse race versus issue airtime are taken from a study commissioned by *USA Today,* as reported in the issue of April 22, 1988.

59. See Christine F. Ridout, "The Role of Media Coverage of Iowa and New Hampshire in the 1988 Democratic Nomination," *American Politics Quarterly* 19 (January 1991): 48–53.

60. William G. Mayer, "The New Hampshire Primary: A Historical Overview," in *Media and Momentum,* ed. Orren and Polsby, 16.

61. Henry E. Brady and Richard Johnston, "What's the Primary Message: Horse Race or Issue Journalism?" in *Media and Momentum,* ed. Orren and Polsby, 128.

62. Nelson W. Polsby, *Consequences of Party Reform* (New York: Oxford University Press, 1983), 67.

63. Wayne, *The Road to the White House 2000.* For more details on viewership, see Kathleen Hall Jamieson et al., "The Public Learned About Bush and Gore from Conventions; Half Ready to Make an Informed Choice" (Annenberg Public Policy Center, August 25, 2000). For a wide-ranging analysis of the role of the press in the 2000 campaign, see Kathleen Hall Jamieson and Paul Waldman, *The Press Effect: Politicians, Journalists, and the Stories that Shape the Political World* (New York: Oxford University Press, 2003).

4 CAMPAIGNS AND CAMPAIGN FINANCE

POLITICAL CAMPAIGNS ARE DIFFICULT TO DESCRIBE for one very good reason: they come in an extraordinary variety of shapes and sizes. Whether there is such a thing as a typical campaign is open to serious doubt. Campaigns will differ depending on the office sought (executive, legislative, or judicial), the level of government (national, state, or local), the legal and political environments (partisan or nonpartisan election, competitive or noncompetitive constituency), and the initial advantages or disadvantages of the candidates (incumbent or nonincumbent, well known or little known), among other things.

The standards by which to measure and evaluate the effectiveness of campaigns are not easy to discover because of the vast number of variables that intrude both on campaign decisions and on voter choice. Does the party that wins an election owe its victory to a superior campaign or would it have won in any case? Data needed to answer the question are elusive. What is evident is that strategies that are appropriate to one campaign may be less appropriate or even inappropriate to another. Tactics that work at one time or in one place may not work under other circumstances. Organizational arrangements that satisfy one party may not satisfy the other. Campaigns are loaded with imponderables. Neither the party organizations nor the candidates have any control over numerous factors in a campaign. In most cases it is not immediately clear when a miscalculation has been made, how serious it may have been, or how best to repair the damage.

Despite the variability and uncertainty that characterize political campaigns, a few general requirements are imposed on all candidates and parties. The candidate making a serious bid for votes must acquire certain resources and meet certain problems. Whatever his perspective of the campaign, the candidate will have to deal with matters of organization, strategy, and finances.

Campaign Organization

Very likely the single most important fact to know about campaign organization is that the regular party organizations are ill equipped to organize and conduct campaigns by themselves. Of necessity, they look to outsiders for assistance in all kinds of party work and for the development and staffing of auxiliary campaign organizations. A multiplicity of organizational units is created in every major election for the promotion of particular candidacies.[1] Some in business will organize to support the Republican nominee and others will organize to support the Democratic candidate. And the same will be true for educators, lawyers, physicians, advertising executives, and even political independents, to mention but a few. At times these groups work in impressive harmony with the regular party organizations (perhaps to the point of being wholly dominated by them), and at other times they function as virtually independent units, seemingly oblivious to the requirements for communication or for coordination of their activities with those of other party or auxiliary units.

The regular party organizations share influence not only with citizen groups but also with the political action committees (PACs) of interest groups. Among the best known are the American Medical Association Political Action Committee, the Realtors Political Action Committee, the Sierra Club Political Action Committee, the National Rifle Association Political Victory Fund, and the AFL-CIO Committee on Political Education. Like other campaign groups, these committees raise funds, endorse candidates, make campaign contributions, and spend money on behalf of candidates. In 2000 PACs contributed $243 million to candidates for Congress, which came to about 25 percent of their total campaign receipts. In addition, PACs spent $21 million independently on presidential and congressional races, nearly double what they spent independently in the 1996 election cycle.[2]

At the top of the heterogeneous cluster of party and auxiliary campaign committees are the campaign organizations created by the individual candidates. Virtually all candidates for important, competitive offices develop personal campaign organizations to counsel them on strategy and issues, assist with travel arrangements and speeches, raise money, defend their interests in party circles, and try to coordinate their activities with those of other candidates and campaign units. The size of a candidate's personal organization is likely to vary according to the significance of the office and the competitiveness of the constituency. The member from a safe congressional district, for example, habituated to easy elections, has less need for an elaborate campaign organization than a candidate from a closely competitive district. Some congressional districts are so safe—at least for the candidate, if not the party—that were it not for having to attend certain district party and civic rites, the incumbent could easily skip campaigning and remain in Washington.

In some campaigns the regular party organization is reduced to the status of just another spectator. Candidates commonly employ professional management firms to direct their campaigns rather than relying on the party organizations to do so.[3] Most facets of American politics today come under the influence of public relations specialists and advertising firms. Possessing resources that the party organizations cannot match, they raise funds; recruit campaign workers; develop issues; gain endorsements; write speeches; arrange campaign schedules; direct the candidate's television appearances; and prepare campaign literature, films, and advertising. Indeed, they often create the overall campaign strategy and dominate day-to-day decision making.

Few features of American politics have changed more dramatically than the way in which candidates contend for office. Barbara G. Salmore and Stephen A. Salmore wrote:

> The role of the party boss has been taken over by the political consultant, that of the volunteer party worker by the paid telephone bank caller. Most voters learn about candidates not at political rallies but from television advertising and computer-generated direct mail; candidates generally gather information about voters not from the ward leader but from the pollster. The money to fuel campaigns comes less from the party organizations and "fat cats" and more from direct mail solicitation of individuals and special-interest political action committees. In short, candidates have become individual entrepreneurs, largely set free from party control or discipline.[4]

Campaign Strategy

The paramount goal of all major party campaigns is to form a coalition of sufficient size to bring victory to the candidate or party. Ordinarily, the early days of the campaign are devoted to the development and testing of a broad campaign strategy designed to produce a winning coalition. In the most general sense, strategy should be seen as "an overall plan for acquiring and using the resources needed for a campaign."[5] In developing a broad strategy, candidates, their advisers, and party leaders must take into consideration a number of factors. These include:

1. the principal themes to be developed during the campaign;
2. the issues to be emphasized and exploited;[6]
3. the candidate's personal qualities to be emphasized;
4. the specific groups and geographical areas to which appeals will be directed;
5. the acquisition of financial support and endorsements;
6. the timing of campaign activities;
7. the relationship of the candidate to the party organization and to factions within it; and
8. the uses to be made of the communications media, particularly television.[7]

To the casual observer, there appear to be no limits to the number of major and minor strategies open to a resourceful candidate. However, important constraints serve to shape and define the candidate's options. For example, campaign strategy is affected by the political, social, and economic environments. Among the factors that intrude on campaign strategy are the competitiveness of the district, the nature of the electorate, the quality and representativeness of the party ticket, the unity of the party, the presence of an incumbent, the election timetable (for example, presidential or off-year election), and the predispositions and commitments of political interest groups. Although difficult to weigh its significance, the temper of the times also affects the candidate's overall plan of action. Whatever the impact of these constraints on campaign strategy, most are beyond the control of the candidate; they are simply conditions to which the candidate must adjust and adapt. The overall strategy that the candidate fashions or selects must be consonant with the given restrictions of the campaign environment.[8]

Do Campaigns Matter?

Some evidence suggests that the campaign environment matters so much that it all but renders the campaign itself meaningless. The earliest studies of political behavior showed that very few people actually changed their vote intention from the beginning of the campaign to the end. Almost without exception, those who said in September that they planned to vote for Dwight D. Eisenhower or Adlai Stevenson actually voted for Eisenhower or Stevenson in November.[9] This behavior held in 1980 as well.[10] Indeed, a number of economists and political scientists have devised relatively simple econometric models that can predict election outcomes based on economic performance. For example, political scientists Michael Lewis-Beck and Tom Rice have predicted the winner of eleven of the past fourteen presidential contests—and ten of eleven before 1992—using data collected months before the campaigns ever began.[11]

Nevertheless, campaigns are far from meaningless. In the same way that well-known consumer brands like Coca-Cola and McDonald's advertise vigorously, well-known political candidates take their campaigns seriously. If they fail to engage the public, they also are likely to lose market share to their competitors. In that sense, it is important to realize that campaigns are designed to do much more than changing people's voting intentions. Instead, the most important goal of a political campaign is to *get core supporters out to vote*. Campaigns need to reinforce the existing predispositions of regular voters. A great many elections are won or lost depending on the turnout of the party faithful. Campaigns must take great pains to fire up their base, something that negative advertising, in particular, can accomplish quite successfully.[12]

Second, candidates must *activate latent support*. Successful campaigns often turn on the ability of the candidate to activate potential voters among the groups that ordinarily support his party.[13] For the Democratic candidate, this means that special efforts must be directed to involve such segments of the population as

Catholics, Jews, African Americans, Hispanics, blue-collar workers, union members, urban residents, women, and members of low-income households. For the Republican candidate, this rule dictates a similar effort to activate Protestants (especially evangelical Christians), whites, suburban or rural residents, and professional, business, and managerial elements. Efforts may also be made to catalyze powerful single-issue groups, such as those in the pro-choice and pro-life movements. It is important to minimize defections to third party candidates among this group as well. Indeed, had Al Gore received even a tiny portion of the more than ninety thousand votes cast for Ralph Nader in Florida, he would have been elected president in 2000.

The third general strategy, though the one that produces the weakest results, is to *change the opposition*.[14] While a large number of Democrats voted for Richard Nixon in 1972 and Ronald Reagan in 1984, and a large number of Republicans bolted from their party to vote for Lyndon B. Johnson in 1964, massive party defections have become less numerous recently as voters have come to see important differences between the parties. Although many partisans cast ballots for third party candidate Ross Perot in 1992 and 1996, few voted for the other major party nominee.[15] In terms of major party voters, the winning party can generally count on the support of about 90 percent of its identifiers while the losing party generally gets the vote of around 85 percent of its partisans. In 2000, even in a three candidate race, 87 percent of Democrats voted for Al Gore and 90 percent of Republicans voted for George W. Bush.[16]

Given the close balance between Republicans and Democrats in the electorate today, even small events may turn out to be meaningful. In examining presidential campaigns, specifically, Daron R. Shaw demonstrates that a number of campaign events, such as debates, gaffes, party conventions, and campaign appearances, significantly affect a candidate's standing in the polls.[17] If a candidate does well in a debate or makes an embarrassing mistake on the campaign trail, his support in the polls will increase or decrease in some degree. Indeed, at least one astute political observer boldly declared that Gore's excessive sighing during his first debate with Bush in 2000 cost him the election.[18] Similarly, if a presidential candidate makes an appearance in a state, his poll standing will increase there as a result. While events affect subsequent poll results immediately more than they do election outcomes, Shaw confirms that they still affect the final results. Recent experience also suggests that appearances by a popular president on behalf of nonpresidential candidates can prove quite helpful. Most pundits believe that Bush's decision to travel to states like Georgia, North Carolina, New Hampshire, Texas, Missouri, and Colorado in 2002 helped Republicans win several very close races, which in turn produced a Republican majority in the Senate. Wherever Air Force One touched down, Republican candidates' poll numbers jumped in response.

No one is really certain what does and does not work from campaign to campaign. Myths and facts are mixed in about equal proportion in the lore of campaign strategy. Indeed, it is scarcely ever apparent in advance which strategies are likely to be most productive and which least productive or even counterproductive. However disciplined and well managed campaigns may appear to those who stand on the outskirts, they rarely are so in reality. A common mistake of postmortems is to assert that a certain event or a stand or mannerism of a candidate caused him to win or lose. Often no one knows whether the election result was because of this factor or despite it. Spectacular events, whether a dramatic proposal, an attack, or something in the news outside the campaign, are like a revolving door. They win some votes and lose others.[19]

Campaign decisions may be shaped as much by chance and the ability of the candidate to seize on events as by the careful formulation of a broad and coherent plan of attack. Consider the decision of John F. Kennedy in the 1960 presidential campaign to telephone Coretta Scott King to express his concern over the welfare of her husband, the Reverend Dr. Martin Luther King Jr., who had been jailed in Atlanta following a sit-in in a department store. There is no evidence that Kennedy's decision—perhaps as critical as any of the campaign—was based on a comprehensive assessment of alternatives or possible consequences. Instead, according to Theodore H. White, the decision came about this way:

> The crisis was instantly recognized by all concerned with the Kennedy campaign. . . . [The] suggestion for meeting it [was made by] Harris Wofford. Wofford's idea was as simple as it was human—that the candidate telephone directly to Mrs. King in Georgia to express his concern. Desperately Wofford tried to reach his own chief, Sargent Shriver, head of the Civil Rights Section of the Kennedy campaign, so that Shriver might break through to the candidate barnstorming somewhere in the Middle West. Early [the next] morning, Wofford was able to locate Shriver . . . and Shriver enthusiastically agreed. Moving fast, Shriver reached the candidate [as he] was preparing to leave for a day of barnstorming in Michigan. The candidate's reaction to Wofford's suggestion of participation was impulsive, direct, and immediate. From his room at the Inn, without consulting anyone, he placed a long-distance telephone call to Mrs. Martin Luther King, assured her of his interest and concern in her suffering and, if necessary, his intervention. . . . The entire episode received only casual notice from the generality of American citizens in the heat of the last three weeks of the Presidential campaign. But in the [African American] community the Kennedy intervention rang like a carillon.[20]

In contrast to the presidential level, congressional campaigns and election outcomes carry few surprises. Candidates win where they are expected to win and lose where they are expected to lose. Incumbent House members who lose in their bids to retain office are almost as rare as some entries on the endangered species list. Senators have more reason to worry over what the voters will deal them, but they too campaign from a position of strength. Congressional campaigns go as expected for three major reasons. First, incumbents enjoy overwhelming advantages. Among other things, they have a public record to which they can point, resources that permit them to assist constituents with their problems, the franking privilege, generous travel allowances, and a staff and offices.

Voters are more familiar with them than with their challengers. By contrast, congressional challengers cannot bank on a large and attentive public audience. No matter how tirelessly they transmit their messages, much of what they say is lost on a public preoccupied with other things.

Second, members of Congress campaign year-round. Their staffs handle constituent problems, and members return home weekend after weekend. Everyone in the member's entourage knows that reelections are won in non-election years.

Third, incumbents have a much easier time raising money than challengers typically do. In 2000, for example, the average House incumbent raised and spent more than four times as much money as did the average House challenger.[21] The fact that greater campaign resources translate into easy victories for incumbent members of Congress provides further evidence that campaigns do, in fact, matter. When campaign resources are more evenly balanced, as in presidential elections, victory is uncertain. When one side has more, it almost always triumphs.

Issues and Campaigns

Donald Stokes distinguishes between two types of campaign issues: *position* and *valence*.[22] Position issues are those on which the parties have taken differing stances on policy questions, such as government spending on programs that benefit the poor or support for affirmative action. Modern election campaigns, however, are dominated by valence issues—"issues on which the voters distinguish parties and candidates not by their real or perceived differences on position issues but by the degree to which they are linked in the voters' minds with conditions, symbols, or goals that are almost universally approved of or disapproved of by the electorate, such as economic prosperity, public corruption, and resolute leadership."[23]

The development of specific stands on positional issues is of somewhat limited importance in designing campaign strategy. For one thing, voters frequently are unable to identify the positions of the candidates, and this is particularly true in congressional elections.[24] Also, though some voters are sensitive to the specific issues generated in a campaign, many others are preoccupied with the candidate's image, personality, and style. Candidates are often judged less by what they say than by how they say it, less by their achievements than by their personalities. Voters' perceptions of a candidate's character are highly important, perhaps especially in presidential contests. Scandals in government typically have a major impact on the strategies of subsequent campaigns, serving to heighten the significance of the candidate's alleged personal virtues—particularly those of honesty and sincerity—and to diminish the significance of positional issues. "I don't think issues mean a great deal about whether you win or lose," observes a U.S. senator. "I think issues give you a chance to [demonstrate] your honesty and candor."[25] Along the same line, a Democratic media consultant contends, "I don't think inflation is an issue.

Who's for it? . . . The real issue is which of the two candidates would best be able to deal with [it]."[26]

According to polls conducted by the Voter News Service in 2000, voters supporting Bush or Gore cited sharply different reasons for their choices. Those who supported Bush stressed the issues of taxes and world affairs, while Gore voters focused on Medicare and Social Security, the economy and jobs, and health care. Although voters favored Gore over Bush in five of the seven issue domains, Gore nevertheless lost, further illustrating the limited import of some position issues. In contrast, Bush had a large advantage in voters' evaluations of the candidates' personal traits, especially those closely linked to vote choice. Evaluating the qualities of the candidates, voters who preferred Bush emphasized his honesty (noted by 24 percent of voters, by far the highest percentage), leadership, and likeability, and those drawn to Gore singled out his experience and understanding of the issues (see Table 4-1).[27] Bush's higher character ratings are part of a larger pattern of the public's perception of Republican candidates as being more trustworthy.

To the extent that issues matter, they are driven less by the specifics of the plans of competing candidates and more by people's general views about the parties' ability to solve different types of problems. Voter preference for the Republican candidate on taxes, foreign affairs, and morality, and for the Democratic candidate on social welfare issues and the environment has been consis-

Table 4-1 Sources of the Presidential Vote

	Percentage Mentioning	Percentage Voting for		Contribution to Vote of	
		Gore	Bush	Gore	Bush
Issue					
Economy/jobs	18	59	37	12	8
Education	15	52	44	9	8
Social Security	14	58	40	9	6
Taxes	14	17	80	3	13
World affairs	12	40	54	5	7
Health care	8	64	33	6	3
Medicare/prescription drugs	7	60	39	5	3
Totals				49	48
Traits					
Honest	24	15	80	4	21
Experienced	15	82	17	13	3
Strong leader	14	34	64	5	10
Deal with complexity	13	75	19	10	3
Good judgment	13	48	50	7	7
Cares about people	12	63	31	8	4
Likeable	2	38	59	1	1
Totals	93			48	48

Source: Gerald Pomper, *The Election of 2000: Reports and Interpretations* (New York: Seven Bridges Press, 2001), 146.

tent over the last three decades. John Petrocik refers to this constancy as *issue ownership*.[28] Bill Clinton's support for the Family and Medical Leave Act of 1993 illustrated his empathy and George Bush's stance on possible war with Iraq demonstrated his toughness. In this interpretation, elections are decided by which candidate is best able to bring his party's issues to the top of the campaign agenda. If Republicans can focus elections on national defense and strength abroad, they will do well—as was evidenced by their strong showing in the 2002 midterm elections when homeland security dominated the campaign agenda. If Democrats can make elections turn on protecting social welfare programs, as Clinton did in 1996 with Social Security and Medicare, they will do well.

The broad point is that in a candidate-centered, television-dominated era, voters' evaluations of candidates' personal characteristics have a much larger effect on their vote choices than do issues.[29] Politics today is framed to a great extent in terms of the candidates' personal strengths and weaknesses, such as their competence, trustworthiness, and ability to lead. Issues tend to be a convenient indicator that the media, particularly television, use to analyze and assess the personal attributes of the candidates.[30] Many observers find it problematic that voters rely more on the candidates' personal characteristics than on issues, since candidates can more easily manipulate their images than they can their positions on issues. Others are less concerned because they argue that issues are ever changing while character is not.[31] When images displace policy in voter decisions, parties obviously are not well served.

Campaign Money

Of all the requirements for successful campaigns, none may be more important than a strong infusion of money. Campaign costs have risen steadily over the years. In 1952 expenditures for the nomination and election of public officials at all levels of government came to about $140 million. By 1968 this figure had climbed to $300 million. Candidates and parties spent approximately $1.8 billion in 1984, $3.2 billion in 1992, and just under $4 billion in 2000.[32]

The spiraling costs of running for office result from a number of factors. The steady increase in the general price level is one: inflation affects campaign costs as well as everything else. The growth in population and the enlargement of the electorate also make campaigning more expensive. The utilization of new techniques, such as computerized mailings, has proved costly. The substitution of presidential primaries for caucus-convention systems appears to have increased campaign expenditures. Candidates spend considerable sums hiring political consultants to direct their campaigns. And the availability of private money in large quantities, particularly from the political action committees of interest groups,[33] encourages candidates to add to their campaign treasuries. Congressional incumbents believe that the best way to discourage challengers is to amass a large campaign fund well in advance of the next election. Thus, it is common for members of Congress to solicit and accept funds even when they have no serious competition. Some members use surplus funds to make contributions to the campaigns of colleagues.[34]

Broadcast advertising in particular has driven up campaign costs. Television, critics contend, is the real culprit. David Broder has estimated that U.S. Senate candidates allocate 70 to 80 percent of their funds to paid television, turning them, as one senator put it, into "bag men for the TV operators."[35] Frank Greer, a Democratic media consultant, contends that 75 to 80 percent of the budgets in competitive campaigns is earmarked for television.[36] Paul S. Herrnson suggests, however, that the numbers often cited by critics are greatly inflated. He notes that, on average, about 17 percent of House campaign budgets and 30 percent of Senate campaign budgets are spent on television ads.[37] Of course, these percentages are significantly higher in very competitive races and significantly lower in uncompetitive races.

Spending campaign money intelligently is problematic to say the least. Candidates spend as heavily as they do because neither they nor their advisers know which expenditures are likely to produce the greatest return in votes. Lacking systematic information, they jump at every opportunity to contact and persuade voters—and every opportunity costs money. As one political consultant is reported to have said, "Half of all the money spent on political campaigns is wasted; the problem is we don't know which half."

Political money does not lend itself to easy analysis. Tracing how it is raised and how it is spent is far from simple. In a federal and fragmented system campaign money is collected and spent by many competing political actors and institutions. If there is a fashion at all, it is helter skelter. In addition, the effects of money on elections, political behavior, and public policy are not fully understood. One point about which there is substantial agreement, however, is that campaign spending has grown dramatically in recent years.

Congressional campaigns provide a good example. In 1978 House and Senate candidates collectively spent about $195 million. By 1992 congressional campaign spending had jumped to $678 million,[38] and in 2000 it cleared the $1 billion mark.[39] Put another way, over a twenty-year period spending on congressional elections experienced a five-fold increase. Early indications are that spending in 2002 would reach more than $900 million, making it the most expensive midterm election ever.[40]

Some observers argue that it is useful to examine these numbers relative to money spent on advertising by private firms. For example, Anthony Gierzynski notes that Apple Computer spent $100 million on one week's worth of advertising for its iMac computer.[41] Frank J. Sorauf claims that Sears had an advertising budget of $1.4 billion in 1990.[42] And, in a different twist, Bradley Smith observes that Americans spend two times as much on potato chips every year as candidates spend on political campaigns.[43]

Relative to past spending, however, current expenditures by winning congressional candidates have grown rapidly. Figure 4-1 presents data on House

Figure 4-1   Total Spending by Winning Congressional Candidates: 1982–2000

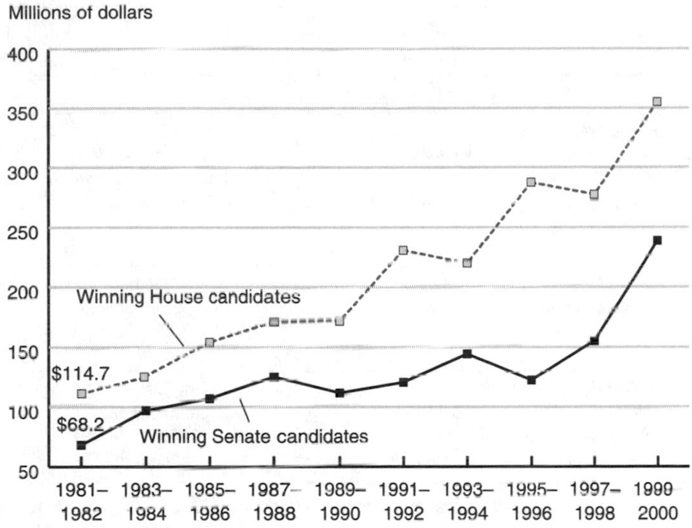

Millions of dollars

Source: Press release, Federal Election Commission, January 9, 2001.

Note: Spending is for all campaigns, including primaries, runoffs, and general elections. An election cycle is for two years, the election year and the year preceding.

and Senate spending by winning candidates from 1982 to 2000. Over this eighteen-year period, expenditures by successful House candidates more than tripled, and expenditures by winning Senate candidates jumped by three-and-a-half times.

Spending is particularly heavy in the most competitive races, including those in which open seats are at stake. In the House elections of 2000, for example, winning Republican challengers had median expenditures of almost $1 million in defeating Democratic incumbents, whose median expenditures were $1.3 million. The median expenditures for successful Democratic challengers were $1.96 million, as contrasted with $1.92 million for losing Republican incumbents (see Table 4-2).

Several broad conclusions can be drawn concerning spending in House campaigns. First, the most expensive races involve incumbents who think or know they are in trouble with the voters. Campaigns costing in excess of $1.5 million are common for anxious House incumbents. Of the fifty most expensive House campaigns in 2000, twenty-six were run by incumbents; each spent in excess of $1.8 million. Even incumbents who expect to win and do win easily often have campaign expenditures of a half-million or more. Second, with not many exceptions, incumbents outspend their challengers, many of whom are severely underfinanced; numerous House challengers, in fact, spend less than $50,000 on

Table 4-2   Spending to Defeat Incumbents and to Win Open Seats and Close Races, U.S. House Elections: 2000

No. of Districts	Median Expenditures			Median Expenditures
	Winning Challengers and Losing Incumbents			
2	Winning Republican challengers	$980,070	Losing Democratic incumbents	$1,332,829
4	Winning Democratic challengers	$1,962,618	Losing Republican incumbents	$1,917,756
	Open Seats			
25	Winning Republicans	$1,115,338	Losing Democrats	$650,578
7	Winning Democrats	$1,091,752	Losing Republicans	$998,403
	Close Races[a]			
19	Winning Republican incumbents	$1,123,854	Losing Democratic challengers	$1,055,513
21	Winning Democratic incumbents	$1,540,830	Losing Republican challengers	$984,857

Source: Adapted from data in press release, Federal Election Commission, May 15, 2001.

[a]Winners received less than 55 percent of the vote.

their campaigns. Third, challengers who win or make a good showing generally are well financed. Fourth, spending in campaigns for open seats is usually heavy, particularly in competitive districts. Fifth, the costs of some House campaigns border on the scandalous. For example, Rep. James Rogan (R-Calif.) spent $6.9 million in 2000 in his failed effort to hold his seat against Democrat Adam Schiff, who spent $4.3 million. Put another way, the two candidates combined spent nearly $20 on each eligible voter in the district.

In several Senate races in 2000, spending was extremely high. Indeed, two races, one in New Jersey and one in New York, broke records for the most expensive campaigns ever. In New Jersey, billionaire investment banker Jon Corzine (D-N.J.) won a Senate seat by spending more than $60 million of his own money to defeat Republican Bob Franks, who spent about a tenth as much. In New York, former first lady Hillary Rodham Clinton (D-N.Y.) spent $30 million to defeat Rep. Rick Lazio (R-N.Y.), who spent $40.6 million. In addition, Maria Cantwell (D-Wash.), a tech-sector millionaire, spent more than $10 million of her own money to defeat an incumbent, Slade Gorton. Plainly, congressional campaign politics is not a poor person's game, at least not for candidates who want to be taken seriously.

The Regulation of Campaign Finance

The public has long been restive over the role of money in American politics. Dissatisfaction focuses on three main complaints. The first is simply that campaign costs have risen to such an extent that candidates with limited resources are seriously disadvantaged in the electoral process. The doubt persists that some talented people never seek public office because they lack financial support or are unwilling to solicit funds from others because of the risk of incurring political indebtedness and of compromising their independence. Moreover, the high cost of elections may mean that the public hears only one side of the campaign—that of the candidate with access to large sums of money.

The second complaint is that the individuals, families, and groups that contribute lavishly to parties and candidates are suspected of buying influence and gaining preferments of some kind in return for the money they channel into campaigns. Whether or not this is true may not be as important as the fact that the public believes it to be true. In some measure, public suspicion about campaign financing contributes to public suspicion of government.

The third, as a result of the Watergate exposé, a heightened awareness exists of the potential for corruption and abuse when huge sums of money are collected and spent for political purposes. Federal and state laws, moreover, increase the probability that irregularities and "sewer money" will be detected and publicized.

To deal with a variety of maladies associated with the financing of federal political campaigns, Congress passed the Federal Election Campaign Act of 1971 (FECA). This act, the first serious attempt since 1925 to reform campaign financing, is of unusual importance. Adopted prior to the Watergate incident, the act anticipated public financing of federal election campaigns by providing that taxpayers could earmark $1 on their personal income tax returns for use in the 1976 presidential election. This represented the first effort at public funding of political campaigns. Of at least equal importance, the act provided for rigorous disclosure requirements concerning campaign contributions, expenditures, and debts. Finally, the act carried a provision to stimulate private contributions to political campaigns. Under a tax-incentive system, taxpayers were permitted to deduct small campaign contributions from their tax obligations. In retrospect, the extraordinary dimensions of the 1972 presidential election scandal would not have been uncovered without the disclosure requirements for political contributions and expenditures contained in the law.

Crisis is often a spur to legislative action. Largely in response to Watergate, Congress in 1974 passed comprehensive amendments to the Federal Election Campaign Act.[44] Designed to curtail the influence and abuse of money in campaign politics, these amendments placed tight restrictions on contributions, expenditures, disclosure, and reporting. Most important, the 1974 legislation provided for at least partial public financing of presidential primaries, elections, and nominating conventions. In 1979 Congress passed an additional amendment to the FECA allowing political parties to spend an unlimited sum of hard dollars on certain grassroots activities—a provision designed to enhance the parties' role in campaigns.[45] The main features of the nation's campaign finance law, including changes adopted in the McCain-Feingold legislation of 2002, are included in Table 4-3.

Table 4-3   Major Provisions for the Regulation of Campaign Financing in Federal Elections

Contribution Limits

- No individual may contribute more than $2,000 plus COLA (cost-of-living adjustment) to any candidate or candidate committee per election. (Primary, runoff, and general elections are considered to be separate elections.)
- Individual contributions to a national party committee are limited to $25,000 per calendar year plus COLA and to any other political committee to $5,000 per calendar year. (The total contributions by an individual to all federal candidates in a two-year election cycle cannot exceed $95,000.)
- A multicandidate committee (one with more than fifty contributors that makes contributions to five or more federal candidates) may contribute no more than $5,000 to any candidate or candidate committee per election, no more than $15,000 to the national committee of a political party, and no more than $5,000 to any other political committee per calendar year.
- The national committee and the congressional campaign committee may each contribute up to $5,000 to each House candidate, per election; the national committee, together with the senatorial campaign committee, may contribute up to a combined total of $35,000 to each Senate candidate for the entire campaign period (including a primary election).
- Political action committees formed by businesses, trade associations, or unions are limited to contributions of no more than $5,000 to any candidate in any election. No limits apply to their aggregate contributions.
- Banks, corporations, and labor unions are prohibited from making contributions from their treasuries to federal election campaigns. Government contractors and foreign nationals are similarly restricted. Contributions may not be supplied by one person but made in the name of another person. Contributions in cash are limited to $100.

Expenditure Limits

- Candidates are limited to an expenditure of $10 million each plus COLA in all presidential primaries (in 2000 each candidate could spend up to $45.6 million in all presidential primaries), provided they accept public funding.
- Major party presidential candidates may spend no more than $20 million plus COLA in the general election (a total of $67.6 million each in 2000).
- Presidential and vice-presidential candidates who accept public funding may spend no more than $50,000 of personal funds in their campaigns.
- Each national party may spend up to two cents per voter on behalf of its presidential candidate.
- In addition to making contributions to candidates, the national committee, together with congressional and senatorial campaign committees, may make expenditures on behalf of House and Senate candidates. For each House member—in states with more than one district—the sum is $10,000 plus COLA. (The amount in 2000 was $33,780.) For each Senate candidate the sum is $20,000 plus COLA or two cents for each person in the state's voting-age population, whichever is greater. (Under the second formula, party committees could spend $3.2 million on behalf of a California Senate candidate in 2000.) State party committees may make expenditures on behalf of House and Senate candidates up to the same limits.
- As a result of the *Buckley v. Valeo* decision, there are no limits on how much House and Senate candidates may collect and spend in their campaigns (or on how much they may spend of their own or their family's money).
- Also in the wake of *Buckley v. Valeo*, there are no limits on the amount that individuals and groups may spend on behalf of any presidential or congressional candidate so long as the expenditures are independent—that is, not arranged or controlled by the candidate.
- As a result of the Supreme Court's 1996 decision in *Colorado Republican Federal Campaign Committee v. FEC*, political parties can now make unlimited independent expenditures on behalf of their candidates for federal office as long as these expenditures are not coordinated with the candidates or their campaigns and the party uses "hard" money. "Independent" expenditures, in other words, are entitled to First Amendment protection and are not to be treated as indirect campaign contributions subject to regulations.

Table 4-3   (*continued*)

Public Financing

* Major party candidates for the presidency qualify for full funding ($20 million plus COLA) prior to the campaign, the money to be drawn from the federal income tax dollar checkoff. In 2000 the Democratic and Republican nominees each received $67.6 million in campaign funds. Candidates may decline to participate in the public funding program and finance their campaigns through private contributions. Candidates who accept public funding may not accept private contributions.
* Minor party and independent candidates qualify for lesser sums, provided their candidates received at least 5 percent of the vote in the previous presidential election. New parties or parties that received less than 5 percent of the vote four years earlier qualify for public financing after the election, provided they drew 5 percent of the vote.
* Matching public funds up to $5 million (plus COLA) are available for presidential primary candidates, provided that they first raise $100,000 in private funds ($5,000 in contributions of no more than $250 in each of twenty states). Once that threshold is reached, the candidate receives matching funds up to $250 per contribution.
* Presidential candidates who receive less than 10 percent of the vote in two consecutive presidential primaries become ineligible for additional campaign subsidies. Subsidies are renewed if the candidate receives 20 percent in a subsequent primary.
* Optional public funding of presidential nominating conventions is available for the major parties, with lesser amounts for minor parties.

Disclosure and Reporting

* Each federal candidate is required to establish a single, overarching campaign committee to report on all contributions and expenditures on behalf of the candidate.
* Frequent reports on contributions and expenditures are to be filed with the Federal Election Commission.

Enforcement

* Administration of the law is the responsibility of a six-member, bipartisan Federal Election Commission. The Commission is empowered to make rules and regulations, to receive campaign reports, to render advisory opinions, to conduct audits and investigations, to subpoena witnesses and information, and to seek civil injunctions through court action.

Source: Federal Election Commission.

The constitutionality of the 1974 provisions relating to the presidential electoral process was promptly tested in the courts. In *Buckley v. Valeo,* decided in 1976, the Supreme Court held that the act's limitations on expenditures (either those of the candidate[46] or of individuals or groups spending independently on behalf of a candidate) were unconstitutional because they interfered with the right of free speech under the First Amendment. Political money, the Court ruled, is political speech. The Court upheld the limitations on contributions to campaigns, the disclosure requirements, and the public-funding provisions for presidential primaries and elections. In 1996 the Court extended its protection of hard-money independent expenditures to political parties, ruling that parties have a First Amendment right to spend without limit on their candidates as long as the spending is done independently of the candidates.[47] In another recent case, the Court reaffirmed the constitutionality of reasonable contribution limits.[48]

No provision is made for the public financing of campaigns for Congress, which has put increasing pressure on candidates to raise vast sums of money from individuals and organized interests. Many members of Congress have become weary of the struggle to raise funds. As David L. Boren, a former senator from Oklahoma, observed, "To raise $4 million means that for every single week for six years without exception a member of the Senate would have to figure out how to raise $15,000 in campaign contributions."[49] Obviously, the time spent engaging in fund-raising takes significant time away from members' ability to legislate.

As Sen. Robert C. Byrd (D-W.V.) observed:

> The present system does not even allow the incumbents with new ideas to get them into place. We are too busy out there engaging in the money chase. We cannot be here in the committees, we cannot be here on the floor doing our work. . . . We are kept so busy out there knocking on doors all over the country, seeking money, asking for money, begging for money, getting on our hands and knees for money, we do not have time to give thought to new ideas and to be putting them into creative legislation.[50]

In addition, the pressure to raise large sums of campaign money drives parties and candidates to cut corners and to engage in questionable (if not illegal) practices.[51] Following the 1996 election, for example, it was discovered that the White House had been rewarding and beguiling Democratic party contributors by letting them spend a night in the Lincoln Bedroom; that numerous White House coffees had been held for prospective big donors; and that Vice President Al Gore had placed various fund-raising telephone calls from the White House, in possible violation of a law that prohibits soliciting funds on federal property. Evidence of illegal foreign donations to the Democratic party from Indonesia and China also surfaced. Topping it off, the Democratic National Committee had to return a number of suspicious or illegal donations because their true source could not be established. Special access, money-hustling, favor-seeking, and buying influence were the central themes in story after story involving the White House's unusual efforts to raise money to compete with the Republican party's highly successful money chase. Moreover, these charges continued to dog Gore during his run for president in 2000. Republican attacks on Gore's honesty often centered on his role in questionable fund-raising practices in 1996.

Soft Money

Discontent over the parties' fund-raising practices derives not only from concern over sleazy behavior but from the perception that campaign finance laws are riddled with loopholes. Consider the matter of contribution limits. One of the major purposes of the FECA was to place sharp restrictions on the amount of money that could be given to federal campaigns by individuals and organizations. These limits are easily evaded, however. Wealthy individuals, corporations, and unions have found a way around them by making donations of "soft money" to the political parties, not to the candidates. What makes this money "soft" is that it is not subject to the "hard" or strict limitations of the FECA. Up through the 2002 election cycle, individuals, corporations, and labor unions could make contributions of unlimited size to party soft money accounts.[52]

The soft money loophole emerged from several Federal Election Commission rulings during the 1970s that allowed state and national political parties to use soft money to finance the nonfederal portion of generic party activities and expenses.[53] By 1980, the national parties were taking advantage of these rulings, using soft money to pay for the nonfederal share of many activities that benefited the entire party ticket. By 1996, however, the national parties began more fully exploiting the soft money loophole by using these funds to finance so-called "issue advocacy advertisements"—ads identical to most candidate ads but that fail to meet the Supreme Court's definition of "express" advocacy.

Specifically, during the 1996 presidential race the Democratic party, quickly copied by the Republican party, began to air "issue advocacy" advertisements that supposedly were produced independently of the Clinton campaign. Issue ads showing images of the candidates are legal, the Supreme Court has ruled, as long as they stop short of using words such as "elect," "vote for," or "vote against"—even though an election message is clearly being conveyed. The nonuse of these so called "magic words" is not particularly meaningful in distinguishing issue advocacy from outright electioneering. A study by Craig Holman and Luke McLoughlin of the 2000 elections showed that a mere 10 percent of advertisements produced by congressional candidates, advocating their own election, actually used these "magic words."[54] In short, issue advocacy ads accomplished virtually everything that a candidate's campaign ads could accomplish.

Not surprisingly, the amount of soft money raised and spent by parties exploded with the 1996 election. As recently as the 1992 election cycle, the parties combined brought in less than $100 million in soft money. In the 2000 election cycle, they raised nearly $500 million (see Figure 4-2). Ordinarily, fundraising increases in presidential years and declines in off-year elections. However, the parties actually raised more soft money in the 2002 election cycle than they did in the previous presidential election year. In the 2002 election cycle, the Democrats collected $246 million in soft money, the Republicans $250 million—overall, more than twice that raised in 1995–1996. As Ellen Miller of the Center for Responsive Politics observed, "The parties find it a lot easier to raise $100,000 in soft money with one call to a corporation than to try to collect $1,000 donations from individuals."[55]

From whom did this money come? Since soft money was not regulated by the FECA, it could come from any source including individuals, corporations, or labor unions. As the data in Figure 4-3 show, the finance, real estate, and insurance industries provided the most soft money to campaigns in the 2000 election cycle. They contributed $107.8 million, 57 percent of which went to Republicans and 42 percent to Democrats. Other miscellaneous businesses contributed more than $58 million in soft money, 60 percent of which went to Republicans. Labor organizations were also heavy contributors ($30.4 million in 2000), with almost all of it earmarked for Democrats.

Figure 4-2   Soft Money Party Receipts Reported to the FEC through Twenty Days after the General Election: 1992–2002

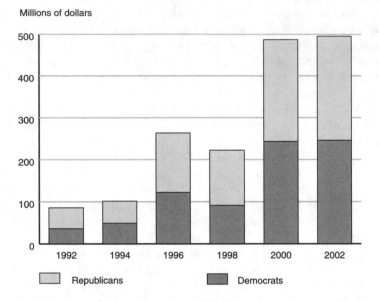

Source: Press release, Federal Elections Commission, December 18, 2002.

Soft money represented a huge boon to the parties, perhaps as much as $250 million to each party. Yet parties did not use this money to create a significantly more party-centered electoral environment. Instead, they chose to use it to further candidate-centered elections. According to the Brennan Center for Justice, only 8.3 percent of soft money in 2000 was spent on party building, get-out-the-vote campaigns, and voter education efforts. In contrast, 38 percent was spent on issue advocacy ads, and even these were not party centered. Fully 99.8 percent mentioned a specific candidate's name, while only eight percent identified a political party.[56] Moreover, the parties focused their efforts strategically on a small number of competitive races to get the biggest bang for their buck. In 2000, for example, the parties aired their "issue ads" in only forty-eight House races, concentrating fully one third of their overall spending in six of them.[57]

In sum, no fund-raising practice provided a more direct assault on the mission of the FECA than soft money. The FECA of 1974 had sought to limit the influence of wealthy interests by limiting individuals to $1,000 contributions per candidate per election, or $5,000 for a PAC. The emergence of soft money reopened the door to big, potentially corrupting, influences. A soft money contribution to a party of several hundred thousand dollars, or even a million or two, captures the attention of the beneficiary in a way quite distinct from that of a $5,000 PAC gift.

Figure 4-3 Soft Money by Sector in 2000

Industry	Total	To Democrats	To Republicans
Agribusiness	$20,832,099	23%	77%
Communications/ electronics	$67,806,433	55	45
Construction	$10,197,926	34	66
Defense	$4,403,486	34	66
Energy and natural resources	$29,707,654	23	78
Finance, Insurance, and real estate	$107,816,843	42	57
Health	$25,000,928	34	66
Lawyers and lobbyists	$23,510,832	81	19
Transportation	$20,935,824	28	72
Misc. business	$58,702,760	39	60
Labor	$30,368,895	99	1
Ideological/ single-issue	$10,385,773	54	42
Other	$11,310,480	47	53

Source: Center for Responsive Politics, opensecrets.org.

Note: Totals reflect contributions made by individuals associated with that company as well as official company contributions based on data released by the Federal Election Commission.

Total	$436,552,264
To Democrats	$201,370,879 (46%)
To Republicans	$232,881,316 (53%)

Reformers sought to eliminate the soft money loophole with increasing urgency after 1996. In 2002, they ultimately succeeded, with the passage of what has become known popularly as the McCain-Feingold Campaign Finance Reform Act, named for Sens. John McCain (R-Ariz.) and Russell Feingold (D-Wis.), the two driving forces behind its passage.

Campaign Finance Reform: McCain–Feingold

The McCain-Feingold Campaign Finance Reform Act was signed into law in March 2002 by President George W. Bush. In the 2000 presidential campaign, Bush, like most Republicans, opposed any significant changes to the campaign finance system, under which Republicans consistently outperformed Democrats. His opponents repeatedly challenged him on the issue. McCain's identification with the issue certainly contributed to his early primary victory in reform-minded New Hampshire. Al Gore declared that McCain-Feingold would be the first bill he would sign if elected. Following the series of corporate scandals in 2001 involving big political contributors like Enron and Global Crossing, Bush bowed to public pressure and signed the reform bill.

Although the measure has numerous provisions, three in particular stand out. First, and most important, it banned the national parties, congressional committees, and federal officeholders from raising and spending soft money. Parties are now limited to hard money contributions from individuals and PACs.

Second, to help compensate for the lost revenue from the soft money ban, hard money contribution limits were in some cases raised and indexed for inflation. One of the major problems with the 1974 FECA amendments was that contribution limits were set relatively low, with no provision for increases. McCain-Feingold sought to mitigate this problem by raising the individual contribution limit to $2,000 per candidate, per election, which would rise with inflation. The limit on individual contributions to parties was also increased from $20,000 to $25,000, and was also indexed for inflation. Finally, McCain-Feingold raised the total amount that individuals could contribute to federal candidates, parties, and PACs during a two-year election cycle from $50,000 to $95,000, with these sums to grow at the pace of inflation.

Third, the law placed new restrictions on corporations, labor unions, and nonprofit groups from running soft money financed "issue ads" within sixty days of a general election or thirty days of a primary election.[58] These ads had been criticized in particular for distorting the records of candidates so close to election day that they lacked adequate time to respond to them. The ways in which the reform legislation altered the flow of money is depicted in Figure 4-4.

In the weeks following its passage, McCain-Feingold came under attack both from the Federal Election Commission—the regulatory agency charged with its administration—and political opponents who sought to invalidate several of its key provisions through the courts. One challenge, involving the Republican National Committee, among others, was directed toward the soft money ban, arguing that it violated the free speech provisions laid out in *Buckley v. Valeo*. The ban on issue advertising within sixty days of the election was also challenged on free speech grounds. Although it is difficult to predict how the courts will decide these matters, many experts believe that the ban on soft money will be upheld while the prohibition on issue advertising will be struck down. Even so, it is hard to imagine that this law can completely shut down the $500 million industry that soft money had become by the end of the 2002 election cycle. Whether funneled through organizations at the state and local level or through some other route, soft money, probably in diminished amounts, is almost sure to wiggle back into federal elections.

Sources of Campaign Financing under FECA

Most of the cost of American elections is borne by private individuals and groups. Only in presidential elections is public financing (that is, funding from

Figure 4-4   How McCain-Feingold Campaign Finance Bill Alters Money Flow

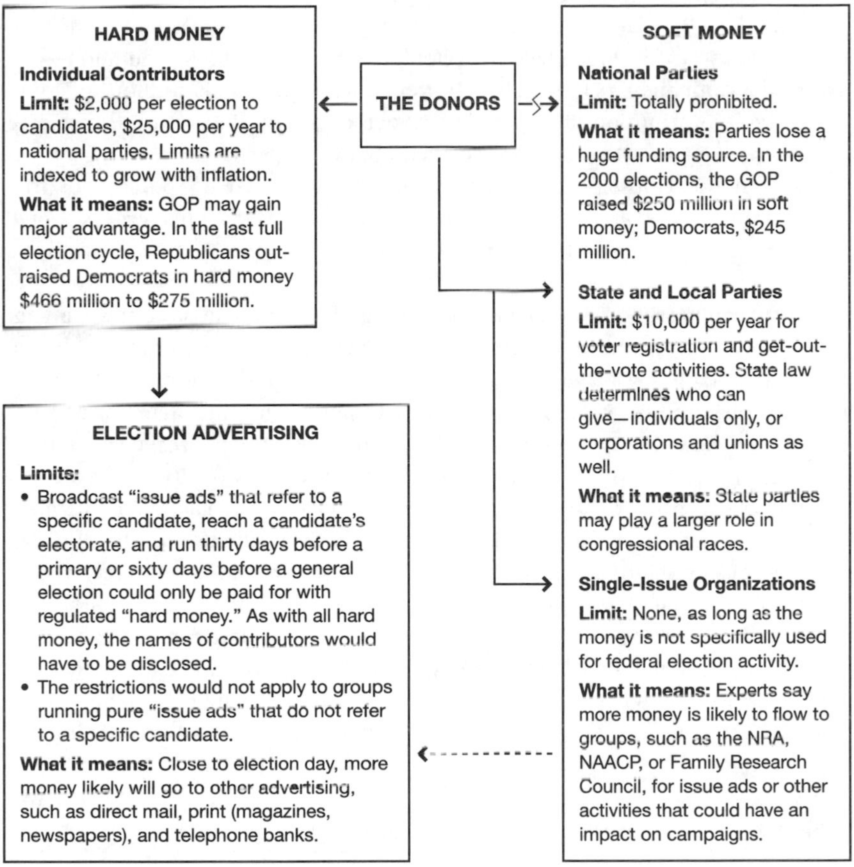

HARD MONEY

Individual Contributors

Limit: $2,000 per election to candidates, $25,000 per year to national parties. Limits are indexed to grow with inflation.

What it means: GOP may gain major advantage. In the last full election cycle, Republicans out-raised Democrats in hard money $466 million to $275 million.

← **THE DONORS** →

SOFT MONEY

National Parties

Limit: Totally prohibited.

What it means: Parties lose a huge funding source. In the 2000 elections, the GOP raised $250 million in soft money; Democrats, $245 million.

ELECTION ADVERTISING

Limits:

- Broadcast "issue ads" that refer to a specific candidate, reach a candidate's electorate, and run thirty days before a primary or sixty days before a general election could only be paid for with regulated "hard money." As with all hard money, the names of contributors would have to be disclosed.
- The restrictions would not apply to groups running pure "issue ads" that do not refer to a specific candidate.

What it means: Close to election day, more money likely will go to other advertising, such as direct mail, print (magazines, newspapers), and telephone banks.

State and Local Parties

Limit: $10,000 per year for voter registration and get-out-the-vote activities. State law determines who can give—individuals only, or corporations and unions as well.

What it means: State parties may play a larger role in congressional races.

Single-Issue Organizations

Limit: None, as long as the money is not specifically used for federal election activity.

What it means: Experts say more money is likely to flow to groups, such as the NRA, NAACP, or Family Research Council, for issue ads or other activities that could have an impact on campaigns.

Source: CQ Weekly, March 23, 2002, 800.

the government) available. Under amendments to the FECA, candidates for the presidential nomination can qualify for matching public funds. Once the nominations have been settled, the candidates can elect to receive full federal funding in the general election campaign. Even so, private money dominates the financing of political campaigns at all levels of government.

Because of the restrictions placed on contributions to presidential campaigns, perhaps the best way to begin the analysis of money in national political campaigns is to examine the sources from which congressional candidates secure funds. Several features of the money hustle of the 2000 election (covering the two-year election cycle and including primary, runoff, and general elections) stand out. First, the contributions of individuals represent the major source of campaign money for congressional candidates. In 2000 individual contributions made up 51 percent of the funds received by House candidates and 55 percent of those raised by Senate candidates.

Second, PACs have also been a major source of money for congressional candidates. In the 1999–2000 election cycle, PACs contributed $244 million to congressional campaigns ($128 million to Republicans and $116 million to Democrats). PAC contributions amounted to 32 percent of receipts for all House races and 14 percent for all Senate races. Incumbents in particular depend on PAC money. In the House, Democratic incumbents received 45 percent of their receipts from PACs, and Republican incumbents received 39 percent. Although they are less dependent on interest groups, Senate incumbents nevertheless raised 25 percent of their funds from PACs.[59]

Third, congressional campaign fund-raising is, purely and simply, an incumbent-dominated system. Challengers do not fare nearly as well in the PAC sweepstakes. (See Table 4-4.) Overall, 75 percent of all PAC funds in 2000 (both parties, both chambers) were given to incumbents,[60] 11 percent to challengers, and 14 percent to candidates for open seats. The average House incumbent received $370,000 from PACs, whereas the average challenger received $26,000. Thirty-two House candidates (twenty-two Republicans and ten Democrats) each accepted over three quarters of a million dollars from PACs. Ten House incumbents reported PAC gifts in excess of $1 million, including Speaker Dennis Hastert (R-Ill.), who received the most. In the Senate, twenty-two candidates received more than $1 million from PACs, with the top ten recipients all Republicans. Forty Senate candidates accepted more than half a million dollars from PACs, with Spencer Abraham (R-Mich.) leading the way with PAC gifts of about $2.5 million, followed by Rick Lazio (R-N.Y.) with $2.4 million, and John Ashcroft (R-Mo.) with $2.0 million.[61] Interestingly, all three lost, proving once again that money can't buy happiness!

Table 4-4   The Sources of Funding for 2000 Congressional Candidates

	Individual Contributions	PAC Contributions	Candidate Contributions	Candidate Loans	Other Loans
House					
Dem. incumbents	51%	48%	*	*	*
Dem. challengers	60	19	2	18	1
Dem. open seats	52	22	2	23	*
Rep. incumbents	57	41	*	1	*
Rep. challengers	60	14	2	23	*
Rep. open seats	46	19	3	32	*
Senate					
Dem. incumbents	63	23	11	3	*
Dem. challengers	46	9	19	25	1
Dem. open seats	35	4	0	61	0
Rep. incumbents	68	30	0	2	0
Rep. challengers	84	11	*	3	1
Rep. open seats	89	11	0	*	0

Source: Calculated from data in press release, Federal Election Commission, May 15, 2001.

*Less than one percent.

The overall growth of PAC contributions has been substantial. (See Table 4-5.) PACs contributed nearly five times as much money to House and Senate candidates in 2000 as they did in 1980. The numbers themselves are instructive: a total of $55 million was contributed in the 1980 election cycle and $243.2 million in the 2000 election cycle.

Political action committees target their gifts carefully, taking into consideration such key factors as incumbency, party, and legislative position. In 2000 labor PACs contributed $51.5 million to congressional candidates, with 92 percent given to Democrats. Corporate PACs gave $67.5 million to congressional candidates, with 79 percent given to Republicans.[62] Committee chairs and party leaders are major beneficiaries of interest group largesse.[63] Committee membership is also taken into consideration. Members of the tax and commerce committees, for example, invariably receive more PAC money than members of the judiciary or foreign policy committees. The pattern of contributions is illustrated by these observations:

The main goal is to support our friends who have been with us most of the time.
—an official of the UAW

The prevailing attitude is that PAC money should be used to facilitate access to incumbents.
*—the director of governmental and political participation for
the Chamber of Commerce of the United States*

We're inclined to support incumbents because we tend to go with those who support our industry. We are not out looking to find challengers. Our aim is not to change the tone of Congress.
—a spokesperson for the Lockheed Good Government Program

We're looking especially for members who serve on key committees, and people who help us on the floor.
—a spokesperson for the Automobile and Truck Dealers Election Action Committee[64]

Table 4-5 The Contributions of Political Action Committees to Congressional Campaigns in Presidential Election Years: 1980–2000 (in millions of dollars)

	1980	1984	1988	1992	1996	2000
Total PAC contributions	$55.2	$105.4	$147.9	$180.5	$201.4	$243.2
All House campaigns	37.9	75.7	102.3	128.6	155.8	192.8
All Senate campaigns	17.3	29.7	45.6	51.9	45.6	50.4
PAC percentage of funds raised by						
All House candidates	26%	34%	37%	33%	31%	32%
All Senate candidates	17	17	23	20	16	14

Sources: Data from press releases, Federal Election Commission, May 16, 1985; February 24, 1989; April 9, 1989; March 4, 1993; April 14, 1997; and May 15, 2001.

In addition to making direct contributions to candidates, PACs are permitted to make unlimited *independent* expenditures for or against candidates, but they are prohibited from consulting candidates concerning these expenditures. In 2000 such independent expenditures by PACs totaled $15 million, with $11 million spent on behalf of candidates and $4 million spent against them.[65] Under the FECA, direct PAC contributions to any candidate in a federal election are limited to $5,000. Independent spending is a way to circumvent this restriction.

So popular are PACs that many members of Congress have created their own political action committees—informally known as "leadership PACs"—to raise and disburse campaign funds. The thrust of some leadership PACs is simply to help reelect partisan or ideological allies. But for most leadership PACs the dominant purpose appears to be self-promotion. The most active congressional PACs are those created by members with aspirations for the presidency, the speakership, and a range of other positions, such as floor leader, whip, or committee chair. These PACs distribute campaign funds to candidates as a way of building good will and creating support for the sponsoring member and his goals. Indeed, with the demise of the seniority system for choosing party leaders and top committee chairs, leadership PACs have become increasingly important for those hoping to occupy leadership positions in Congress.[66] For presidential hopefuls in particular, having one's own PAC is invaluable in meeting the expenses of political travel necessary to capture public attention or to campaign for other congressional candidates.[67]

The availability of PAC money makes life easier for incumbents. They and their aides understand the PAC network and know how to curry favor with PACs (or at least how to avoid their enmity), how to solicit funds from them, and how to respond to their initiatives. Members are largely comfortable in this world of organization money, even though they resent the amount of time required to raise funds and worry over possible obligations to their benefactors. Nonetheless, access to PAC money is not the most important advantage of incumbents. Their main advantages are simply the opportunities and resources that are attached to holding congressional office: the franking privilege; a public record; name recognition; generous travel allowance; opportunities to make news; opportunities to take credit for "pork" brought into the constituency; and, perhaps most important of all, a large staff, many of whom are assigned to the district or state. "The Hill office," wrote David R. Mayhew, "is a vitally important political unit, part campaign management firm and part political machine."[68] The office is a political unit financed by the U.S. Treasury Department, and the contributions to incumbents are substantial. Michael Malbin estimates that House incumbents enjoy perquisites of office, supporting constituent contact, worth at least $1 million over the period of a two-year term ($400,000 for constituent service staff; $400,000 for district office expenses, travel, phones, computers, and the like; and $250,000 for unsolicited mailings to constituents).[69] (Indeed, it might be argued that the United States *has* publicly funded congressional campaigns—but only for incumbents.) Hence the heavy support of political action committees is simply icing on the cake—double rich.

Raising campaign money is a relentless pursuit for members of Congress and their aides. House and Senate rules permit each office to have at least one staff member assigned to receive campaign contributions. Additionally, many members hire professional fund-raisers who advise them on the techniques for soliciting money (to ask for the "right" amount—not too much, not too little) and who travel around the country with them to court contributors. Increasingly, the money hunt has prompted members to seek funds from sources outside their home states. Fund-raising events at Washington watering holes occur night after night (cost of admission: usually $500 on the House side and $1,000 or more on the Senate side), attracting lobbyists and assorted contributors who know that gifts are acknowledged with the promise of access. Members solicit and accept out-of-state political money, first, because it is readily available, and second, because it is easier than asking their own constituents and perhaps offending them.[70]

After individuals and PACs, the political party is the third most important source of campaign funds for congressional candidates, but it is destined to become less important because of the passage of McCain-Feingold. The party's role is limited by the FECA, both in terms of how much money it is permitted to contribute directly to candidates and how much it can spend on their behalf. In making *direct* contributions to House candidates, national party committees—the national committee and the party's congressional campaign committee—are each limited to $5,000 per candidate per election. Candidates for the Senate can receive up to $17,500 in combined direct contributions from the national committee and the senatorial campaign committee in a calendar year. State and local committees also make limited contributions to congressional campaigns. Direct contributions by national party committees do not amount to much; Democratic national committees contributed $1.4 million to the party's congressional candidates in 2000, Republicans, $2.3 million.[71]

Much more important are national party expenditures made on behalf of congressional candidates—so-called *coordinated* expenditures. Permitted only in the general election, coordinated expenditures are made by party committees alone, though the committees may consult with the candidates' organizations to decide how the money should be spent. Based on state voting-age population, the amounts permitted are sizable for Senate campaigns in populous states. In California, for example, each party in 2000 could spend $1.6 million on behalf of each of its senatorial candidates; in New York, $929,000; in Texas, $967,000; in Pennsylvania, $617,000; and in thirteen relatively small states, $67,000. For House candidates in 2000, coordinated expenditures were limited to $33,780 (except in states with only one member, where the limit was $67,560).[72] In addition, fortified by a Supreme Court ruling,[73] a state party committee can transfer its spending authority to the national committee, which effectively doubles the expenditures the national party can make on behalf of its candidates. These agency agreements have been a boon to the spending plans of the Republican party in particular.

Party support for congressional candidates is important.[74] In 2000 coordinated expenditures totaled more than $29 million for the Republican party and $21 million for the Democratic party.[75] In addition, the Republican party transferred an additional $129.9 million in soft money to its state parties, much of which was used to boost the fortunes of congressional candidates. The Democratic party similarly transferred $149.8 million to its state parties. Gary C. Jacobson estimates that national party committees can supply one fourth of the money necessary for a serious House campaign and, in some states, up to half of the funds necessary for a full-scale Senate campaign.[76] Nevertheless, the parties do not stack up particularly well in comparison with PACs, especially now that soft money has been banned by McCain-Feingold. If the behavior of officeholders is influenced by campaign money, as Herbert E. Alexander has observed, the parties do not have an especially strong claim for preference, given the contributions to legislators by individuals and PACs.[77]

Evaluating the Campaign Finance System

At this point it is useful to take stock of what has happened since the adoption of the FECA and its subsequent amendments. Experience with the campaign finance law for three decades provides support for a number of observations concerning its impact on citizens, parties, candidates, and the political system.[78] While it has been effective in some ways, it has failed to meet the expectations of reformers in some of the most important areas.

One of the main goals of the FECA was to limit the cost of campaigns. In this regard, it has failed miserably. The Supreme Court's 1976 ruling in *Buckley v. Valeo* that restrictions on the personal and total expenditures of candidates for Congress were unconstitutional led to an explosion of spending. Winning candidates for the Senate in 1976 spent a total of $20 million; in 2000 they spent $238 million, more than eleven times as much as was spent in 1976. Winning candidates for the House in 1976 spent a total of $38 million; in 2000 they spent $355 million, more than nine times as much. In 2000 thirty-five Senate candidates spent more than $3 million on their campaigns; twenty-two spent more than $5 million. Fifty House candidates spent more than $1.8 million each.[79] Today campaigns are significantly more expensive, not less.

The FECA has also failed in its effort to curtail the influence of organized interests. Indeed, much of the spending increase is the direct result of the increased activity of PACs. The impact of interest groups is especially pronounced at the congressional level. In 1974 PACs made campaign contributions of about $12.5 million to congressional candidates. In 2000 their contributions totaled $260 million—more than twenty times as much. Currently there are just under four thousand PACs, nearly seven times as many as there were in 1974.

The FECA also sought to increase the involvement of ordinary citizens in the financing of campaigns. At first, it appeared that citizen participation would proliferate. In 1976 sixteen percent of Americans reported having made a contribution to help a campaign, twice the percentage recorded just ten years earlier.[80] In addition, 29 percent of all taxpayers took advantage of the federal income tax checkoff option in 1980, earmarking $1 of their taxes to the public funding of presidential campaigns. By 1992, however, this percentage had dropped below 20 percent, where it has remained each year since. The low point was 1996, when only 12 percent of taxpayers participated in the income tax checkoff. In fact, the declining percentage of taxpayers willing to earmark a dollar of their taxes for this purpose necessitated an increase to $3 for the checkoff box in 1993 to maintain the fund's solvency. Mirroring the decline in the income tax checkoff, only nine percent of Americans reported that they contributed money to help a campaign in 2000, about half the percentage reported in 1976.[81]

The direct influence of wealthy contributors on electoral politics has declined, though not as much as reformers had hoped. After McCain-Feingold, the contributions of an individual to federal candidates are limited to $2,000 for each election and to a total of $95,000 in a two-year election cycle. In reality, these are not stringent limitations. Only direct contributions to federal candidates are effectively limited. As a result of the *Buckley* decision, wealthy individuals can spend an unlimited amount of money to help elect a candidate if the money is spent *independently* of the candidate's campaign. In addition, individuals can contribute $5,000 to state parties—all fifty if they like—knowing that this money will help the overall ticket, and they can also contribute $25,000 per year to the national parties. Thus, it is a myth that strict limitations govern contributions to federal campaigns. McCain-Feingold's soft money ban will, however, limit how much wealthy interests can donate to the national parties. In the decade before its passage, it was not uncommon for well-heeled contributors to write $100,000 checks, some reaching into the millions of dollars. People and groups will have to find different ways to inject these monies into the political system, and undoubtedly they will.

The matching fund system for funding presidential primaries was also intended to increase the influence of small contributors. As provided by the FECA, matching federal funds become available for presidential primary and caucus candidates who first raise $100,000 in small sums—by obtaining $5,000 in contributions of $250 or less in each of twenty states. Once a candidate has reached the $100,000 threshold, the government matches the first $250 of any individual contribution. This encourages candidates to raise money in smaller chunks, something that ordinary people might be able to afford. To receive federal matching funds, however, presidential candidates must agree to certain spending limits. In 2000, for example, candidates who accepted public funds could not spend more than $45.6 million during the primary season. In addition, they had to grapple with state spending ceilings, which are determined by population. In 2000 candidates had to limit themselves to $675,000 in a small state like New Hampshire and to $13.1 million in California, the largest state.[82]

To avoid these limitations, presidential candidates have increasingly begun to eschew federal funding and to raise their funds from private or personal sources. George W. Bush demonstrated that such an approach could be successful. He spent nearly $100 million during the primaries, more than twice the limit for those who accepted federal matching funds. As a result, Bush was able to build strong political organizations in all fifty states, which ultimately allowed him to grind down the challenge of John McCain. While McCain was scrambling for money after his strong early showings, the well-funded Bush relied on his nationwide organization to deliver victories in the March primaries, thus forcing McCain out of the race. Bush's success will almost certainly cause some future candidates to ignore federal funding, with its emphasis on small donors.

In at least one area, the FECA has not been a complete failure. Opportunities to misuse money in federal elections have been constricted to some extent. The risks of detection are greater as a result of timely and comprehensive disclosure provisions, requirements for centralized accounting of contributions and expenditures, curbs on cash contributions, and the existence of a full-time agency—the Federal Election Commission—to administer the law and to investigate alleged infractions of it. Some minor provisions in McCain-Feingold should increase the government's regulatory power. Every major presidential candidate organization has numerous accountants and lawyers to analyze and monitor the candidate's financial activities. Bookkeeping has thus become a major feature and expense of campaigns for federal office, congressional as well as presidential. Still, the knowledge that legal action by the chronically understaffed and underfunded Federal Election Commission will not be taken until well after the election doubtlessly tempts some candidates to play fast and loose with the rules on campaign finance.

In terms of the parties, the FECA has aided them in some respects and weakened them in others. Among the provisions of the Federal Election Campaign Act that benefit the parties are:

1. individual contributors can give more money to the parties ($25,000) than they can to candidates ($2,000);
2. each national party can spend money on behalf of its presidential and congressional candidates (coordinated expenditures);
3. both national and state party committees can make direct contributions to House and Senate candidates;
4. public funds are available to defray the costs of presidential nominating conventions; and
5. at least until the adoption of McCain-Feingold, the parties could raise and spend unlimited sums of soft money on the nonfederal portion of generic party-building activities.

Other features of the law, however, do not serve the party interest. The parties' impact on presidential elections has been diminished. The public funds made available in the nominating and election phases go directly to the candidates instead of to the parties; in fact, each major party candidate received $67.6 million in 2000. In this major feature, the law is plainly candidate centered. With the passage of McCain-Feingold, the parties are limited in the amounts they can contribute to their candidates and in the amounts they can spend on their behalf. Especially if the Supreme Court strikes down the limits on soft money–financed ads run by nonparty entities and upholds the soft money ban on parties, as many experts believe will occur, individuals and interest groups will hold much more sway than parties in the campaign finance game. And, as noted, direct contributions by PACs to candidates for Congress have increased substantially in recent years. On the whole, the campaign finance law has increased the influence of nonparty groups in American politics. No one apparently planned for that to happen.

Although FECA places certain restrictions on the parties in raising and spending funds, the parties' role in campaigns is nevertheless growing in importance. In accounting for both hard and soft money, the three Republican national committees (national, senatorial, and congressional) raised $691.8 million in 2000, and the corresponding Democratic committees raised $513.0 million.[83] Compared with the 1970s and 1980s, when the Republican party often outraised the Democratic party by five to one, the gap has narrowed considerably, though Republicans still maintain a substantial advantage. As Table 4-6 demonstrates, the main reason for the Democrats' improved fund-raising performance was their ability to attract soft money. In 2000, for example, soft money made up 47 percent of the Democrats' total receipts but only 35 percent of the Republicans'.[84] At least in the short run, the soft money ban under McCain-Feingold figures to hurt the Democrats more than the Republicans.

Table 4-6   Party Fund-Raising, Hard and Soft Money: 1992–2002 (in millions of dollars)

	Presidential Year			Off Year		
	1992	1996	2000	1994	1998	2002
Democrats						
Hard money	$155.5	$210.0	$269.9	$121.1	$153.4	$220.2
Soft money	36.3	122.3	243.1	49.1	91.5	245.8
Total	191.8	332.3	513.0	170.2	244.9	466.0
Republicans						
Hard money	$266.3	$407.5	$447.4	$223.7	$273.6	$402.1
Soft money	49.8	141.2	244.4	52.5	131.0	250.0
Total	316.1	548.7	691.8	276.2	404.6	652.1
Republican advantage	$124.3	$216.4	$178.8	$106	$159.7	$186.1

Source: Press release, Federal Election Commission, December 18, 2002.

By removing nearly $500 million in soft money from the parties' revenue stream, McCain-Feingold may, to some degree, undermine the parties' ability to make meaningful contributions to their candidates. However, it is worth noting that the parties became significantly better at attracting hard as well as soft money donations in the 1990s. Between 1992 and 2000, the Democrats increased their hard money receipts by 74 percent, and the Republicans increased theirs by 68 percent. Moreover, the increase in the contribution limits to parties under McCain-Feingold, and the fact that these limits will grow with inflation, should help the parties continue to play a meaningful, if somewhat diminished, role.

Neither the adoption of the FECA and its amendments nor McCain-Feingold has solved all the problems of financing American elections. Inequities, confusion, and uncertainties persist. Have campaigns become too costly? Some close observers argue that they are underfinanced.[85] Should congressional as well as presidential campaigns be publicly financed? Thus far, Congress has said no. In theory, the public supports the concept, but Americans have expressed no desire to pay for public funding. And what of interest groups, now spending with a vengeance and undoubtedly gaining improved access to policy makers and securing questionable preferments? How much regulation of independent expenditures by interest groups will the Supreme Court permit? Is it realistic to think of passing new campaign finance legislation that makes elections more competitive by diminishing the advantages of incumbents over their challengers? As it stands, the massive advantages of office for incumbents, who are benefited additionally by one-sided PAC campaign support, ordinarily leave challengers with no more than an outside chance of winning, particularly in House elections. Both law and practice have combined to build a comprehensive incumbent-protection system. Can campaign finance legislation be designed to strengthen the parties, and should this be a public policy goal? These are some of the questions that will inform debate on campaign finance and its reform. Answers are not easy to fashion. The consequences of change, moreover, are difficult to anticipate. Protecting the status quo is the best single safeguard against the unanticipated outcomes that invariably accompany change.[86]

The manner in which political campaigns are financed has long been a source of controversy. Devising acceptable public policy on the subject has proved to be difficult, as it usually is on complex questions. But the objectives of regulation have been clear: to increase public confidence in the political process by curbing the abusive uses of political money, to enhance the opportunities for citizens to participate in politics by running for public office or contributing to political campaigns, and to reduce the vulnerability of candidates and public officials to the importunings and pressures of major benefactors. The campaign finance law has contributed only marginally to the achievement of these objectives. A solid majority of the public thinks that the government is run for a small number of big interests rather than for the nation as a whole, and large contributors still dominate the fund-raising system. Overall, the FECA has created some new problems, accentuated certain old ones, conferred advantages on incumbent politicians and disadvantages on challengers, and, arguably, done more to weaken the parties than to strengthen them.

NOTES

1. For an analysis of these party networks, see John F. Bibby, "National-State Integration, Allied Groups, and Issue Activists," in John C. Green and Daniel Shea, eds., *The State of the Parties: The Changing Role of Contemporary Parties* (Lanham, Md.: Rowman and Littlefield, 1999).

2. Press release, Federal Election Commission, May 31, 2001.

3. For an early analysis of campaign style, particularly in terms of the role of campaign management firms, see Robert Agranoff, *The New Style in Election Campaigns* (Boston: Holbrook Press, 1972). For more recent analyses, see Paul S. Herrnson, *Congressional Elections: Campaigning at Home and in Washington*, 3d ed. (Washington, D.C.: CQ Press, 2000); and Dennis W. Johnson, *No Place For Amateurs: How Political Consultants Are Shaping Democracy* (New York: Routledge, 2001).

4. Barbara G. Salmore and Stephen A. Salmore, *Candidates, Parties, and Campaigns* (Washington, D.C.: CQ Press, 1989), 215–216.

5. David A. Leuthold, *Electioneering in a Democracy* (New York: Wiley, 1968), 3. Leuthold's study of congressional campaigns shows that "the problems of acquisition are more significant than the problems of using the resources. As a result, the decision on making an appeal for the labor vote, for example, will depend not only on the proportion of the constituency which is labor-oriented, but also on the success that the candidate has had in acquiring such resources as the support of labor leaders, the money and workers needed to send a mailing to labor union members, and information about issues important to labor people."

6. A study of women's and men's campaigns for the U.S. House of Representatives shows that they have more similarities than differences. The most important difference is that women are more likely than men to stress social issues, such as children, poverty, and education. Kirsten la Cour Dabelko and Paul S. Herrnson, "Women's and Men's Campaigns for the U.S. House of Representatives," *Political Research Quarterly* 50 (March 1997): 121–135. For a complete treatment of gender differences in campaigns, see Kim Fridkin Kahn, *The Political Consequences of Being a Woman: How Stereotypes Influence the Conduct and Consequences of Political Campaigns* (New York: Columbia University Press, 1996).

7. Daniel Shea, *Campaign Craft: The Strategies, Tactics, and Art of Political Campaign Management* (Westport, Conn.: Praeger, 1996).

8. Salmore and Salmore, *Candidates, Parties, and Campaigns*; Shea, *Campaign Craft*. For an interesting argument that negative campaigning is not necessarily bad campaigning, see William G. Mayer, "In Defense of Negative Campaigning," *Political Science Quarterly* 111 (fall 1996): 437–455.

9. Just how minimal the effect of campaigns is depends on the study. Paul Lazarsfeld, Bernard Berelson, and Hazel Gudet, *The People's Choice* (New York: Columbia University Press, 1944), find it to be between five and eight percentage points. Steven E. Finkel, "Reexamining the 'Minimal Effects' Model in Recent Presidential Campaigns," *Journal of Politics* 55 (March 1993): 1–21, finds a similar effect in a more contemporary study. Larry M. Bartels, "Electioneering in the United States," in *Electioneering: A Comparative Study of Continuity and Change*, ed. David Butler and Austin Ranney (New York: Oxford University Press, 1992), finds the effect of political campaigns to be only about two percentage points.

10. Finkel, "Reexamining the 'Minimal Effects' Model in Recent Presidential Campaigns."

11. See, for example, Michael Lewis-Beck and Tom Rice, *Forecasting Elections* (Washington, D.C.: CQ Press, 1992); and Steven J. Rosenstone, *Forecasting Presidential Elections* (New Haven: Yale University Press, 1983).

12. Stephen Ansolabehere and Shanton Iyengar, *Going Negative* (New York: Free Press, 1995).

13. Bartels, "Electioneering in the United States."

14. Lewis A. Froman Jr., "A Realistic Approach to Campaign Strategies and Tactics," in *The Electoral Process,* ed. M. Kent Jennings and L. Harmon Zeigler (Englewood Cliffs, N.J.: Prentice Hall, 1966), 7–8.

15. See Marc J. Hetherington, "The Effect of Political Trust on the Presidential Vote," *American Political Science Review* 93 (June 1999): 311–326.

16. 2000 Voter News Service Exit Poll.

17. Daron R. Shaw, "A Study of Presidential Campaign Event Effects from 1952–1992," *Journal of Politics* 61 (May 1999): 387–422. Also see Daron R. Shaw, "The Effect of TV Ads and Candidate Appearances on Statewide Presidential Votes, 1988–96," *American Political Science Review* 93 (June 1999): 345–362; Thomas Holbrook, *Do Campaigns Matter?* (Beverly Hills: Sage University Press, 1996); and John G. Geer, "The Effects of the Presidential Debates on the Electorate's Preferences for Candidates," *American Politics Quarterly* 16 (May 1988): 486–501.

18. Charles Cook of the Cook Political Report is the political analyst in question. It is worth noting that Gore had a several-point lead in the polls in the days leading up to this debate but trailed from then until election day.

19. Stimson Bullitt, *To Be a Politician* (Garden City, N.Y.: Doubleday, 1961), 72–73.

20. From Theodore H. White, *The Making of the President, 1960* (New York: Atheneum, 1961), 322–323. For analysis of the major models of campaign decision making, see Karl A. Lamb and Paul A. Smith, *Campaign Decision-Making: The Presidential Election of 1964* (Belmont, Calif.: Wadsworth, 1968).

21. Press release, Federal Election Commission, May 15, 2001.

22. Donald E. Stokes, "Spatial Models of Party Competition," *American Political Science Review* 57 (June 1963): 368–377.

23. John J. Dilulio Jr., "Valence Voters, Valence Victors," in *The Election of 1996,* ed. Michael Nelson (Washington, D.C.: CQ Press, 1997), 172.

24. Salmore and Salmore, *Candidates, Parties, and Campaigns,* 113.

25. "Campaign Consultants: Pushing Sincerity in 1974," *Congressional Quarterly Weekly Report,* May 4, 1974, 1105.

26. Salmore and Salmore, *Candidates, Parties, and Campaigns,* 113.

27. Voter News Service exit poll.

28. John R. Petrocik, "Issue Ownership in Presidential Elections, with a 1980 Case Study," *American Journal of Political Science* 40 (August 1986): 825–850.

29. A large number of studies make this point, notably George E. Marcus, "The Structure of Emotional Response: 1984 Presidential Candidates," *American Political Science Review* 82 (September 1988): 737–761; Wendy M. Rahn, John H. Aldrich, Eugene Borgida, and John L. Sullivan, "A Social-Cognitive Model of Candidate Appraisal," in *Information and Democratic Processes,* ed. John A. Ferejohn and James H. Kuklinski (Urbana, Ill.: University of Illinois Press, 1990), 136–159.

30. Roderick P. Hart, *Seducing America* (New York: Oxford University Press, 1994).

31. For an example of this line of argument, see Samuel Popkin, *The Reasoning Voter,* 2d ed. (Chicago: University of Chicago Press, 1994).

32. See Herbert E. Alexander, *Financing the 1980 Election* (Washington, D.C.: CQ Press, 1983); William J. Crotty and Gary C. Jacobson, *American Parties in Decline* (Boston: Little, Brown, 1980), 816–823; and Frank J. Sorauf, *Money in American Elections* (Glenview, Ill.: Scott Foresman/Little, Brown, 1988), 186–221. The 1988, 1992, and 1996 estimates are by Herbert E. Alexander; the 2000 estimates are by Candice J. Nel-

son, "Spending in the 2000 Elections," in *Financing the 2000 Elections*, ed. David J. Magleby (Washington, D.C.: Brookings Institution, 2002).

33. See an article by Frank J. Sorauf that examines the organizational lives of PACs, the role of donors to PACs, and PAC accountability: "Who's in Charge? Accountability in Political Action Committees," *Political Science Quarterly* 99 (winter 1984–1985): 591–614. Also see the studies of PAC goals, organization, and decision making by Theodore J. Eismeier and Philip H. Pollock III, "An Organizational Analysis of Political Action Committees," *Political Behavior* 7, no. 2 (1985): 192–216; and "Strategy and Choice in Congressional Elections: The Role of Political Action Committees," *American Journal of Political Science* 30 (February 1986): 197–213. The authors distinguish three PAC roles: *accommodationist* (seek access in Congress through gifts to incumbents); *partisan* (basically financial auxiliaries of the major parties); and *adversary* (seek to defeat members whom they regard as hostile to their interests).

34. Paul S. Herrnson, "Money and Motives: Spending in House Elections," in Lawrence C. Dodd and Bruce I. Oppenheimer, eds., *Congress Reconsidered*, 6th ed. (Washington, D.C.: CQ Press, 1997).

35. *Washington Post*, June 15, 1987.

36. We should note that, of course, most House races are strikingly uncompetitive.

37. Herrnson, *Congressional Elections*, 81–82. Herbert E. Alexander also believes that television costs in overall political spending are not as great as critics contend. He observes that only about one half of the candidates for the U.S. House of Representatives ever purchase television time.

38. Press release, Federal Election Commission, March 4, 1993.

39. Press release, Federal Election Commission, May 15, 2001.

40. Press release, Federal Election Commission, January 2, 2003.

41. Anthony Gierzynski, *Money Rules: Financing Elections in America* (Boulder, Colo.: Westview Press, 2000), 8.

42. Frank J. Sorauf, *Inside Campaign Finance: Myths and Realities* (New Haven, Conn.: Yale University Press, 1992), 187.

43. Bradley A. Smith, *Unfree Speech, The Folly of Campaign Finance Reform* (Princeton, N.J.: Princeton University Press, 2001), 42.

44. Many states also passed campaign finance reform legislation following Watergate. Campaign finance regulations in the states vary widely. Some states, such as Virginia, have virtually no regulations on political money, while others, such as Wisconsin, have strict campaign finance regulations. For an excellent analysis of state campaign regulation, see Michael J. Malbin and Thomas L. Gais, *The Day After Reform: Sobering Campaign Finance Lessons from the American States* (Albany, N.Y.: The Rockefeller Institute Press, 1998). Also see Joel A. Thomas and Gary F. Moncrief, eds., *Campaign Finance in State Legislative Elections* (Washington, D.C.: CQ Press, 1998).

45. Larry J. Sabato and Bruce Larson, *The Party's Just Begun*, 2d ed. (New York: Longman, 2002), 72.

46. *Buckley v. Valeo*, 424 U.S. 1 (1976). The Court struck down provisions that limited the spending of personal funds by candidates ($35,000 for Senate candidates and $25,000 for House candidates) and those that limited total expenditures. Senate candidates were to be limited to total expenditures of no more than $100,000 or eight cents per eligible voter (whichever is greater) in primaries, and $150,000 or twelve cents per voter (whichever is greater) in general elections. Fund-raising costs of up to 20 percent of the spending limit could be added to these amounts. House candidates were to be limited to no more than $70,000 in primaries and $70,000 in general elections (plus fund-raising costs of up to 20 percent of the spending limit).

47. *Colorado Republican Federal Campaign Committee v. Federal Election Commission*, 518 U.S. 604 (1996).

48. *Nixon v. Shrink Missouri Government PAC*, 528 U.S. 377 (2000).

49. U.S. Congress, Senate, *Congressional Record,* daily ed., 101st Cong., 1st sess., May 11, 1990, S6037.

50. U.S. Congress, Senate, *Congressional Record,* daily ed., 101st Cong., 1st sess., May 11, 1990, S6038.

51. What campaign money buys for nonincumbents is voter recognition. See Gary C. Jacobson, "The Effects of Campaign Spending in Congressional Elections," *American Political Science Review* 72 (June 1978): 469–491; Gary C. Jacobson, "Money in the 1980 and 1982 Congressional Elections," in *Money and Politics in the United States: Financing Elections in the 1980s,* ed. Michael J. Malbin (Washington, D.C.: American Enterprise Institute for Public Policy Research, 1984), 60–63; Gary C. Jacobson, "The Effects of Campaign Spending in House Elections: New Evidence for Old Arguments," *American Journal of Political Science* 34 (May 1990): 334–362; and Donald P. Green and Jonathan S. Krasno, "Rebuttal to Jacobson's 'New Evidence for Old Arguments,'" *American Journal of Political Science* 34 (May 1990): 363–372. Also see Scott J. Thomas, "Do Incumbent Campaign Expenditures Matter?" *Journal of Politics* 51 (November 1989): 965–976. Thomas argues that incumbent expenditures do make a difference: "The principal effect of incumbent spending is to win back voters who would have voted for the incumbent in the absence of the receipt of challenger (negative) advertisements." Quotation on p. 973.

52. The best treatment of soft money is Anthony Corrado, "Party Soft Money," in *Campaign Finance Reform: A Sourcebook,* ed. Anthony Corrado, Thomas E. Mann, Daniel R. Ortiz, Trevor Potter, and Frank J. Sorauf (Washington, D.C.: Brookings, 1997), 165–224.

53. See Sabato and Larson, *The Party's Just Begun,* 73, 99, n.16. Also see Anthony Corrado, "Party Soft Money," in Richard Briffault, "Soft Money Reform and the Constitution," *Election Law Journal* 1 (2002): 343–372.

54. Craig B. Holman and Luke P. McLoughlin, *Buying Time 2000: Television Advertising in the 2000 Federal Elections* (New York: Brennan Center for Justice, 2002).

55. *New York Times,* September 8, 1996.

56. Press release, Brennan Center for Justice, July 3, 2001.

57. Holman and McLoughlin, *Buying Time 2000: Television Advertising in the 2000 Federal Elections.*

58. Importantly, by creating a new category of political advertisement called "electioneering communications," McCain-Feingold essentially broadened the Supreme Court's definition of what constitutes an express advocacy (election) advertisement. According to the McCain-Feingold legislation, an electioneering communication is any "broadcast, cable, or satellite communication [that] refers to a clearly identified candidate within 60 days of a general election or 30 days of a primary election [and] is made to an audience that includes members of the electorate for such an election."

59. Calculated from press release, Federal Election Commission, May 16, 2001.

60. See especially the scholarly dialogue between Jonathan S. Krasno and Donald Philip Green on the one hand and Gary C. Jacobson on the other in assessing the effect of incumbent spending. Specifically, Donald Philip Green and Jonathan S. Krasno, "Salvation for the Spendthrift Incumbent: Reestimating the Effects of Campaign Spending in House Elections," *American Journal of Political Science* 32 (November 1988): 884–907; Jonathan S. Krasno and Donald Philip Green, "Preempting Quality Challengers in House Elections," *Journal of Politics* 50 (November 1988): 920–936; and Gary C. Jacobson, "The Effects of Campaign Spending in House Elections," *American Journal of Political Science* 34 (May 1990): 334–362. Also see Alan I. Abramowitz, "Incumbency, Campaign Spending, and the Decline of Competition in U.S. House Elections," *Journal of Politics* 53 (February 1991): 34–56.

61. Press release, Federal Election Commission, May 31, 2001.

62. Press release, Federal Election Commission, May 31, 2001.

63. Kevin B. Grier and Michael C. Munger, "Comparing Interest Group Contributions to House and Senate Incumbents, 1980–1986," *Journal of Politics* 55 (1992): 615–643.

64. *Congressional Quarterly Weekly Report,* April 8, 1978, 850–851; and November 11, 1978, 3260–3262.

65. Press release, Federal Election Commission, May 31, 2001.

66. See Sabato and Larson, *The Party's Just Begun,* 84–88; Bruce A. Larson, "Incumbent Contributions to the Congressional Campaign Committees, 1990–2000," *Political Research Quarterly,* forthcoming.

67. *Congressional Quarterly Weekly Report,* August 2, 1986, 1751–1754.

68. David R. Mayhew, *Congress: The Electoral Connection* (New Haven: Yale University Press, 1974), 84.

69. *Wall Street Journal,* September 24, 1986.

70. See an interesting account, "Don't Look Homeward," in *National Journal,* June 16, 1990, 1458–1460.

71. Press release, Federal Election Commission, May 15, 2001.

72. Press release, Federal Election Commission, March 1, 2000.

73. *Federal Election Commission v. Democratic Senatorial Campaign Committee,* 454 U.S. 27 (1981).

74. For a study that finds that national party contributions to congressional candidates enhance their party loyalty, see Kevin M. Leyden and Stephen A. Borrelli, "Party Contributions and Party Unity: Can Loyalty Be Bought?" *Western Political Quarterly* 43 (June 1990): 343–365.

75. Press release, Federal Election Commission, May 15, 2001.

76. Gary C. Jacobson, "Party Organization and Distribution of Campaign Resources: Republicans and Democrats in 1982," *Political Science Quarterly* 100 (winter 1985–1986): 611.

77. Herbert E. Alexander, "Political Parties and the Dollar," *Society* 22 (January/February 1985): 49–58.

78. For a discussion of some of these themes, see an insightful essay by F. Christopher Arterton, "Political Money and Party Strength," in *The Future of American Political Parties,* ed. Joel Fleishman (Englewood Cliffs, N.J.: Prentice Hall, 1982), especially 116–122.

79. Press release, Federal Election Commission, May 15, 2001.

80. American National Election Study, Cumulative File, 1948–2000.

81. American National Election Study, Cumulative File, 1948–2000.

82. Anthony Corrado, "Financing the 2000 Elections," *The Election of 2000: Reports and Interpretations,* ed. Gerald M. Pomper (New York: Chatham House, 2001), 92–124.

83. Press release, Federal Election Commission, December 18, 2002.

84. Press release, Federal Election Commission, December 18, 2002.

85. Alexander, "Political Parties and the Dollar," 49–58.

86. For insight into the reform question, see Michael J. Malbin, "Looking Back at the Future of Campaign Finance Reform: Interest Groups and American Elections," in *Money and Politics in the United States,* 232–270.

5 THE CONGRESSIONAL PARTY AND THE FORMATION OF PUBLIC POLICY

THE TASKS THAT CONFRONT THE AMERICAN major party are formidably ambitious. From one perspective, the party is a wide-ranging electoral agency organized to make a credible bid for power. Here and there a party organization is so stunted and devitalized that it seldom can make an authentic effort to win office. Where it is not taken seriously, the party finds it difficult to develop and recruit candidates, to gain the attention of the media, and to attract financial contributors. Elections may go by default to the dominant party as the second party struggles merely to stay in business. But throughout most of the country the parties compete on fairly even terms—if not for certain offices or in certain districts, at least for some offices or in a state at large. Presidential elections are vigorously contested virtually everywhere. As electoral organizations, the parties recruit candidates, organize campaigns, develop issues, and mobilize voters. Typical voters get their best glimpse of the workings of party when they observe the "party in the electorate" during political campaigns.

From another perspective, the party is a collection of officeholders who share in some measure common values and policy orientations. In the broadest sense, its mission is to take hold of government, to identify national problems and priorities, and to work for their settlement or achievement. In a narrower sense, the task of the "party in the government" is to consolidate and fulfill promises made to the electorate during the campaign. How it is organized to achieve this aim, and how it does it, is the concern of this chapter. The focus is the party in Congress.

Congressional Elections

In the study of congressional elections, scholars have found ample evidence to support Tip O'Neill's adage that "all politics is local." The two most important variables in the election of members of Congress are, in fact, local political conditions—incumbency status and party affiliation.[1] Although less important than local conditions, national political conditions, such as economic performance and the popularity of the president, also help determine how well the president's party does in a given year.[2]

Congressional incumbents have numerous advantages in elections. The offices and staffs of members are basic units in their campaign organizations. Voters are much more likely to recognize the name of the incumbent than that of the challenger. Some voters will have benefited from the many services that members regularly perform for their constituents. The franking privilege permits members to send mail to their constituents at government expense. And, of major importance, incumbents ordinarily find it much easier than challengers to raise campaign funds, particularly from interest groups. It is not surprising, then, that incumbents are difficult to defeat. It is rare for less than 90 percent of all House incumbents seeking reelection to be successful; this has happened only twice since 1968—in 1974 and 1992. Most often, the reelection rate surpasses 95 percent, as it did in 2002 when 98 percent were returned to office. Although Senate incumbents usually face stronger competition, they also win with great regularity. In 2000, a tough year for Senate incumbents, 79 percent were still reelected, and in 2002, 85 percent won another term.[3]

Party affiliation is also a key factor in congressional elections. In the typical state, some districts nearly always elect Democratic legislators and some districts nearly always elect Republican legislators. Some districts are so thoroughly dominated by one party that the second has virtually no chance of winning. For example, with few exceptions House districts in major cities are securely Democratic, irrespective of the incumbency factor. In other suburban, small-town, and rural districts Democratic candidates may face insurmountable odds in election after election. Districts do not often switch from one party to the other. In only two elections since 1968—1974 and 1994—did as many as 10 percent of the 435 seats switch party control.[4] Often the percentage is much lower than that.

Incumbency and party combine to yield a great many one-sided elections, especially in the House. Districts are typically won by a vote of 60 percent or more. In 2002, only 44 House races out of 435 saw the winner receive 55 percent of the vote or less.[5] In fact, both parties are accustomed to having a number of House races in which their candidates face no major party opposition.

While party competition for congressional seats is generally minimal, national conditions conducive to the party opposite the president have the potential to unseat more incumbents than usual. Indeed, with a still floundering economy in 1938, Franklin D. Roosevelt's party lost a whopping seventy-one seats in the House and six in the Senate. A recession in 1958 cost Dwight D. Eisenhower's Republicans forty-eight seats in the House and thirteen in the Senate. Richard Nixon's Watergate-induced unpopularity cost the Republicans forty-nine House seats and four Senate seats in 1974. And an unpopular Bill Clinton saw his party lose fifty-four House and ten Senate seats in 1994. The reason for these big losses is that high-quality challengers, such as those who have previously held some elected office, decide to run when conditions are favorable to them. When national conditions are not favorable, they decide to wait.[6]

It is important to note, however, that such large party-oriented changes are significantly less likely to occur now than they had been a generation or more ago. Indeed, the decline of party competition for congressional seats is one of the most conspicuous features of contemporary American politics. The most compelling explanation is that Democratic and Republican state legislators cooperate to protect each party's incumbents: they draw congressional district lines (along with their own) in such a way as to create as many safe districts as possible. As evidence, fewer than fifty House seats were even considered marginally competitive in 2002, the year directly after a redistricting when House seats are typically most up for grabs.[7] Redistricting's influence is also evident in the decreasing number of congressional districts that vote for a member of Congress of one party and a presidential candidate of the other. In the 1972 election fully 44 percent of districts provided split results. In 2000 only 20 percent did, the lowest percentage since the early 1950s. While increasing partisanship in the electorate is part of the explanation, the fact that electoral boundaries today put such a safe percentage of Democrats or Republicans in a district all but precludes the other party from winning.

In addition to redistricting, David R. Mayhew contends that incumbents have become more skillful in "advertising" their names, in "claiming credit" for federal governmental programs that benefit their districts, and in "position taking" on key issues of concern to their constituents. And they have large and talented staffs to help them cultivate their constituents.[8] Another study finds that information on the candidates is an important factor. If it is not available on both candidates, voters "are likely to vote for incumbents, whom they already like and may have voted for, faced with challengers they know little, if anything, about."[9]

It is hard to say exactly how public policy is affected by the relatively stable membership of both houses of Congress. Conventional wisdom holds that opportunities for major policy change are limited by a membership that remains largely intact election after election. Alternatively, members today have the luxury of pursuing more ideological ends in Congress, especially in the House, since their districts are now so safe that they feel little pressure to moderate their voting records. Strong ideological tendencies could lead to fundamental changes in a political system that has generally been characterized by its moderation.

Party Representation in Congress

Figures 5-1 and 5-2 show the representation of the parties in each house over the past seventy years, from 1932 to 2002. The broad picture is one of Democratic dominance with brief interludes of Republican control of one or both chambers. But party fortunes changed sharply in 1994. The Republicans gained an extraordinary fifty-four seats in the House and ten in the Senate,[10] winning control of Congress for the first time since the mid-1950s. More important, they have held these majorities for five consecutive elections, the longest period of Republican dominance in Congress since the 1920s.[11] Indeed, the 2002 election is noteworthy because it, along with those of 1902 and 1934, is one of only three in the last century in which the president's party increased its strength in both houses in a midterm election.[12]

Several explanations for the new Republican success have been advanced by Gary Jacobson. First, the reallocation of House seats following the 1990 and 2000 census rewarded those regions, such as the South and the West, that are favorable to the Republican party. Second, the creation of majority-minority districts had the effect of bunching African American voters into a few districts and at the same time making the surrounding areas relatively more Republican.[13] Third, with the retirement of many southern Democrats, the Republicans began to win seats that, given their characteristics, should have been Republican all along. Fourth, the Democrats' minority status in Congress, stemming from the 1994 debacle, prompted a number of members to retire in 1996, thus giving the Republicans an opportunity to win open seats in districts disposed toward their party.[14] Fifth, the Republicans' capture of Congress in 1994 upset the pattern of political action committee (PAC) contributions; since 1996 Republican Senate candidates have collected about twice as much money from PACs as their Democratic opponents. And sixth, the Democrats' loss of majority control in 1994 made it more difficult for them to recruit quality candidates to challenge Republican incumbents. So fundamental are these developments, Jacobson contends, that the best opportunity for Democrats to recapture Congress will occur when voters become disillusioned with some future Republican administration.[15]

Party membership is a major factor not only in determining who is elected to Congress but also in influencing members' behavior once they have taken office. The fact that party cohesion collapses on certain issues that come before Congress does not alter the general proposition that party affiliation is a major explanation of voting behavior. In fact, party is more important in a congressperson's voting behavior today than it has been for decades.[16] Members recognize that there are advantages to going along with the leadership and voting in agreement with their party colleagues. An examination of party voting follows an analysis of congressional party organization.

Figure 5-1 Democratic Strength in Senate Elections: 1932–2002

Number of seats

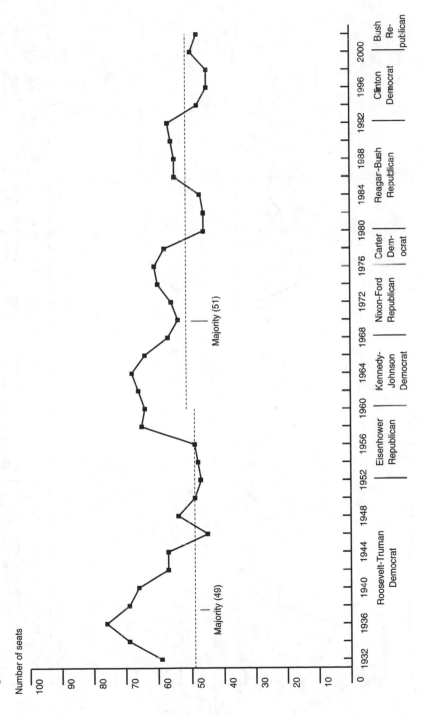

Figure 5-2 Democratic Strength in House Elections: 1932–2002

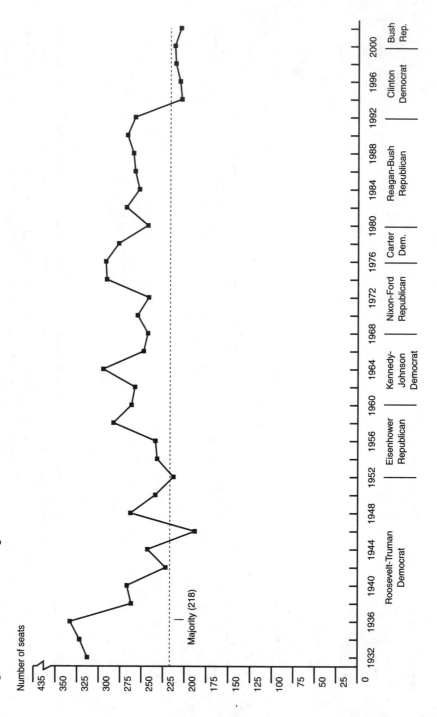

Party Organization in Congress

Party Conferences

The central agency of each party in each chamber is the conference or caucus. All those elected to Congress automatically become members of their party's caucus. During the early twentieth century, and particularly during the Wilson administration, the House majority party caucus was exceptionally powerful. Following World War I, disillusionment with the caucus became manifest, and members came to question the right of the caucus to bind them to a course of action. The power of the caucus declined sharply in the 1920s, and soon its functions were limited to the selection of party leaders such as the Speaker of the House, the floor leaders, and the whips.

For all intents and purposes, the caucus was moribund for the next half century. In 1969, after years of somnolence, the Democratic caucus began to hold regular monthly meetings to examine proposals for reforming the House. In the early 1970s, the caucus made several modifications to the seniority system, the most important of which provided for secret ballots on nominees for committee chairs. In 1973 it created the Steering and Policy Committee to formulate legislative programs and to participate in the scheduling of legislation for floor consideration.

The power of the Democratic caucus was dramatically demonstrated at the opening of the Ninety-fourth Congress in 1975 when, among other things, the caucus voted to remove three committee chairs from their positions, transferred to the Steering and Policy Committee the power to make committee assignments from the Democratic members of the Ways and Means Committee, and made a number of changes involving nominations and subcommittee procedures. Included in these changes was a provision to empower the Speaker, subject to caucus approval, to nominate the Democratic members of the powerful Rules Committee. The key test in filling vacancies on this committee now appears to be the member's allegiance to the leaders. Major disciplinary action by the Democratic caucus occurred again at the start of the Ninety-eighth Congress (1983–1984). In an unusual action, the caucus voted to remove Phil Gramm, then a Democratic House member from Texas, from the Budget Committee because in the previous Congress he had worked closely with the administration in the design of President Ronald Reagan's budget strategy.[17]

The Democratic party in the 1970s and 1980s did much to centralize control of the House in the leadership. The Republicans who took control of Congress after the 1994 midterm elections did much more. According to Steven S. Smith and Gerald Gamm, Rep. Newt Gingrich (R-Ga.), who was elected Speaker after engineering the Republican takeover, used his standing to pick committee chairs, who were only later endorsed by the party conference, and several subcommittee chairs, who were only later appointed by committee chairs. Gingrich even reviewed the appointment of top committee staffers.[18] His successful efforts to centralize power made him the most powerful Speaker in eighty years. Ultimately, however, his imperious style wore thin with the independent-minded rank-and-file members of his party, leading to his ouster as Speaker less than four years after he won the position. Following Gingrich's departure, the trend toward centralization slowed, though both parties have remained remarkably unified in their voting behavior nonetheless.

In the end, caucus power collides with the nagging reality of all legislative politics: the individual member's electoral security, and thus his primary interest, lies in the constituency. For many members of the House, the attractions of a cohesive party are not nearly so great as the attractions of independence, with all the opportunities it affords the legislator to concentrate on constituency interests and problems. Party leaders and committee leaders, moreover, usually take a dim view of caucus involvement in policy questions. As Speaker Thomas P. "Tip" O'Neill Jr. (D-Mass., 1977–1986), observed, "I don't like any of these [policy] matters coming from the caucus on a direct vote." A similar view was expressed by Rep. Richard Bolling (D-Mo.) during his long tenure in the House: "I think [members] would have an awful time if they tried [to set party policy in the caucus]. It's better left to the committee system."[19] The cards are stacked against centralized power in any form. The independence of today's members makes a return to the earlier days when "King Caucus" reigned over the House all but impossible.

The Speaker of the House

The most powerful party leader in Congress is the Speaker of the House. In the early twentieth century, the Speaker's powers were almost beyond limit, the House virtually his private domain. It is scarcely an exaggeration to say that legislation the Speaker favored was adopted and that legislation he opposed was defeated. The despotic rule of Speaker Joseph G. ("Uncle Joe") Cannon (R-Ill., 1903–1911) eventually proved his undoing. In 1910 Democrats and rebellious Republicans formed a coalition to challenge his leadership. After a struggle of many months, it succeeded in instituting a number of rules changes to curb the Speaker's powers. Cannon was removed from membership on the Rules Committee, which he had chaired; his power to appoint and remove members and chairs of the standing committees was eliminated; and his power to recognize, or not to recognize, members was limited. Although the "revolution of 1910–1911" fundamentally altered the formal powers of the Speaker, it did not render the office impotent. Since then, a succession of Speakers—men disposed to negotiate rather than to command—has helped to rebuild the powers of the office. What a Speaker like Joseph Cannon secured through autocratic rule, today's Speakers secure through persuasion and the astute exploitation of the bargaining advantages inherent in their positions.

The Speaker's formal powers are wide ranging, though not especially significant in themselves. The presiding officer of the House, the Speaker announces the order of business, puts questions to a vote, refers bills to committees, rules on points of order, interprets the rules, recognizes members who desire the floor, and appoints members to select and conference committees. The Speaker also has the right to vote and enter floor debate. Ordinarily he exercises these rights only in the case of major, closely contested issues.

Although difficult to delineate with precision, the informal powers of the Speaker are far more impressive. As the foremost leader of his party in Congress, he is at the center of critical information and policy-making systems. No one is in a better position than the Speaker to obtain and disseminate information, to shape strategies, or to advance or frustrate the careers of members. Perhaps the principal tangible preferment the Speaker has at his disposal is the influence he can exert to secure favorable committee assignments for members of the major-ity party. The Speaker's good will is important to majority-party members anx-ious to move ahead in the House.

As Joseph Cooper and David W. Brady note, however, the Speaker faces many limits. Today's party leaders, they write, "function less as the commanders of a stable party majority and more as brokers trying to assemble particular majorities behind particular bills."[20] Similarly, David W. Rohde observes, "In their day, Speakers such as Reed or Cannon ordered and punished the members at will. But it is . . . inconceivable to think of this in the modern Congress. The members now tell the leaders what to do, and the leaders do it."[21]

The ultimate failure of the Gingrich speakership illustrates the need to be a negotiator, not a commander. In addition to enhancing his personal role in appointing committee and subcommittee chairs, Gingrich was not shy about punishing those who did not toe his line. For example, he removed Rep. Mark Neumann (R-Wis.) from a plum Appropriations subcommittee in favor of a less desirable post because Neumann had repeatedly voted against the caucus lead-ership. A band of junior caucus members mutinied, forcing Gingrich to provide Neumann a coveted spot on the Budget Committee to make amends.[22] Since Gingrich's resignation from the speakership after the Republicans' poor showing in the 1998 midterm elections,[23] his successor, Dennis Hastert (R-Ill.), has employed a much softer touch with the party membership. As a result, the genial former high-school wrestling coach has been a much more popular, not to men-tion longer serving, Speaker.

The Floor Leaders

In addition to the Speaker of the House, the key figures in the congressional party organizations are the House and Senate floor leaders, who are chosen by party caucuses in their respective chambers. The floor leaders serve as the prin-cipal spokespersons for party positions and interests and as intermediaries in both intraparty and interparty negotiations. The floor leaders of the party that controls the presidency also serve as links between the president and his con-gressional party. Because floor leaders are obliged to play several roles at the same time—for example, representatives of both the congressional party and the president—it is not surprising that role conflicts develop. Serving the inter-ests of their congressional party colleagues or perhaps those of their constituents is anything but a guarantee that they will be serving presidential interests.

Floor leaders have a potpourri of informal, middling powers. Their availability, however, does not ensure that they can lead their colleagues or strongly shape the legislative program. By and large, their influence is based on their willingness and talent to exploit these powers steadily and imaginatively in their relations with other members. They can, if they choose:

1. influence the allocation of committee assignments (not only rewarding individual members but also shaping the ideological makeup of the committees);
2. help members to advance legislation of particular interest to them;
3. assist members in securing larger appropriations for their committees or subcommittees;
4. play a major role in debate;
5. intercede with the president or executive agencies on behalf of members (perhaps to assist their efforts to secure a federal project in their state or district);
6. make important information available to members;
7. help members to secure campaign money from a congressional campaign committee or from the political action committee of an interest group;
8. campaign on behalf of individual members; and
9. focus the attention of the communications media on the contributions of members.

Much of the influence of floor leaders, like that of the Speaker, is derived from informal powers, in particular from opportunities afforded them to advance or protect the careers of party colleagues. In solving problems for them and in making their positions more secure, floor leaders increase the prospects of gaining their support on critical questions. By the same token, floor leaders can in some measure hamper the careers of those members who continually refuse to go along with them. At the center of active floor leaders' powers is the capacity to manipulate rewards and punishments.

An important function and a major source of power for the majority floor leader, particularly in the Senate, is the scheduling of bills on the floor. (In the House, the Rules Committee dominates the agenda.) However pedestrian the scheduling function may sound, it is a surprisingly important source of power. The majority leader who fails to keep lines of communication clear, who misjudges the sentiments of members, who neglects to consolidate the majority by winning over undecided members or by propping up wavering members, or who picks the wrong time to call up a bill can easily go down to defeat. Prospective majorities are much more tenuous and much more easily upset than might be supposed. Support can be lost rapidly as a result of poor communications, missed opportunities for negotiation and compromise, and bad timing. The effective leader builds his power base by tending to the shop; ordering priorities; having a sense of detail that overlooks nothing; taking account of the demands placed on members; sensing the mood of congressional opinion, especially that of key members; and exhibiting skill in splicing together the legislative elements necessary to fashion a majority.

Given the heterogeneous nature of the nation as a whole, floor leaders necessarily face a difficult task, especially in the Senate, where the rank and file tends to be more independent minded than in the House. Former Senate majority leader Trent Lott (R-Miss.) likened his job to "putting bullfrogs in a wheelbarrow," and Sen. George Mitchell (D-Maine), one of Lott's predecessors, compared it to "herding cats."[24] Indeed, consider the number of factions that Sen. Bill Frist (R-Tenn.), the majority leader elected for the 108th Congress (2003–2004), faces. He must balance the wishes of southern social conservatives, northeastern moderates, business-oriented midwesterners, and pro-gun, low-tax westerners. The first month of Frist's leadership was successful in this regard, because he held all fifty-one members of his caucus together on a series of tough appropriations votes. But this task will undoubtedly grow more difficult after his honeymoon is over.

The principal power of the floor leader is the power of persuasion. As a former Democratic leader of the Senate, Lyndon B. Johnson (D-Texas), once observed, "The only real power available to the leader is the power of persuasion. There is no patronage; no power to discipline; no authority to fire Senators like a President can fire his members of Cabinet."[25] To be persuasive, a leader must know the members well. He must know what they want and what they will settle for, and what concessions they can and cannot make, given their constituencies. In addition, it requires good lines of communication into the other party to pick up support when elements of the majority party appear likely to wander off the reservation. Members prefer to support their leader and the party position rather than the opposing forces. The task of the leader is to find reasons for them to do so and conditions under which they can.

The development of a legislative program requires the majority leader to work closely with the key leaders in his party, particularly the chairs of the major committees. As Johnson observed during his tenure as Senate majority leader, "You must understand why the committee took certain actions and why certain judgments were formed."[26] His successor, Sen. Mike Mansfield (D-Mont.), observed, "I'm not the leader, really. They don't do what I tell them. I do what they tell me. . . . The brains are in the committees."[27] The effective leader works with the resources available—in essence, the power of persuasion. Relations between the leader and the committee chairs are never characterized by a one-way flow of mandates. On the contrary, the leader must be acutely sensitive to the interests of the chairs, adept at recognizing their political problems, and flexible in negotiations with them. Bargaining is the key characteristic of the relationships between the majority leader and the committee chairs.

Party management in Congress has become increasingly difficult in recent years. Several reasons help to explain this situation. First, the adoption of "sunshine" rules in both houses has made Congress a much more open institution. For the most part, committee, subcommittee, and even party caucus meetings are now open to the public. Second, combined with the new visibility of congressional actions, the growing power of interest groups, stemming particularly from their campaign contributions, has made members more vulnerable to outside pressures and, at the same time, increasingly resistant to the influence of party leaders. Third, the weakening of the electoral parties has been accompanied by an extraordinary growth in candidate-centered campaigns. Members who are elected to Congress largely on their own efforts have less reason to concern themselves with party objectives and less reason to defer to the wishes of party leaders. For example, despite Democratic party leaders' efforts to present a unified image to the country in 2003, Rep. Charlie Stenholm (D-Texas) led a number of southern conservatives in voting against Rep. Nancy Pelosi (D-Calif.) for House Minority Leader. It is always good politics in conservative west Texas, Stenholm's home district, to oppose a liberal from San Francisco.

Finally, internal changes have contributed to the further decentralization of congressional power. Subcommittees have grown both in number and in independence. The influence of committee chairs has declined as that of subcommittee chairs has grown. In addition, both chambers now limit the number of committee and subcommittee chairs that a member may hold, the effect of which has been to spread leadership positions (thus power) among more members. The presence of a large number of specialized policy caucuses may also have made it more difficult for the parties to integrate policy making. Singly and in combination, these changes have diminished the capacity of the parties to build majorities and to mobilize their members for concerted action.

The more individualistic Congress becomes, the more difficult it becomes for the party leadership to play a decisive role. As former Senate majority whip Alan Cranston (D-Calif.) observed, "A lot of leadership is just housekeeping now. Occasionally you have an opportunity to provide leadership, but not that often. The weapons to keep people in line just aren't there."[28] Rarely was this dilemma more clear than in 2001, when Sen. Zell Miller (D-Ga.) not only supported but actually cosponsored the tax cut on which Republican George W. Bush had campaigned in 2000. This badly undercut the efforts by Minority Leader Tom Daschle (D-S.D.) in the evenly split Senate to either defeat, or at least significantly change, the president's initiative. In the end, the tax package that passed included almost everything the president had proposed, thanks in large part to Miller. After the tax vote, Miller remained highly popular in conservative Georgia. In stark contrast, fellow Georgian senator Max Cleland, a Democrat who opposed Bush on the tax bill, lost his reelection bid in 2002.

Several important constraints shape the positions of the floor leaders. They are not free to fashion their role as they might like to see it. The limited range of powers available to them, their personality, their relationship to the president, and their skills in bargaining—all affect in some measure the definition of their role. Moreover, no two leaders are likely to perceive their roles in exactly the same light. In addition, the nature of the floor leaders' position is strongly influenced by the nature of the legislative parties. Persistent cleavages within both parties make it necessary for leaders to play mediating roles. Leaders are middlemen in the sense that they are more or less steadily involved in negotiations with all major elements within their party, and also in terms of their voting record.[29] In the passage of much legislation, the test is not so much the wisdom of the decision as it is its political feasibility. Leaders identified with an extreme group within their party would find it difficult to work out the kinds of compromises necessary to put together a majority. They are, first and foremost, brokers. Candidates for leadership positions whose voting records place them on the ideological edges of their party ordinarily are less likely to be elected than those whose voting records fall within the central range of party opinion.

Nevertheless, exceptions to this rule of moderation occur from time to time. In the 108th Congress (2003–2004), House Republicans chose one of their most conservative members, Rep. Tom Delay (R-Tex.), as majority leader, while House Democrats picked one of their most liberal members, Rep. Nancy Pelosi (D-Calif.), as minority leader. The election of these leaders, drawn from the wings of their parties, reflects the growing polarization of the congressional parties in the House.

The Whips

Another unit in the party structure of Congress is the whip organization. Party whips are selected in each house by the floor leaders or by other party agencies. Many assistant whips are required in the House because of the large size of the body. On the Democratic side, for example, more than one quarter of all members are now in the whip organization, making it a "mini-caucus every week."[30] Working to enhance the efforts of the leadership, the whips carry on a number of important functions. They attempt to learn how members intend to vote on legislation; relay information from party leaders to individual members; work to ensure that a large number of "friendly" members will be present at the time of voting; and attempt to win the support of those party members who are in opposition, or likely to be in opposition, to the leadership. The influence of the Speaker and the majority leader supplement the pressure of the whips. As described by one chief staff assistant to the majority whip, whips apply "the heavy party loyalty shtick. Then it's more personalities than issues. There are some members who can only be gotten by the Speaker or the majority leader."[31]

The central importance of the whip organization is that it forms a communications link between the party leadership and rank-and-file members. The whips are charged with discovering why members are opposed to certain legislation and how that legislation might be changed to gain their support. The intelligence the whips supply sometimes spells the difference between victory and defeat on a major issue. On some issues no amount of activity on the part of the leadership can bring recalcitrant members into the fold. If the outlook for a bill is unpromising following a "whip check" of members' sentiments, the leadership will often postpone its floor consideration. Whip checks can thus protect the leadership from embarrassing losses.

The Policy Committees

Few proposals for congressional reform have received as much attention as those designed to strengthen the role of political parties in the legislative process. The Joint Committee on the Organization of Congress recommended in its 1946 report that policy committees be created for the purpose of formulating the basic policies of the two parties. Although this provision was later stricken from the reorganization bill, the Senate independently created such committees in 1947. The House Republicans established a policy committee in 1949, though it did not become fully active for another decade.[32] Rounding out the list, the rejuvenated House Democratic caucus voted to establish a policy committee in 1973.

The high promise of the policy committees as agencies for enhancing party responsibility for legislative programs has never been realized. Neither party leaders nor rank-and-file members agree on the functions of the policy commit-tees. The policy committees are so in name only. Those in the Senate "have never been 'policy' bodies, in the sense of considering and investigating alternatives of public policy, and they have never put forth an overall congressional party pro-gram. The committees do not assume leadership in drawing up a general legisla-tive program . . . and only rarely have the committees labeled their decisions as 'party policies.' "[33]

It is not surprising that the policy committees have been unable to function effectively as agencies for the development of overall party programs. An author-itative policy committee would constitute a major threat to the scattered and rel-atively independent centers of power within Congress. Committee chairs would undoubtedly find their influence over legislation diminished if the policy com-mittees were to assume a central role in defining party positions. The independ-ence of the committee system would be affected adversely, and many individual members would suffer an erosion of power. If the policy committees had func-tioned as planned, a major reshuffling of power in Congress would have resulted. To those who hold the keys to congressional power, this is scarcely an appealing idea. However attractive the proposal for centralized committees empowered to speak for the parties in Congress, these committees are unlikely to emerge so long as the parties are decentralized and fragmented, composed of members who represent a wide variety of constituencies and ideological positions.

Such limitations do not render them useless. Both parties require forums for the discussion of issues and for the negotiation of compromises, and for these activities the policy committees are well designed. Moreover, the staffs of the committees have proved to be helpful for individual members seeking research assistance. Most important, the policy committees have served as communica-tions channels between the party leaders and their memberships.

The policy committees are an ambitious attempt to deal with the persistent problem of party disunity. If they have generally failed in this respect, they have nonetheless succeeded in others. As clearinghouses for the exchange of party information and as agencies for the reconciliation of at least some intraparty differences, they have made useful contributions.

Informal Party Groups and Specialized Congressional Caucuses

In addition to the formal party units in Congress, several informal party organizations meet more or less regularly to discuss legislation, strategy, and other questions of common interest. Among these organizations are the Blue Dog Democrats (conservative), New Democrat Coalition (moderate), Progressive Caucus (Democratic, liberal), Republican Study Committee (conservative), and Wednesday Group (Republican, moderate). Formed to promote the policy positions of a faction within the party, these groups are major sources of information for their members. They focus primarily on the congressional agenda, drafting and introducing legislation and amendments as well as seeking to attract the interest and support of other members and outside forces. Extending their reach, some of these groups have sought to influence the content of party platforms.

Informal party groups compete and cooperate with dozens of other specialized policy caucuses organized to advance particular interests. These relatively narrow-gauge groups are formed around geographic, economic, race, gender, and assorted concerns. Included in this far-flung policy network are such caucuses as the Northeast-Midwest Congressional Coalition and the Steel, Coal, Textile, Travel and Tourism, Farm Crisis, Wine, Mushroom, Port, Human Rights, Black, Blue Collar, Hispanic, Sunbelt, Border, Congresswomen's, Rural, Suburban, Crime, Arts, and Drug Enforcement Caucuses. Groups such as these have come to play a significant role in the policy process through problem identification, member mobilization, and coalition building. They are centers for information exchange.[34] At the same time, they reflect the fragmentation of power in Congress. Whether they enhance or inhibit the capacity of party leaders to control the policy-making process is an empirical question. But whatever the answer, it is not likely that these mechanisms of representation will disappear.

Factors Influencing the Success of Party Leaders

The cohesiveness of the parties in Congress can never be taken for granted. The independence of the committees and their chairs, the rudimentary powers of elected leaders, the importance of constituency pressures, the influence of political interest groups, and the disposition of members to respond to parochial impulses—all, at one time or another, contribute to the fragmentation of power in Congress and to the erosion of party unity. The member who ignores or is oblivious to leadership cues, or who builds a career as a party maverick, is far more common than might be supposed. In the end the leadership can do little to bring refractory members into line. For example, neither the Republican leadership nor President Bush has been able to stop Sen. John McCain (R-Ariz.) from sponsoring legislation that the party has opposed, such as campaign finance reform or a patient's bill of rights.

Research on the Democratic party in the House by Lewis A. Froman Jr. and Randall B. Ripley identifies a number of conditions under which leadership influence on legislative decisions is either promoted or inhibited.[35] First, leadership success is likely to be contingent on a high degree of agreement among the leaders themselves. Ordinarily the Speaker, majority leader, and whip are firm supporters of their president's legislative program; frequently, however, other key leaders, such as committee chairs, are allied with opponents. When unity among the leaders breaks down, prospects for success fall sharply. Second, leadership success in gathering the party together tends to be affected by the nature of the issue under consideration—specifically, whether it is procedural or substantive. On procedural issues (for example, election of the Speaker, adoption of rules, and motions to adjourn), party cohesion is ordinarily much higher than on issues that involve substantive policy. Third, the efforts of party leaders are most likely to be successful on issues that are not highly visible to the general public. When issues gain visibility conflicting pressures emerge, and the leaders must commit greater resources to keep party ranks intact. Fourth, the visibility of the action to be taken has a bearing on the inclination of members to follow the leadership. Not all forms of voting are equally noticeable. Roll-call votes on final passage of measures are highly conspicuous—the member's "record" on a public question is firmly established at this point. On the one hand, voting with the leadership on the floor may seem to the member to pose too great a risk. On the other hand, supporting the leadership in committee or on a key amendment is less risky, because these actions are not as easily brought into public focus. Fifth, and perhaps most important, members are most likely to vote with their party when the issue at stake does not stir up opposition in their constituencies. Party leaders know full well that they cannot count on the support of members who feel that they are under the thumb of constituents on a particular issue—for example, some southern members on certain questions relating to civil rights. Finally, support for the leadership is likely to depend on the activity of the state delegations. Leadership victories are more likely when individual state delegations are not involved in bargaining with leaders over specific demands.

These conditions, then, constitute the background against which leaders try to mold their party into a unit. Party loyalty, it should be emphasized, is more than a veneer. By and large, members prefer to go along with their party colleagues. But they will not queue up in support of their leaders if the conditions appear wrong, or if it appears that more is to be lost than gained by following the leadership. For example, dozens of Republicans eventually voted in favor of the McCain-Feingold campaign finance reform effort in 2002 despite the objections of their party leadership because of the issue's popularity at home. Members guard their careers by taking frequent soundings within their constituencies and among their colleagues and by making careful calculations of the consequences that are likely to flow from their decisions.

National Party Agencies and the Congressional Parties

In theory, the supreme governing body of the party between one national convention and the next is the national committee, which is composed of representatives from each state. In the best of all worlds, from the perspective of those who believe in party unity and responsibility, close and continuing relationships would be maintained between the national committee of each party and fellow party members in Congress. Out of such associations, presumably, would come coherent party policies and a heightened sense of responsibility among members of Congress for developing a legislative program consistent with the promises of the party platform. The tone and mood that dominate relations between the national committees and the congressional parties, however, are as likely to be characterized by suspicion as by cooperation. Congressional leaders in particular are little disposed to follow the cues that emanate from the national committees or, for that matter, from any other national party agency.

Not only do national party leaders have a minimal impact on congressional decision making, but they are also largely excluded from the process of nominating congressional candidates. Although the National Republican Congressional Committee sometimes enters House primary fights, giving funds to the Republican candidate it prefers, the practice is not common. The Democratic Congressional Campaign Committee does not make funds available to primary candidates.[36]

National party leaders seldom become involved in the congressional nominating process because state and local leaders are likely to resent it. Occasionally an intrepid president has sought to influence congressional nominations, as Franklin D. Roosevelt did in 1938. As it turned out, nearly all of the lawmakers marked for defeat won easily, much to the chagrin of the president. Twelve years later President Harry S. Truman met the same fate when he endorsed a candidate in the Democratic senatorial primary in Missouri. The state party organization rallied to the other side, and the president lost. Richard Nixon also failed in his efforts to defeat a number of liberal Republicans in 1970. Although a few presidential "purges" have succeeded, most attempts have not. The lesson seems evident: congressional nominations are regarded as local matters, to be decided in terms of local preferences.

The national party is concerned with the election of members who are broadly sympathetic to its traditional policy orientations and its party platform. In counterpoise, local party organizations aim to guarantee their own survival as independent units. Occasional conflict between the two is predictable. The principal consequence of local control over congressional nominations is that all manner of men and women get elected to Congress. Those who find it easy to accept national party goals rub elbows with those who are almost wholly out of step with the national party. The failure of party unity in Congress is due as much as anything to the folkway that congressional nominations are local questions to be settled by local politicians and voters according to preferences they alone establish.

Do the Parties Differ on Public Policies?

Party affiliation is the cutting edge of congressional elections. Ordinarily few surprises occur on election day: Democratic candidates win where they are expected to win, and Republican candidates win where they are expected to win.[37] The public at large may continue to believe that each election poses an opportunity for the outs to replace the ins, but this happens infrequently. The chief threat to an incumbent legislator is a landslide presidential vote for the other party, one so great that congressional candidates on the winning presidential ticket are lifted into office on the presidential candidate's coattails. Even landslide votes, however, do not disturb the great majority of congressional races.

If party affiliation largely determines who goes to Congress, does it also significantly influence their behavior once in office? The answer for most legislators—for majorities within each party—is yes. Party affiliation is the most important single variable in predicting how members will respond to questions that come before them. Indeed, the key fact to be known about any member is the party to which he belongs—it influences the choice of friends; group memberships; relations with lobbies, other members, and the leadership; and, most important, policy orientations. Party loyalty does not govern the behavior of members; neither is it taken lightly.

The proportion of roll-call votes in Congress in which the parties are sharply opposed is moderately large, and it has been on the increase lately. The standard that congressional scholars use to measure party unity is the percentage of votes that a majority of one party votes against the majority of the other party. In the early 1970s, it was common for both houses to have fewer than 40 percent party unity votes and occasionally the percentage fell below 30. In contrast, between 1992 and 1996 about 60 to 65 percent of all roll-call votes in both houses found party majorities arrayed against each other. One reason for the increase in party voting is the changes in the wings of both parties. The more liberal eastern wing of the Republican party and the more conservative wing of the Democratic party have been atrophying over the last two decades.[38] This leaves more homogenous party memberships, which are more often in agreement.

As a result of the short-lived bipartisanship that grew out of the September 11, 2001, terrorist attacks and the party leadership's desire to postpone divisive votes on domestic policy until after the 2002 elections, the percentage of party unity votes dropped below 50 percent in the first two years of the Bush administration. Most experts, however, expect these scores to increase markedly in the future, especially given the Republicans' narrow majority in both houses. Narrow majorities place a premium on party unity.[39]

What factors appear to promote partisan cleavage? Examining a recent thirty-five-year period, Samuel C. Patterson and Gregory A. Caldeira found that party voting in the House increases significantly when external party conflict is high—in particular, during periods when sharp differences exist between the national parties on central issues of the economy, labor-management questions, and the distribution of wealth. Interparty conflict also escalates when the presidency and House are controlled by the same party. In the Senate, where party voting is somewhat less common, presidential leadership is the key factor; specifically, when the Senate majority is of the same party as the president, party voting increases. Surprisingly, in view of conventional interpretations, the election of many new members does not lead to markedly greater increases in partisan cleavages.[40]

In her research on party voting in the House from 1946 to 1990, Mary Alice Nye finds that the best explanation for altering levels of partisanship is the changing voting patterns of members who continue from one Congress to the next; that is, they vote differently in response to the events and circumstances—"period effects"—of a particular session of Congress, and conversion takes place. Nye finds little evidence that changing party support is explained by generational change (e.g., newly elected members are more or less partisan than those they replaced) or by the life-cycle hypothesis that members tend to stray from their party as their tenure increases. The importance of period effects may reflect such factors as party leadership—particularly the role of the Speaker—and the party caucus.[41]

Important issues are often at stake when party lines do form. In general, Democrats have been much more likely than Republicans to support expanded health and welfare programs, legislation advantageous to labor and low-income groups, government regulation of business, higher taxes on the wealthy, the use of federal funds for family planning, reductions in the defense budget, federal assistance for cities, and a larger role for the federal government.

The Parties and Liberal-Labor Legislation

The current policy orientations of the parties in Congress are not distinctly different from those they have held over the past half-century. The positions of the parties (and the wings within them) on proposals of interest to the AFL-CIO in the 107th Congress are presented in Table 5-1. A member voting in agreement with the AFL-CIO would have supported such measures as a prescription drug benefit under Medicare; an increase in public school construction; a patient's bill of rights; and an extension of collective bargaining rights for firefighters, police officers, and emergency medical professionals.

Table 5-1 shows two broad patterns of congressional voting on issues of concern to organized labor. First, the parties are not altogether cohesive in voting on this legislation. Northern Democrats are somewhat more supportive of labor legislation than are southern Democrats, though southern Democrats are still clearly pro-labor as well. Among Republicans, those from the East are significantly less hostile than those from other regions, particularly the South. In fact, all but one southern Republican member of the 107th Congress (2001–2002)

Table 5-1   House and Senate Support for Labor Legislation, by Party and Region, 107th Congress, First Session (percent prolabor votes)

	House				Senate			
	0–25%	26–50%	51–75%	76–100%	0–25%	26–50%	51–75%	76–100%
Democrats								
Southern	2	7	13	78	0	0	22	78
Northern	0	1	3	96	0	0	0	100
Republicans								
Noneastern	95	5	0	0	84	16	0	0
Eastern	63	37	0	0	43	29	29	0
Southern	99	1	0	0	100	0	0	0

Source: Developed from data in *AFL-CIO Report on the 2001 Congress* (Washington, D.C., 2002).

Note: House members are ranked by the percentage of votes they cast in accordance with the positions of the AFL-CIO. The South is defined as the eleven states of the Confederacy plus Kentucky and Oklahoma. Noneastern Republicans are all northern members except those from eastern states.

provided less than 25 percent support for labor legislation. In contrast, more than half of Republican senators from the East provided at least moderate (25 to 75 percent) support. Second, despite certain intraparty divisions, substantial differences between the parties are apparent. Democrats in general give overwhelming support to labor objectives,[42] while Republicans are much less supportive, no matter the region. Even conservative southern Democrats are much more prolabor than liberal eastern Republicans.

To assess the policy differences of the congressional parties more generally, it is useful to examine the range of attitudes in the Senate during the first session of the 107th Congress (2001) on issues deemed important by the liberal-oriented Americans for Democratic Action (ADA) and the conservative-oriented American Conservative Union (ACU). (See Figure 5-3.) Senators are located on the diagram according to the percentage of votes they cast in agreement with the positions of each political interest group. Sens. Barbara Boxer (D-Calif.), Jon Corzine (D-N.J.), Ted Kennedy (D-Mass.), and Mark Dayton (D-Minn.) emerge as the most liberal members of the upper house. At the conservative pole are such senators as Jesse Helms (R-N.C.), Jim Bunning (R-Ky.), Richard Shelby (R-Ala.), and John Kyl (R-Ariz.).

The data in Figure 5-3 reinforce the conclusions reached earlier. Significant differences separate the majorities of the two parties. Nearly all of the Republican senators are found on the right-hand side of the diagram, indicating their agreement with the ACU and disagreement with the ADA, whereas nearly all of the Democratic senators are on the left side, showing agreement with ADA policy objectives and disagreement with those of the ACU. The only Democrat who is more conservative than the most liberal Republicans on these two dimensions is Sen. Zell Miller (D-Ga.), and the only Republican more liberal than the most conservative Democrats is Sen. Lincoln Chafee (R-R.I.). This scatterplot also reveals that a small handful of eastern Republicans—Sens. Susan

Figure 5-3 Support for Positions Held by Americans for Democratic Action (ADA) and by American Conservative Union (ACU) by Selected Senators, 107th Congress, First Session

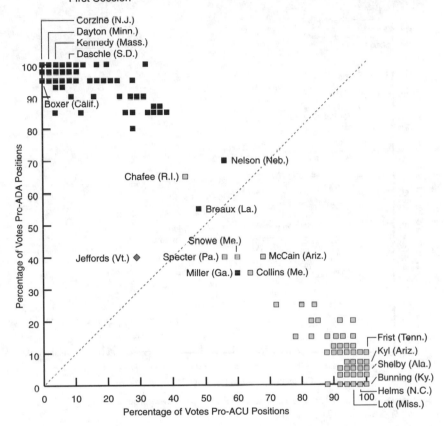

Sources: Developed from data appearing in www.adaction.org and www.conservative.org.

Note: ■ Democrat;   ▢ Republican;   ◆ Independent

Collins (R-Maine), Olympia Snowe (R-Maine), and Arlen Specter (R-Pa.)— are significantly more moderate than the rest of the caucus. Sens. Ben Nelson (D-Neb.) and John Breaux (D-La.) grade out as significantly more moderate than the rest of the Democratic caucus. The main point, however, is one of intraparty homogeneity.

This separation between the parties is a relatively recent development. Compare the scatterplot in Figure 5-3 with that in Figure 5-4, which performs the same analysis, only using ACU and ADA scores from 1985, just a decade and a half earlier. While a number of changes are evident, the most important is the higher level of intraparty heterogeneity in 1985. In stark contrast to the 2001 data, many members had moderate scores, in the forty to sixty range, from both

Figure 5-4   Support for Positions Held by Americans for Democratic Action (ADA) and by American Conservative Union (ACU) by Selected Senators, 99th Congress, First Session

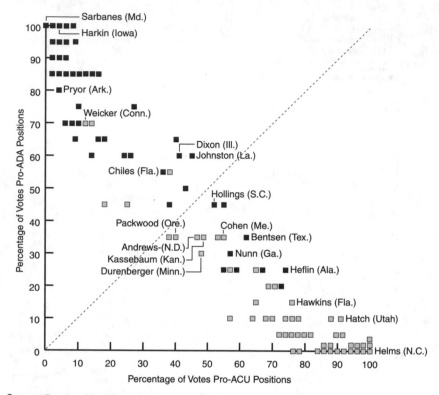

Sources: Developed from data appearing in www.adaction.org and www.conservative.org.

Note: ■ Democrat;   □ Republican

the ACU and the ADA. Moreover, many Republicans had voting records that were more liberal than the most conservative Democrats and many Democrats had more conservative voting records than the most liberal Republicans. If data were available to perform this analysis for Congresses in the late 1960s and early 1970s, the degree of intraparty heterogeneity and ideological overlap between the parties would be even more pronounced. From a historical perspective, the Congress of today has an extraordinarily high degree of ideological polarization between the parties.

When partisanship in Congress was weaker, the formation of biparty coalitions was commonplace. The most important was the so-called "conservative coalition"—an informal league of southern Democrats and northern Republicans. Whereas this coalition commonly would emerge on as many as one hundred votes per session in the 1960s and 1970s, the recent increase in intraparty homogeneity has caused it almost to disappear. In fact, the coalition was decisive on only two votes in the 107th Congress.[43] When it does appear, the coalition's success rate is impressive. In only two sessions since 1961 (the first two years of Johnson's Great Society, 1965 and 1966) did the coalition win fewer than 50 percent of the roll calls on which it appeared. In twenty-seven of the thirty-six sessions, the batting average of the coalition exceeded 60 percent. Recently the coalition has won nine out of every ten appearances.[44] Today, however, it appears on only rare occasions.

Weak Party Leadership but Strong Parties in Government

Our earlier discussion detailed the relatively weak formal powers available to party leaders in Congress. The fragmentation of the congressional parties has often been attributed to the absence of a strong, central party leadership. Yet party cohesiveness has increased dramatically over the last two decades. While some of the centralizing reforms in the congressional caucuses in the 1970s and 1980s have contributed to this development, they are only a partial explanation for the increase in party based voting in Congress.

David W. Rohde demonstrates that the realignment of southern politics played the crucial role.[45] Although the South is perhaps the most ideologically conservative region of the country, there was no Republican party to speak of in the region until the 1950s because southerners held Republicans responsible for the harsh post–Civil War Reconstruction. The Democrats' embrace of civil rights legislation changed this picture considerably. Beginning with Barry Goldwater's campaign in 1964, the South started to vote regularly for southern presidential candidates. Moreover, when conservative southern Democratic congressmen retired, even more conservative Republicans replaced them. If ideology, rather than race, had been the guiding factor in the decades before the civil rights movement, many of these seats would have been won by Republicans long before. Instead, it took until 1994 for the Republicans to win a majority of House seats in the states of the former Confederacy, and this percentage has increased with each succeeding election.

Similarly, since passage of the Voting Rights Act of 1965, African Americans have entered southern state electorates in great numbers, and their participation has driven Democratic incumbents and challengers to adopt more liberal positions on certain domestic policy questions. African American voters in southern Democratic primaries are now in a much better position to influence the behavior and policy stances of Democratic congressional candidates. The behavior of white voters also enters the calculus. Richard Fleisher writes, "In districts with large minority populations and white constituents [who] show a willingness to support progressive Democratic candidates, representatives in Congress respond with liberal voting and party support similar to that of northern Democrats."[46]

Constituency change in the South has been critical. In responding to changes in their constituencies, Stanley P. Berard argues, Southern Democrats have become increasingly partisan in their voting behavior in Congress. Three factors have contributed to this new partisanship: urbanization, the mobilization of African American voters, and the rise of Republican electoral competition. In short, these factors have led to the "northernization" of southern Democratic politics.[47]

The redrawing of congressional district boundaries to reflect shifts in population after each census has served to harden divisions between the parties as well. Mapmakers of both parties typically draw district lines to protect as many incumbents as possible, creating districts in which it is almost impossible for a challenger to win.[48] And since challengers tend to take strongly ideological positions on issues, their odds for winning are further reduced. A recent study by Stephen Ansolabehere, James Snyder, and Charles Stewart shows that almost all Republican candidates for Congress in 1996 were more conservative than almost all Democratic candidates nationally; moreover, the ideological gap between Republican and Democratic challengers was often quite large.[49] Under these circumstances, challenger victories are uncommon. Voters in safe Republican districts are unlikely to elect generally liberal Democratic challengers, and voters in safe Democratic districts are unlikely to elect generally conservative Republican challengers.

Finally, John H. Aldrich suggests that the nature of the parties themselves also helps to explain the emergence of ideologically polarized parties.[50] When patronage-driven party machines dominated the political scene, winning elections was much more important than advancing ideological interests. Government jobs and other spoils were given to the winners. As reforms in the political process all but eliminated patronage, Aldrich argues, ideological activists came to play a key role in each party. Because their jobs did not depend on electoral outcomes, they were more willing to lose an election here and there to maintain the ideological purity of the party.

This discussion exposes an interesting paradox in the study of congressional party leadership.[51] Since the apparent strength of party leadership is a function of the loyalty of rank-and-file members, leadership appears strongest when it is actually least important. Irrespective of the strength of the leadership, party members in Congress today are likely to vote consistently with their caucuses because the parties' policy goals match the ideological preferences of the individual members. Ordinarily, no arm-twisting is necessary to secure the votes of conservatives for Republican objectives or of liberals for Democratic objectives. Party mavericks are far less numerous today than in the past.

The President and the Congressional Party

Presidential power appears more awesome at a distance than it does at close range. Although the Constitution awards the president a number of formal powers—for example, the power to initiate treaties, to make certain appointments, and to veto legislation—his principal everyday power is simply that to persuade.

The president who opts for an active role in the legislative process, who attempts to persuade members of Congress to accept his leadership and his program, encounters certain obstacles in the structure of American government. Foremost among these is the separation of powers. This arrangement of "separated institutions sharing powers"[52] not only divides the formal structure of government, thus creating independent centers of legislative and executive authority, but it also contributes to the fragmentation of the national parties. The perspectives of those elements of the party for whom the president speaks are not necessarily the same as those for whom members of his congressional party speak. Policy that may suit one constituency may not suit another. Indeed, the chances are high that the presidential constituency and the constituencies of individual members of his party in Congress will differ in many important respects, thus making inevitable a certain amount of conflict between the branches.

Limits on Presidential Influence

The separation of powers is not the only constraint that faces the activist president who hopes to move Congress to adopt his program. The limited influence of party leaders on Congress, the insulation and independence of members that stem from the substantial staff and other office resources they enjoy,[53] the relative independence of committees and subcommittees, the difficulty of applying sanctions to wayward legislators, and the parochial cast in congressional perceptions of policy problems all converge to limit presidential influence. Moreover, electoral arrangements and electoral behavior may make executive leadership difficult. Off-year elections are nearly always more damaging to the president's party than they are to the out party.[54] In off-year elections from 1926 to 2002, for example, the president's party gained seats in only three House elections (1934, 1998, and 2002) and in only four Senate elections (1934, 1962, 1970, and 2002). Losses can be severe. In 1994 the Democratic party lost an extraordinary fifty-four seats in the House and ten in the Senate—the worst loss in any off-year election since 1946. The president has every reason to fear the worst when these elections roll around; the next two years are almost certain to be more difficult.

Finally, the root of the president's legislative difficulties may lie with the voters themselves. The election that produces a president of one party may yield a Congress dominated by the other party or one with a different ideological coloration. Different coalitions form around offices. The coalition that elected Bill Clinton in 1996, for example, had a much different cast from the one that produced a Republican majority in the House of Representatives. A disproportionate number of Clinton voters were females (58 percent), African Americans/Hispanic Americans (24 percent), white Catholics (32 percent), and people earning less than $50,000 annually (66 percent). The Republican House majority, by contrast, was elected by a coalition of males (53 percent), whites (92 percent), religious right (24 percent), and people earning more than $50,000 annually (44 percent). Additionally, the Clinton and Republican coalitions clashed on their views of the role of government. Sixty percent of the Clinton voters believed that government "should do more," and 73 percent of the voters who supported Republican House candidates believed that government "should do less." Optimism about life in the future also was reflected in the two coalitions. Seventy-five percent of the Clinton voters held that life would be better, contrasted with 60 percent of the Republican coalition who thought it would be worse.[55] With two different coalitions making claims on the executive and legislative branches, it would be altogether surprising if the relationships at key points were not contentious, conflictual, muddled, or reflective of some class concerns.

A measure of the legislative success enjoyed by presidents from 1953 to 2002 is presented in Figure 5-5. This analysis shows how frequently Congress voted in accordance with positions taken by each president during his administration. Lyndon Johnson achieved the highest rate of success of any of these ten presidents; in 1965 his position prevailed 93 percent of the time. The major reason for his success was undoubtedly that the Democratic party controlled both houses by such large margins that even the defections of southern members had minimal impact on outcomes. Ronald Reagan's 82 percent success rate in 1981 ranks among the highest in the preceding thirty years. Moreover, his overall party support scores were higher than those of any other president since 1953.

George H. W. Bush, whose success rate averaged only 51.8 percent over his term, produced the lowest score of any president since 1953. Perhaps not surprisingly, Bush lost to Bill Clinton in 1992. During each of Clinton's first two years in office, when Democrats held a majority in both houses, he had an impressive 86 percent success score. But his third year in office, following the Republican takeover in the 1994 election, was a disaster. His legislative success rate fell to 36 percent, the lowest score of any president since Congressional Quarterly began its survey in 1953. Clinton did, however, increase his success rate later in his administration, but never to the levels achieved in the first two years.

George W. Bush has had remarkable success in passing his agenda through Congress. During the first two years of his administration, he produced success scores of 87 and 88 percent, respectively. Part of his success was due to the fact that he took stands on fewer issues than his predecessors had. By keeping his policy agenda short and focused, he was able to win a high proportion of the time. The bipartisanship that developed out of the September 11 terrorist attacks and his overall popularity also contributed to his success. His approval ratings hit 90 percent right after September 11 and remained above 70 percent for almost a year.

When the opposition party controls one or both houses of Congress, presidential influence is typically constrained. Republican presidents understand this nagging reality better than anyone: every Republican president since Eisenhower has confronted it for at least part of his administration. And, of course, Clinton's success rate fell dramatically when the Democrats became the minority party in the 104th Congress (1995–1996). With both houses in Republican hands for the 108th Congress (2003–2004), George W. Bush stands to continue his remarkable batting average with Congress.

Figure 5-5 Presidential Success on Legislative Votes: 1953–2002

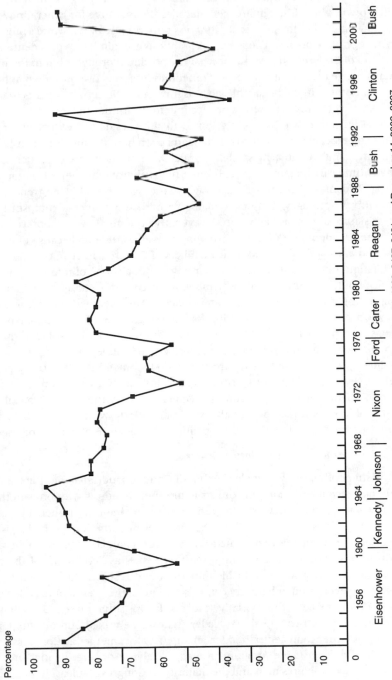

Source: Congressional Quarterly Weekly Report, December 19, 1992, 3896; December 21, 1996, 3427–3431; and December 14, 2002, 3237.

So much has been written about the role of the president as chief legislator that it is easy to lose sight of the fact that members of Congress have power in their own right. Although in recent decades the initiative for generating legislation has shifted to the president, Congress remains one of the world's most powerful legislative bodies. A good many conditions are inimical to presidential domination of Congress. It may adopt what the president proposes but in the process may change the accent and scope. Sometimes it merely disposes of what he proposes. Nothing in the president's plans is inviolable. No certainty exists that Congress will share his perceptions or succumb to his influence. The careers of individual legislators are not tightly linked to the president's, except perhaps for those members from marginal districts, and even here the link is firm only when the president's popularity is high.[56] Indeed, some members of Congress have made their careers more secure through the visibility that comes from opposing the president and his program. Notwithstanding the worldwide trend toward executive supremacy, Congress remains a remarkably independent institution—a legislature almost as likely to resist executive initiatives as to embrace them.

The president and Congress get along as well as they do because of one element that the president and some members of Congress have in common: party affiliation. In substantial measure, party provides a frame of reference, an ideological underpinning, a rallying symbol, a structure for voting, and a language for testing and discussing ideas and policies. The member's constituency has never been the only valid criterion for assessing the wisdom of public policies. Legislators prefer to ride along with their party if it is at all possible, if the costs do not loom too large. Moreover, the president and his legislative leaders are not at liberty to strike out in any direction they feel may be immediately popular with the voters. They are constrained by party platforms, by previous policy commitments, by interest group involvement, and by the need to consult with party officials and members at all levels, particularly with those who compose the congressional wing. Consensus politics is the essence of party processes.

The President and Legislative Leaders

A study of majority party leadership in Congress indicates that the president and party leaders in Congress can structure their relations with one another in many ways. Typically, when the president and the majority leadership in Congress are of the same party and the president assumes the role of chief legislator, relations between the two branches have been characterized by cooperation. Within this pattern leaders tend to see themselves as lieutenants of the president, of necessity sensitive to his initiatives and responsible for his program. However, even though his party controls Congress, the president may decline to play a central role in the legislative process. In this situation, relations between the president and congressional leaders tend to be mixed and nonsupportive. Collegial rather than centralized leadership usually emerges as Congress generates its own legislative program instead of relying on presidential initiative. Finally, when the president and the majority in Congress (at least in one house) are of opposing parties (a so-called "truncated majority"), relations between the president and congressional leaders are often characterized by conflict and opposition. Leadership tends to be highly centralized, but legislative successes are usually few in number. "The leader of a truncated majority has great room for maneuver in the tactics of opposition and embarrassment on the domestic front, if his followers are willing to go along with him, but he must necessarily remain partially frustrated by his inability to accomplish much of his program domestically."[57]

David Truman has described the relationship between the president and the elective leaders of his congressional party as one of "functional interdependence." This system has mutual advantages. The president needs information to make intelligent judgments, and the leaders can supply it. Moreover, they can offer him policy guidance. At the same time, the leaders can perform better if bolstered by the initiatives and leverage of the president. They have no power to give orders. They can only bargain and negotiate, and their effectiveness in doing so, in notable measure, is tied to the president's prestige and political assets.[58] The nature of their jobs makes it important for the president's program to move through Congress. If the president wins, they win; if he loses, they lose.[59]

The Role of the Minority Party in Congress

A study by Charles O. Jones identifies a number of political conditions that individually and in combination help to shape the role the minority party plays in mobilizing congressional majorities and in shaping public policy. Some of these conditions originate outside Congress; others manifest themselves inside Congress. The principal external forces are the temper of the times, such as the presence of a domestic or international crisis; the relative political strength of the minority party in the electorate; the degree of unity within the parties outside Congress; and the power of the president and his willingness to use the advantages inherent in his office. Conditions within Congress that affect minority party behavior are legislative procedures; the majority party's margin over the minority; the relative effectiveness of majority and minority party leadership; the time the party has been in a minority status, perhaps contributing to a minority party mentality; and the relative strength of the party in the other house.[60]

The important point about the behavior of the minority party is that the strategies open to it are determined not simply by the preferences of the leadership or the rank-and-file members, by idiosyncratic circumstances, or by opportunities thrust up from time to time. Rather, what it does is influenced to a significant extent by conditions of varying importance over which it has little or no control. By and large, the conditions most likely to affect the minority party's behavior and shape its strategies are, among the external group, party unity and presidential power, and among the internal group, the size of the margin and the effectiveness of party leaders in both parties. Although restrictive political conditions depress the range of alternatives available to the minority party, a resourceful minority leadership can occasionally overcome them, enabling the minority party to assume an aggressive, creative role in the legislative process. Among recent Congresses, however, this has been the exception, not the rule.[61]

The Party in Congress: Unfavorable Odds

It is as difficult to write about congressional parties without uncertainty as it is to pin a butterfly without first netting it. The party is hard to catch in a light that discloses all its qualities or its basic significance. Party is the organizing mechanism of Congress, and Congress could not do without it. It is hard to imagine how Congress could assemble itself for work, process the claims made on it, lend itself to majority coalition building, or be held accountable in any fashion without a wide range of party activities in its midst. Moreover, there are some sessions of Congress in which the only way to understand what Congress has done is to focus on the performance of the majority party. But that is only part of the story. In the critical area of policy formation, majority party control can slip away, to be replaced by enduring biparty alliances or coalitions of expediency. Party counts, but not predictably—hence the reason for the uncertainty in assessing the role of the congressional party.

Summary arguments may help to establish a perspective on the congressional parties. The indifferent success that sometimes characterizes party efforts in Congress is easy to explain. The odds are stacked against the party. In the first place, members of Congress are elected under a variety of conditions in a variety of constituencies: they are elected in environments where local party organizations are powerful and where they are weak; where populations are homogeneous and where they are heterogeneous; where competition is intense and where it is absent; where the level of voter education is high and where it is low; where income is high and where it is low; where one interest dominates and where many compete. The mix within congressional parties is a product of that within the nation's constituencies. It could scarcely be otherwise. The net result of diversity is that the people who make their way to Congress see the world in different ways, stress different values, and pursue different objectives. A vast amount of disagreement inevitably lurks behind each party's label.

In the second place, the salient fact in the life of a legislator is his career. If he fails to protect it, no one else will. Representatives and senators know that their party can do very little to enhance their security in office and, conversely, very little to threaten it. As a member of Congress put it, "If we depended on the party organization to get elected, none of us would be here."[62] Members are on their own. Whether they are reelected or not depends more on the decisions they make than on those their party makes, more on how they cultivate their constituency than on how their party cultivates the nation, more on the credit they are able to claim for desirable governmental action than on the credit the party is able to claim,[63] and more on the electoral coalition they put together or from which they are able to benefit than on the electoral coalition of their party. Although sweeping electoral tides may carry members out of office from time to time, individual members cannot do much about such movements. Hence typical members concentrate on immediate problems. They take their constituency as it is; if they monitor and defend its interests carefully, they stand a good chance of having a long career in Congress, no matter what fate deals to their party.

The growing importance of party campaign expenditures on behalf of congressional candidates (so-called "coordinated expenditures") may ultimately increase the members' dependence on the party and, accordingly, be reflected in their voting behavior in Congress. But there is little evidence now that members vote one way or another in response to party pressures linked to financial aid in campaigns.[64] Parties are in business to win elections, and each prefers the election of its own mavericks to that of loyal members of the opposition. Members' ability to attract interest group contributions, moreover, gives them additional political space in which to maneuver, free from party controls. What those groups extract from the members is another question.

In the third place, party efforts are confounded by the fragmentation of power within Congress. Those who chair major committees and subcommittees are as likely to have keys to congressional power as are the elected party leaders. Committees go their separate ways, sometimes in harmony with the party leadership and sometimes not. Powerful committees are sometimes under the control of party elements that are out of step with the party's leadership in Congress and with national party goals. No power to command rests with the party leadership, and there is not a great deal it can do to bring into line those members who steadily defy the party and oppose its objectives. In addition, the party caucuses and the policy committees have never in any real sense functioned as policy-shaping agencies. "Parties" within parties, such as the conservative Blue Dog Democrats, bear witness to the lack of party agreement on public policy. Numerous specialized caucuses (coal, cotton, New England, steel, sunbelt, textiles, and the like) also contribute to the decentralization of power in Congress.

In the fourth place, the intricacies of the legislative process make it difficult for the parties to function smoothly and effectively. For the party to maintain firm control, it must create majorities at a number of stages in the legislative process: first in the standing committee, then on the floor, and last in the conference committee. In the House a majority is also needed in the Rules Committee. Failure to achieve a majority at any stage is likely to mean the loss of legislation. Even those bills that pass through the obstacle course may be so sharply changed as scarcely to be recognizable by their sponsors. In contrast, the opponents of legislation have only one requirement: to splice together a majority at one stage in the decision-making process. Breaking the party leadership at some point in the chain may not require great resources or much imagination. For these reasons, the adoption of a new public policy is immeasurably more difficult than the preservation of an old one. All the advantages, it seems, rest with those legislators bent on preserving existing arrangements.

In the fifth place, the congressional party functions as it does because, by and large, it is a microcosm of the party in the electorate, beset by the same internal conflicts. The American political party is an extraordinary collection of diverse, conflicting interests and individuals brought together for the specific purpose of winning office. The coalition carefully put together to make a bid for power comes under heavy stress once the election is over and candidates have become officeholders. Differences ignored or minimized during the campaign soon come to the surface. Party claims become only one input among many that the members consider in shaping their positions on policy questions. Not surprisingly, national party objectives may be disregarded as members sort out their own priorities and take account of those interests, including those of the local party organization, whose support may be essential to reelection.

The astonishing fact about the congressional parties is that they perform as well as they do. One reason is the phenomenon of party loyalty—typical members are more comfortable when they vote in league with their party colleagues than when they oppose them. Another is that most members within each party represent constituencies that are broadly comparable in makeup; in "voting their district" they are likely to be in harmony with the general thrust of their party. A third reason is found in the informal powers of the elected leaders. Members who respond to their leadership may be given assistance in advancing their pet legislation, awarded with an appointment to a prestigious committee, or armed with important information. There are advantages to getting along with the leadership. Lastly, presidential leadership seems to serve as a unifying force for the president's party in Congress. Members may not go along with the president gladly, but many do go along, and even those who do not give his requests more than a second thought.

NOTES

1. For an analysis of the literature on congressional elections, see Peverill Squire, "Candidates, Money, and Voters—Assessing the State of Congressional Elections Research," *Political Research Quarterly* 48 (December 1995): 891–917. Also see Jonathan Krasno and Donald Philip Green, "Preempting Quality Challengers in House Elections," *Journal of Politics* 50 (1988): 920–936; Richard Born, "Strategic Politicians and Unresponsive Voters," *American Political Science Review* 80 (1986): 599–612; and Jon Bond, Cary Covington, and Richard Fleisher, "Explaining Challenger Quality in Congressional Elections," *Journal of Politics* 47 (1985): 510–529.

2. See, for example, John R. Hibbing and John R. Alford, "Electoral Impact of Economic Conditions: Who Is Held Responsible?" *American Journal of Political Science* 25 (1981): 423–439; Gerald H. Kramer, "Short-Term Fluctuations in U.S. Voting Behavior, 1896–1964," *American Political Science Review* 65 (1971): 131–143; and Edward Tufte, "Determinants of the Outcomes of Midterm Congressional Elections," *American Political Science Review* 62 (1975): 812–826. For a review, see Richard G. Niemi and Herbert F. Weisberg, *Classics in Voting Behavior* (Washington, D.C.: CQ Press, 1993), especially section IV.

3. For the most part, these data come from Norman J. Ornstein, Thomas E. Mann, and Michael J. Malbin, *Vital Statistics on Congress, 2001–2002* (Washington, D.C.: American Enterprise Institute, 2002).

4. Ibid.

5. *CQ Weekly,* November 9, 2002, 2934.

6. This theory is articulated by Gary C. Jacobson and Samuel Kernell, *Strategy and Choice in Congressional Elections*, 2d ed. (New Haven: Yale University Press, 1983).

7. See, for example, Richard Born, "Partisan Intentions and Election Day Realities in the Congressional Redistricting Process," *American Political Science Review* 79 (1985): 305–319; Charles Bullock, "Redistricting and Congressional Stability, 1962–1972," *Journal of Politics* 37 (1975): 569–575; Amihai Glazer, Bernard Grofman, and Marc Robbins, "Partisan and Incumbency Effects of 1970s Congressional Redistricting," *American Journal of Political Science* 30 (1987): 680–707; and Michael Lyons Michael and Peter F. Galderisi, "Incumbency, Reapportionment, and U.S. House Redistricting," *Political Research Quarterly* 48 (December 1995): 857–871.

8. David R. Mayhew, *Congress: The Electoral Connection* (New Haven: Yale University Press, 1974), especially 49–77. For a sampling of other studies that bear on the decline of competitive seats, see John C. McAdams and John R. Johannes, "Constituency Attentiveness in the House: 1977–1982," *Journal of Politics* 47 (November 1985): 1108–1139; Glenn R. Parker and Suzanne L. Parker, "Correlates and Effects of Attention to District by U.S. House Members," *Legislative Studies Quarterly* 10 (May 1985): 223–242; Albert D. Cover, "The Electoral Impact of Franked Congressional Mail," *Polity* 17 (summer 1985): 649–663; and Melissa P. Collie, "Incumbency, Electoral Safety, and Turnover in the House of Representatives, 1952–1976," *American Political Science Review* 75 (March 1981): 119–131.

9. Lyn Ragsdale, "Incumbent Popularity, Challenger Invisibility, and Congressional Voters," *Legislative Studies Quarterly* 6 (May 1981): 215. When accused of corruption, House incumbents and challengers are likely to be defeated 25 percent of the time, according to a study by Susan Welch and John R. Hibbing, "The Effects of Charges of Corruption on Voting Behavior in Congressional Elections, 1982–1990," *Journal of Politics* 59 (February 1997): 226–239. Corruption allegations, in fact, play a significant role in congressional turnover.

10. Two of these ten were the result of Democrats switching their party affiliation after the election.

11. In 2000 the Republicans won fifty seats in the Senate, which made them the majority party because the vice president, in this case Republican Dick Cheney, is constitutionally allowed to break tie votes. The Democrats took the majority in mid-2001, not because of an election result, but rather because Sen. James Jeffords of Vermont switched from the Republican party to independent.

12. Ornstein, Mann, and Malbin, *Vital Statistics on Congress, 2001–2002*.

13. John R. Petrocik and Scott W. Desposato argue that the creation of majority-minority districts through redistricting was not a fundamental reason for the Republican drift. Instead, a general trend in favor of Republicanism was more important. See their article, "The Partisan Consequences of Majority-Minority Redistricting in the South, 1992 and 1994," *Journal of Politics* 60 (August 1998): 613–633. Also see Kevin A. Hill, "Does the Creation of Majority Black Districts Aid Republicans? An Analysis of the 1992 Congressional Elections in Eight Southern States," *Journal of Politics* 57 (1995): 384–401.

14. It is important to note that, while this may have been the case for 1996, the pattern of retirements has not persisted. In addition to becoming fewer in number since 1996, more incumbent Republicans have retired than incumbent Democrats.

15. Gary C. Jacobson, "Congress: Unprecedented and Unsurpassing," in *The Elections of 1996*, ed. Michael Nelson (Washington, D.C.: CQ Press, 1997), 143–167.

16. Keith T. Poole and Howard Rosenthal, "D-NOMINATE after Ten Years: A Comparative Update to *Congress: A Political Economic History of Roll-Call Voting*," *Legislative Studies Quarterly* 26 (February 2001): 5–29.

17. Gramm bolted from the Democratic party after being disciplined, was elected as a Republican, and served in the Senate until his retirement in 2002.

18. Steven S. Smith and Gerald Gamm, "The Dynamics of Party Government in Congress," in *Congress Reconsidered,* ed. Lawrence C. Dodd and Bruce I. Oppenheimer, 7th ed. (Washington, D.C.: CQ Press, 2001), 245–268.

19. *Congressional Quarterly Weekly Report,* April 15, 1978, 875–876.

20. Joseph Cooper and David W. Brady, "Institutional Context and Leadership Style: The House from Cannon to Rayburn," *American Political Science Review* 75 (June 1981): 417.

21. *Congressional Quarterly Weekly Report,* December 30, 1989, 3550.

22. For a more complete treatment of the relationship between Neumann and Gingrich, see Larry J. Sabato and Bruce Larson, *The Party's Just Begun: Shaping Political Parties for America's Future,* 2d ed. (New York: Longman, 2002).

23. Gingrich's role in the 1998 debacle is interesting. Benjamin Highton demonstrates that Gingrich's lack of popularity was decisive in understanding why he lost seats in a midterm election. See Benjamin Highton, "Bill Clinton, Newt Gingrich, and the 1998 Congressional Elections," *Public Opinion Quarterly* 66 (spring 2002): 1–17.

24. *CQ Weekly,* January 4, 2003.

25. "Leadership: An Interview with Senate Leader Lyndon Johnson," *U.S. News and World Report,* June 27, 1960, 88. Also see Ralph K. Huitt, "Democratic Party Leadership in the Senate," *American Political Science Review* 55 (June 1961): 333–344.

26. "Leadership," 90.

27. *New York Times,* July 17, 1961, 11.

28. *Congressional Quarterly Weekly Report,* September 4, 1982, 2181.

29. Concerning the mediating role of the floor leader, see David B. Truman, *The Congressional Party* (New York: Wiley, 1959), 106–116, 205–208; Barbara Hinckley, "Congressional Leadership Selection and Support: A Comparative Analysis," *Journal of Politics* 32 (May 1970): 268–287; and William E. Sullivan, "Criteria for Selecting Party Leadership in Congress," *American Politics Quarterly* 3 (January 1975): 25–44.

30. Burdett A. Loomis, *The New American Politician: Ambition, Entrepreneurship, and the Changing Face of Political Life* (New York: Basic Books, 1988), 175.

31. *Congressional Quarterly Weekly Report,* May 27, 1978, 1304.

32. For a detailed study of this committee, see Charles O. Jones, *Party and Policy-Making: The House Republican Policy Committee* (New Brunswick, N.J.: Rutgers University Press, 1964).

33. Hugh A. Bone, "An Introduction to the Senate Policy Committees," *American Political Science Review* 50 (June 1956): 352. Also see Robert L. Peabody, *Leadership in Congress* (Boston: Little, Brown, 1976), 337–338.

34. Among the studies to consult on this subject are Susan Webb Hammond, "Congressional Caucuses in the 104th Congress," in *Congress Reconsidered,* ed. Lawrence C. Dodd and Bruce I. Oppenheimer (Washington, D.C.: CQ Press, 1997), 274–292; Susan Webb Hammond, Daniel P. Mulhollan, and Arthur G. Stevens Jr., "Informal Congressional Caucuses and Agenda Setting," *Western Political Quarterly* 38 (December 1985): 583–605; Arthur G. Stevens Jr., Daniel P. Mulhollan, and Paul S. Rundquist, "U.S. Congressional Structure and Representation: The Role of Informal Groups," *Legislative Studies Quarterly* 6 (August 1981): 415–437; Burdett A. Loomis, "Congressional Caucuses and the Politics of Representation," in *Congress Reconsidered,* 2d ed., ed. Lawrence C. Dodd and Bruce I. Oppenheimer (Washington, D.C.: CQ Press, 1981), 204– 220; Arthur G. Stevens Jr., Arthur H. Miller, and Thomas E. Mann, "Mobilization of Liberal Strength in the House, 1955–1970: The Democratic Study Group," *American Political Science Review* 68 (June 1974): 667–681; and Kenneth Kofmehl, "The Institutionalization of a Voting Bloc," *Western Political Quarterly* 17 (June 1964): 256–272. Of related interest, see Barbara Sinclair, "State Party Delegations in the U.S. House of Representatives: A Comparative Study of Group Cohesion," *Journal of Politics* 34 (February 1972): 199–222; Richard Born, "Cue-Taking within State Party Delegations in the U.S. House of Repre-

sentatives," *Journal of Politics* 38 (February 1976): 71–94; and Jeffrey E. Cohen and David C. Nice, "Changing Party Loyalty of State Delegations to the U.S. House of Representatives, 1953–1976," *Western Political Quarterly* 36 (June 1983): 312–325.

35. See Lewis A. Froman Jr. and Randall B. Ripley, "Conditions for Party Leadership: The Case of the House Democrats," *American Political Science Review* 59 (March 1965): 52–63.

36. *Congressional Quarterly Weekly Report*, November 1, 1980, 3235.

37. Robert A. Bernstein finds an interesting association between House members' ideological deviation and support for their reelection. At the primary stage, Democratic incumbents lose support for being too conservative, and Republicans for being too liberal. By contrast, in general elections Democratic incumbents lose support for being more liberal than their constituents prefer, whereas Republicans hurt themselves by being more conservative than their constituencies would like. The net impact, in general elections, is that deviation (Democratic incumbents to the right of their constituencies' preferences, Republican incumbents to the left) tends to help reelection prospects. "Limited Ideological Accountability in House Races: The Conditioning Effect of Party," *American Politics Quarterly* 20 (April 1992): 192–204.

38. For excellent discussions of these changes and their effects, see Nicol Rae, *The Decline and Fall of the Liberal Republicans* (New York: Oxford University Press, 1991); and David W. Rohde, *Parties and Leaders in the Postreform House* (Chicago: University of Chicago Press, 1991).

39. For a discussion of these trends and some speculation about the future, see *CQ Weekly*, December 14, 2002, 3240–3250.

40. Samuel C. Patterson and Gregory A. Caldeira, "Party Voting in the United States Congress," *British Journal of Political Science* 18 (January 1988): 111–131. The authors employ the "majority versus majority" concept of a party vote.

41. Mary Alice Nye, "Party Support in the House of Representatives: Generational Replacement, Seniority, or Member Conversion," *American Politics Quarterly* 22 (April 1994): 175–189.

42. See an interesting study of the strong relationship between organized labor and congressional Democrats by Taylor E. Dark, "Organized Labor and the Congressional Democrats: Reconsidering the 1980s," *Political Science Quarterly* 111 (spring 1996): 83–104.

43. *CQ Weekly*, December 15, 2002.

44. Ornstein, Mann, and Malbin, *Vital Statistics on Congress, 2001–2002*.

45. Rohde, *Parties and Leaders in the Postreform House*.

46. Richard Fleisher, "Explaining the Change in Roll-Call Behavior of Southern Democrats," *Journal of Politics* 55 (May 1993): 327–341.

47. See Stanley P. Berard, *Southern Democrats in the U.S. House of Representatives* (Norman, Okla.: University of Oklahoma Press, 2001), especially chapters 5 and 6.

48. See, for example, Richard Born, "Partisan Intentions and Election Day Realities in the Congressional Redistricting Process," *American Political Science Review* 79 (1985): 305–319; Charles Bullock, "Redistricting and Congressional Stability, 1962–1972," *Journal of Politics* 37 (1975): 569–575; Amihai Glazer, Bernard Grofman, and Marc Robbins, "Partisan and Incumbency Effects of 1970s Congressional Redistricting," *American Journal of Political Science* 30 (1987): 680–707; and Michael Lyons Michael and Peter F. Galderisi, "Incumbency, Reapportionment, and U.S. House Redistricting," *Political Research Quarterly* 48 (December 1995): 857–871.

49. Stephen Ansolabehere, James Snyder, and Charles Stewart, "Candidate Positioning in U.S. House Elections," *American Journal of Political Science* 45 (January 2001): 136–159.

50. John H. Aldrich, *Why Parties? The Origin and Transformation of Political Parties in America* (Chicago: University of Chicago Press, 1995).

51. See John H. Aldrich and David W. Rohde, "The Logic of Conditional Party Government: Revisiting the Electoral Connection," in *Congress Reconsidered*, 7th ed., ed. Lawrence C. Dodd and Bruce I. Oppenheimer (Washington, D.C.: CQ Press, 2001), for a rigorous theoretical treatment of this paradox.

52. Richard E. Neustadt, *Presidential Power: The Politics of Leadership* (New York: Wiley, 1960).

53. See a particularly instructive discussion of the insulation of members from party and committee controls in Loomis, *The New American Politician*, chapter 6.

54. For a study that finds that, contrary to conventional wisdom, presidential campaigning in midterm Senate elections helps candidates in close races, particularly through the mobilization of voters, see Jeffrey E. Cohen, Michael A. Krassa, and John A. Hamman, "The Impact of Presidential Campaigning on Midterm U.S. Senate Elections," *American Political Science Review* 85 (March 1991): 165–178.

55. See an assortment of data on the parties' coalitions in the *Washington Post*, November 7, 1996.

56. There is additional evidence that a member's support for the president's policy proposals is influenced by how well the president ran in his district. In essence, the stronger the president runs in the member's district, the more policy support he will receive from that member. Presidential elections thus do more than select winners; they help to shape support patterns in Congress for presidential initiatives. See George C. Edwards III, "Presidential Electoral Performance as a Source of Presidential Power," *American Journal of Political Science* 22 (February 1978): 152–168. For a study that finds that the president's coattails significantly help his party's Senate candidates (covering the years 1972–1988), see James E. Campbell and Joe A. Sumners, "Presidential Coattails in Senate Elections," *American Political Science Review* 84 (June 1990): 513–524.

57. From Randall B. Ripley, *Majority Party Leadership in Congress* (Boston: Little, Brown, 1969), 175.

58. One little-appreciated way that presidents influence members of Congress is to time their announcements of federal projects that benefit members to coincide with presidential and congressional elections. John A. Hamman and Jeffrey E. Cohen, "Reelection and Congressional Support: Presidential Motives in Distributive Politics," *American Politics Quarterly* 25 (January 1997): 56–74.

59. See Truman, *The Congressional Party*, especially 279–319. Long required reading for an understanding of the role of party in the contemporary Congress, *The Congressional Party*'s central conclusions continue to ring true. To examine congressional parties from other perspectives, see Keith T. Poole and R. Steven Daniels, "Ideology, Party, and Voting in the U.S. Congress, 1959–1980," *American Political Science Review* 79 (June 1985): 373–399; Sara Brandes Crook and John R. Hibbing, "Congressional Reform and Party Discipline: The Effects of Changes in the Seniority System on Party Loyalty in the U.S. House of Representatives," *British Journal of Political Science* 15 (April 1985): 207–226; Ross K. Baker, "Party and Institutional Sanctions in the U.S. House: The Case of Congressman Gramm," *Legislative Studies Quarterly* 10 (August 1985): 315–337; David W. Brady, "A Reevaluation of Realignments in American Politics: Evidence from the House of Representatives," *American Political Science Review* 79 (March 1985): 28–49; Burdett A. Loomis, "Congressional Careers and Party Leadership in the Contemporary House of Representatives," *American Journal of Political Science* 28 (February 1984): 180–202; David W. Brady and Barbara Sinclair, "Building Majorities for Policy Changes in the House of Representatives," *Journal of Politics* 46 (November 1984): 1033–1060; Donald A. Gross, "Changing Patterns of Voting Agreement among Senatorial Leadership: 1947–1976," *Western Political Quarterly* 37 (March 1984): 120–142; Jeffrey E. Cohen and David C. Nice, "Changing Party Loyalty of State Delegations to the U.S. House of Representatives, 1953–1976," *Western Political Quar-*

terly 36 (June 1983): 312–325; Charles S. Bullock III and David W. Brady, "Party, Constituency, and Roll-Call Voting in the U.S. Senate," *Legislative Studies Quarterly* 8 (February 1983): 29–43; Thomas H. Hammond and Jane M. Fraser, "Baselines for Evaluating Explanations of Coalition Behavior in Congress," *Journal of Politics* 45 (August 1983): 635–656; Robert G. Brookshire and Dean F. Duncan III, "Congressional Career Patterns and Party Systems," *Legislative Studies Quarterly* 8 (February 1983): 65–78; Richard A. Champagne, "Conditions for Realignment in the U.S. Senate, or What Makes the Steamroller Start?" *Legislative Studies Quarterly* 8 (May 1983): 231–249; William R. Shaffer, "Party and Ideology in the U.S. House of Representatives," *Western Political Quarterly* 35 (March 1982): 92–106; Thomas E. Cavanagh, "The Dispersion of Authority in the House of Representatives," *Political Science Quarterly* 97 (winter 1982–1983): 623–637; Walter J. Stone, "Electoral Change and Policy Representation in Congress," *British Journal of Political Science* 12 (January 1982): 95–115; and Patricia A. Hurley, "Predicting Policy Change in the House," *British Journal of Political Science* 12 (July 1982): 375–384.

60. Charles O. Jones, *The Minority Party in Congress* (Boston: Little, Brown, 1970), especially 9–24.

61. This study by Charles O. Jones identifies eight strategies open to the minority party in the overall task of building majorities in Congress: support of the majority party by contributing votes and possibly leadership, inconsequential opposition, withdrawal, cooperation, innovation, consequential partisan opposition, consequential constructive opposition, and participation (this strategy representing a situation in which the minority party controls the White House and thus is required to participate in constructing majorities). Strategies may vary within a single session of Congress and from one stage of the legislative process to the next. Jones, *The Minority Party in Congress,* 19–24, and chapters 4–8.

62. Charles L. Clapp, *The Congressman: His Work as He Sees It* (Washington, D.C.: Brookings Institution, 1963), 30–31.

63. For an analysis of the "credit claiming" activities of members, see Mayhew, *Congress: The Electoral Connection,* 52–61. The basic assumption of this remarkable little book is that reelection to Congress is the singular goal of members, and its relentless pursuit steadily influences not only their behavior but also the structure and functioning of the institution itself.

64. One study suggests that party contributions have a subtle effect. See Kevin M. Leyden and Stephen A. Borrelli, "An Investment in Goodwill: Party Contributions and Party Unity Among U.S. House Members in the 1980s," *American Politics Quarterly* 22 (1994): 421–452. Other studies, however, demonstrate either little or no effect. See Richard Clucas, "Party Contributions and the Influence of Campaign Committee Chairs on Roll-Call Voting," *Legislative Studies Quarterly* 22 (1997): 179–194; and David M. Cantor and Paul S. Herrnson, "Party Campaign Activity and Party Unity in the U.S. House of Representatives," *Legislative Studies Quarterly* 22 (August 1997): 393–415.

6 PARTY IDENTIFICATION, PARTISANSHIP, AND ELECTIONS

IN THE MID-1950S RESEARCHERS at the University of Michigan undertook the second large-scale academic study of the political attitudes of ordinary American citizens.[1] The result of their research, *The American Voter*, was the most significant book about political behavior published in the last fifty years. The most important political opinion held by individuals, the study discovered, was their party identification. Generations of research have confirmed that the psychological attachment of individuals to one or the other of the major parties (or the absence of such an attachment) reveals more about their political attitudes and behaviors than any other single opinion.

By contemporary standards, this finding may not seem particularly exceptional—that is, that people who think of themselves as Republicans tend to vote Republican and those who think of themselves as Democrats tend to vote Democratic. At the time, however, it was an extraordinary observation because the conventional wisdom concerning voting behavior revolved around social group identification, such as social class, race, religion, and the like.[2] Although the social groups with which people identify are important in influencing their voting decisions, parties are even more important. They organize how most people think about politics.

Party identification, moreover, explains more than simply how people are likely to vote. It often shapes what policy attitudes they are likely to have, how they will interpret new political information, how likely they are to vote, and how they tend to evaluate their political leaders. In short, parties influence in major ways how ordinary people interact with the political world.

The Origins of Party Identification

More than any other group or factor, the party provides cues to voters and gives shape and meaning to elections. Some voters elude party labeling, preferring the role of the independent. Even though their importance cannot be minimized, especially in presidential elections, their consistent impact on politics is less than that of party members. The reason is partly a matter of numbers: about two out of three voters classify themselves as members of one or the other of the two major parties, and another 25 percent lean toward one of them.

Where do these attitudes come from? Most research suggests that party identification is learned early in life and that parents play an influential role in its development. If a child grows up in a household where Republicans are held in high esteem and Democrats are derided, the child will typically grow up to be a Republican. In that sense, people are born into a party, much as they are born into a religion. From very early on in life, most people develop an attachment to a party, not unlike that to a sports team. Moreover, this association tends to grow stronger through the life cycle. Once someone has decided that he is a Red Sox and not a Yankees fan, he does not easily change sides and, in fact, usually becomes a more resolute fan. Similarly, once someone decides that he is a Republican, he usually remains a Republican, and his identification tends to grow stronger over time.

Parental party identification does not completely govern a child's choice of party. Early political experiences also bear on party identification.[3] For example, people who grew up in the shadow of the Great Depression, which was blamed on Republicans, tend to be less Republican than the population as a whole. Their early experiences included both Republican failures with the economy and the Democratic successes with the New Deal. Conversely, those who came of age politically during Democrat Jimmy Carter's failures in the late 1970s and Republican Ronald Reagan's successes in the 1980s are more likely to be Republicans.

Although party identification usually takes hold early in life, it is obviously subject to change. A person's intense interest in an issue, for example, can affect his party identification. Someone who grew up in a Republican household but developed an intense pro-choice position on abortion may shift to the Democratic party or become an independent. While parental partisanship is for most people the most important factor in their own partisanship, issues become increasingly important as people enter their twenties and thirties.[4] In addition, regularly voting for candidates of the opposite party may alter one's party identification.[5] Indeed, vote choice and party identification are not the same thing. Consistent voting for Republican presidential candidates by southern Democrats eventually strengthened their Republican identification.

The Effects of Party Identification

It is more useful to think about the things that party identification affects than the things that affect party identification. It is by far the most stable political attitude, which means that it most often influences other opinions and behaviors rather than being influenced by them.[6] While certain issues, such as abortion, can affect a person's party identification, usually it is party identification that affects his opinions about political issues.

For most people, party provides a useful shortcut for understanding a complicated political world. People have neither the time nor the desire to learn everything they need to know about politics, but party helps them find their way around with less than perfect information. Public opinion research shows that most Americans know very little about politics and government.[7] If asked to identify the chief justice of the Supreme Court, fewer than 10 percent regularly answer correctly. Usually only about one half can identify which party holds a majority in the House of Representatives. About 10 percent cannot identify the vice president by name. The uncomfortable truth is that Americans barely have opinions at all about the issues of the day.

As a result, most people use their attachment to party to decide where they stand on issues. For example, most Americans do not follow politics closely enough to have a well-formed opinion on tax policy. They can use information presented in the mass media, however, to see how political elites analyze tax issues. They might find that Republicans in Congress are supporting deep tax cuts that favor upper income groups and that Democrats are supporting smaller cuts that reward persons with lower incomes. Partisans are then able to use this information to form their own positions.

Because ordinary Americans use partisan cues, public opinion typically follows elite opinion. Consider the question of racial integration in the 1950s and 1960s. The Democratic party's decision to embrace civil rights for African Americans was not the result of an enormous shift in the percentage of people favoring this policy course. Rather, the shift occurred only after the Democratic party took up the issue and signaled its legitimacy.[8] Some southerners abandoned their Democratic identification, but more Americans changed their opinions on racial integration than changed their partisanship. In general, the decisions of party leaders drive the opinions of partisans, not the other way around. Partisans thus tend to align their views with those of their party leaders.

Party identification also acts as an important perceptual screen for incoming political information. Watching exactly the same news broadcast, Republicans and Democrats can often take away completely different impressions. The Monica Lewinsky scandal during Bill Clinton's presidency provides a striking example. As evidence grew that the president had had an affair in the Oval Office with a young intern, Republicans became outraged and called for his removal from office. In contrast, many Democrats supported the president even more intensely, believing that the affair had little or no relevance for his ability to conduct the presidency. Had the president been a Republican, the partisan response almost certainly would have been reversed. For example, when it came to light during the last week of the 2000 presidential campaign that George W. Bush had been arrested for drunk driving in the mid-1970s, Republicans dismissed this transgression as old news. But the same Democrats who claimed Clinton's moral transgressions were irrelevant in 1998 spoke quite differently about Bush's. What happened is that party elites presented these views through the mass media, and partisans in the electorate lined up their opinions accordingly.

The 2000 presidential election provides further evidence of the importance of party identification in shaping perceptions. In assessing the election's outcome, Republicans tended to highlight the fact that George W. Bush had received more legal votes in Florida than had Al Gore. Democrats, by contrast, highlighted the fact that thousands more voters in Florida intended to vote for Gore than for Bush, but that poorly designed ballots and racial discrimination distorted or invalidated their votes and cost Gore the election. Survey data taken by the Gallup Organization paints a very partisan picture of the Florida controversy. More than 90 percent of Republicans criticized Gore's legal efforts in Florida, while more than 80 percent of Democrats approved of it.[9] Democrats and Republicans developed vastly different opinions about a seemingly objective outcome (who won a presidential election), even though they received basically the same information from the mass media. This suggests that party identification matters profoundly in shaping opinions.

The perceptual screen of party identification also affects a range of other opinions, including estimates of how well the president is doing his job. According to a Gallup Poll taken a month before the September 11, 2001, terrorist attacks, Bush's approval rating was 57 percent. But this number obscures substantial partisan differences; 89 percent of Republicans but only 28 percent of Democrats approved of his performance. Bush was doing the same job, but Republicans and Democrats perceived it differently. Even after September 11, with almost all Americans embracing the president, partisan differences persisted. Whereas 98 percent of Republicans gave the president high marks, only 85 percent of Democrats did so. In the months after September 11, approval among Republicans remained around 95 percent, while it declined substantially among Democrats, who followed their party leaders in assessing the president. In the months after the terrorist attacks, no one in Washington dared criticize the president for fear of appearing unpatriotic. As September 11 receded into the past, however, other issues, such as the financial chicanery of certain corporations and a wobbly economy, came to the fore. Democratic leaders turned to these more partisan issues to sharpen their attacks against the president, which, in turn, led to lower approval ratings, mostly among Democrats.

The list of attitudes that party identification affects is impressive. When there is a Republican president, Democratic partisans always view the economy as worse than their Republican counterparts do, and vice versa. In evaluating the personal characteristics of political candidates, Republican partisans always rate the competence, character, and attractiveness of Republican candidates more favorably than do Democrats, and vice versa. In short, party identification structures the political world of partisans more thoroughly than any other attitude or set of attitudes.

The Distribution of Party Identification

To understand partisanship and its intensity, the National Election Study (NES) regularly asks a random sample of Americans a set of questions beginning with:

> Generally speaking, do you usually think of yourself as a Republican, Democrat, an independent, or what?

Tracking responses to this question over time reveals what appears to be an extraordinary change in identification. (See Figure 6-1.) When the NES debuted this question in the early 1950s, 47 percent of Americans classified themselves as Democrats, 28 percent as Republicans, and only 23 percent as independents. By 1984, the percentage of Democrats had dropped by about ten points, the percentage of independents had increased by about the same amount, and the percentage of Republicans remained steady. Based on this apparent dealignment from the parties, scholars published books with titles such as *The Decline of American Political Parties*.[10] In 2000 fully 40 percent of Americans chose the independent label rather than that of one of the major parties.

That the high water mark for partisan independence seems to have occurred in 2000 is strange, given the partisan contentiousness of the campaign, the election, and the election aftermath. Most Americans seemed to care intensely about the outcome—not a characteristic of a largely politically independent electorate.

Figure 6-1   The Distribution of Party Identification in the Electorate: 1952–2000

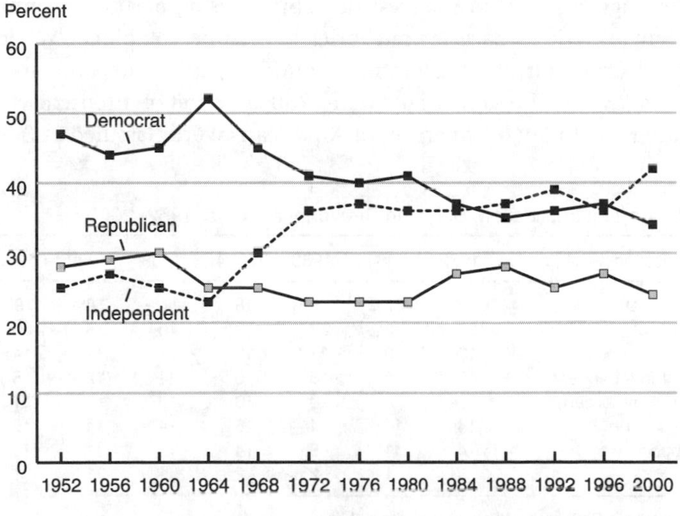

Source: American National Election Study, Cumulative File, 1948–2000.

In fact, an examination of the responses to the other two party identification questions asked by the NES reveals a much different picture of contemporary party identification:

> If a person answers that he is a Republican or Democrat to the first question, he is asked "Would you call yourself a strong or a not very strong Republican/Democrat?"
>
> If a person answers that he is an independent to the first question, he is asked "Do you think of yourself as close to the Republican or Democratic party?"

Public opinion researchers usually combine the responses to these questions to form a seven-point scale, ranging from strong Democrat on one end to strong Republican on the other, with pure independent at the midpoint. Those who fail to fit any of these categories are labeled apoliticals, a group that has never been larger than a percentage point or two. The data showing the seven-point party identification scale from 1952 to 2000 appear in Table 6-1.

The seven-point scale creates three partisan categories for each party: strong partisans, weak partisans, and independents who lean in a partisan direction. Bruce Keith and his coauthors observe that people who call themselves independent but lean toward one of the parties (partisan leaners) behave politically in a manner that is at least as partisan, if not more partisan, than those who are weak partisans.[11] Furthermore, the only group that behaves as if it is truly disconnected from the parties and the political system is the pure independents—those who answer "independent" to the first question and that they do not feel close to either of the parties to the second question. After a surge in the 1970s, the percentage of pure independents is basically the same today as it was in the 1960s. In other words, people today are not nearly as disconnected from the parties as scholars and commentators previously had argued.

The findings of this study suggest that, in assessing partisan alignment and dealignment, the three partisan categories should be combined. When that is done, the distribution of Republicans, Democrats, and independents in 2000 looks almost exactly the same as it did in 1960, a period of intense partisanship. (See Figure 6-2.) In 1960 52 percent of Americans were classified as Democrats,

Table 6-1   Party Identification, Selected Presidential Years: 1952–2000

Party identification	1952	1964	1980	1984	1988	1992	1996	2000
Strong Democrat	22%	27%	18%	18%	17%	18%	19%	19%
Weak Democrat	25	25	23	22	18	18	20	15
Independent Democrat	10	9	11	10	12	14	14	15
Independent-Independent	6	8	13	6	11	12	8	12
Independent Republican	7	6	10	13	13	12	11	13
Weak Republican	14	14	14	15	14	14	15	12
Strong Republican	14	11	9	14	14	11	13	12
Apolitical	3	1	2	2	1	1	1	1

Source: Center for Political Studies, University of Michigan.

Note: Columns may not add to 100 because of rounding.

37 percent as Republicans, and 12 percent as independents. In 2000 the percentages were 50, 37, and 12—statistically indistinguishable from those in 1960.
In this interpretation, the data point to a relatively marked increase in political
independence in the 1970s that, in fact, was short lived.

To examine the durable changes in the strength of party identification, it is
useful to fold the scale at its midpoint. Table 6-2 shows that the percentage of
strong partisans has declined noticeably since the early 1960s. When John F.
Kennedy defeated Richard Nixon in 1960, 36 percent of Americans identified
themselves as strong partisans. By 1976, this figure had dropped by a third, to 24
percent. In 2000 the percentage of strong partisans recovered to 31 percent, but
this level was still well below those achieved in the 1960s. The most sizable
decline has occurred among weak partisans, who held relatively constant in the
high thirties from the 1950s to the early 1980s but dropped sharply to 27 percent in 2000. By contrast, the percentage of partisan leaners has more than doubled since the late 1950s and early 1960s.[12] Since weak and leaning partisans
behave similarly, this change is of somewhat limited consequence.

Party Identification and Voting Behavior

Party identification data beg the question of why Republicans tend to win
presidential elections when Democrats consistently outnumber them in the electorate. Since 1968, Republicans have won six out of nine presidential elections.
Obviously, factors other than party affect election outcomes. Even the authors of
The American Voter, who centered their analysis on party identification, noted the

Figure 6-2   The Distribution of Party Identification in the Electorate, Leaners Included as
Partisans: 1952–2000

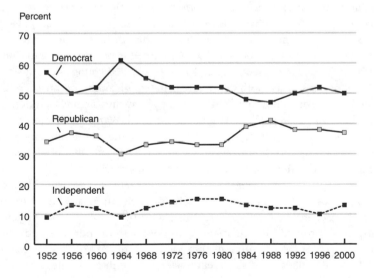

Source: American National Election Study, Cumulative File, 1948–2000.

Table 6-2   Strength of Partisanship, Selected Presidential Years: 1952–2000

	1952	1964	1976	1988	1992	1996	2000
Independent or apolitical	9%	9%	15%	12%	13%	10%	13%
Leaning partisan	17	15	22	25	27	26	28
Weak partisan	39	38	39	32	32	34	27
Strong partisan	35	38	24	31	29	30	31

Source: American National Election Study, Cumulative File, 1948–2000.

importance of the candidates' personal characteristics in vote choice. The Michigan scholars were, of course, writing in the 1950s, when the Democrats' identification advantage was greatest; yet it was also the time when Republican Dwight Eisenhower won two terms by comfortable margins, undoubtedly helped by his war hero status. And, recently, the Republicans have fielded more attractive presidential candidates than the Democrats. Perhaps the most charismatic president of the last several decades was Reagan, and virtually all analyses of the 2000 election stressed Bush's likeability advantage over Gore.[13]

Differences between Republican and Democratic identifiers also help account for Republican presidential successes. First, Republicans are significantly more loyal than Democrats to their candidates. In 2000, for example, 86 percent of self-identified Democrats voted for Gore while 91 percent of self-identified Republicans voted for Bush.[14] This loyalty gap between Republicans and Democrats has often been even wider during the last several decades.

In addition to voting more loyally, Republicans are more likely than Democrats to vote at all. Numerous studies have shown that citizens who are better educated and have higher incomes are more likely to vote than those with limited education and low incomes. In other terms, higher socioeconomic status (SES) encourages turnout, while lower socioeconomic status discourages it. Since upper-SES persons tend to vote Republican, while those with low incomes and low levels of education tend to vote Democratic, it is not surprising to find that, in the 2000 election, 82 percent of Republicans reported voting as contrasted with 77 percent of Democrats. Both figures are inflated, of course, because a relatively high percentage of Americans say they vote when they actually do not. (Voter turnout in 2000 was only about 51 percent.) Indeed, Warren Miller finds that the Republicans' turnout advantage is sufficiently large that about an equal percentage of Republicans and Democrats actually vote in presidential elections—a fact that explains the nation's many close recent presidential elections.[15]

In sum, Republicans are able to overcome the Democrats' party identification advantage because they vote more loyally for their candidates and turn out in greater numbers. In addition, Republicans, with their limited-government philosophy, have profited from their ability to field better candidates and from the general antigovernment sentiment that followed the end of Lyndon Johnson's burst of liberal public policy, the Great Society; the military's failure in Vietnam; and the Watergate crisis.

Emerging Differences in Party Identification: Gender and Religion

For years, the most striking change in party identification was the movement of white southerners away from the Democratic party that began in the 1960s. They turned to the Republicans when they became disillusioned with the liberal thrust of the national Democratic party, particularly its positions on civil rights.

Another dramatic development in party identification is the growing difference between men and women, shown in Figure 6-3. As recently as 1976, men and women identified with the parties in basically the same numbers. But a gender gap in party identification started to develop in 1980. By 2000, data from the NES show that men were seven percentage points more Republican than women, and that women were eight points more Democratic than men. This difference manifests itself in voting behavior as well. In 2000, for example, the Voter News Service exit poll found that 54 percent of women voted for Gore, compared with 43 percent for Bush, while 53 percent of men voted for Bush, compared with only 43 percent for Gore. This twelve-point gender difference in the Democratic vote is about the same as the fourteen-point difference recorded in 1996, the largest gap between the sexes recorded in the survey era.[16]

Although popular analysis tends to focus on women in discussions of the gender gap, the real change in attitudes has occurred among men.[17] In 2000, 34 percent of women identified themselves as Republicans, the same percentage as in 1976. The attitudes of men, by contrast, have changed significantly. Whereas 34 percent of men identified themselves as Republicans in 1976, fully 41 percent

Figure 6-3   Gender Gap in Party Identification: 1976–2000

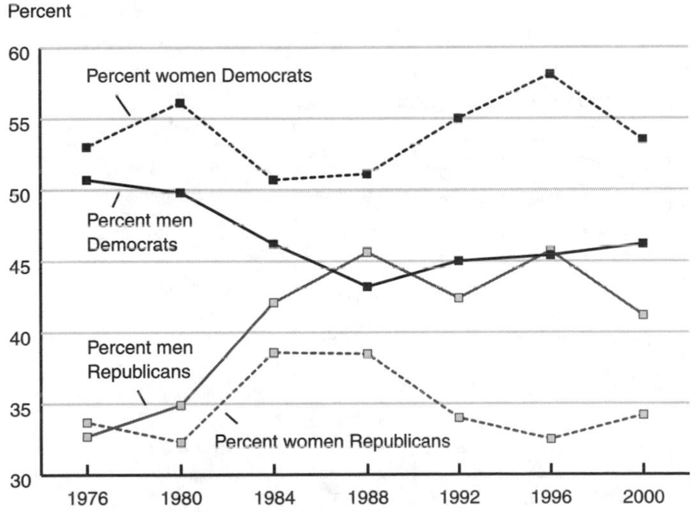

Source: American National Election Study, Cumulative File, 1948–2000.

did so in 2000. The usual stability that characterizes attitudes makes this ten-per-centage-point change nothing short of extraordinary.

Karen Kaufmann and John Petrocik find that gender difference is the result of both disparities in policy attitudes, particularly on social welfare issues, and in the weight that men and women assign these issues. In other words, most of the differences in party identification and voting behavior between men and women stem from the fact that men tend to be more conservative than women on issues such as spending on the poor and on minorities, and they are also more likely to favor a smaller government role in creating jobs and providing for health care. In addition, men tend to place greater emphasis on these issues than women typically do.[18]

In addition to the growing chasm between men and women voters, a major division has developed between those who attend church regularly and those who attend infrequently or not at all. Specifically, those who attend church at least once a week have become stalwarts of the Republican party; those who attend church less often or not at all are now disproportionately Democrats. The trend over time appears in Figure 6-4. According to NES data, church attendance and party identification were basically unrelated in the 1970s. The gap began to emerge in the 1980s, with the election of Reagan, who was closely identified with Reverend Jerry Falwell and the Christian Right movement. Although the gap disappeared in 1988, it became even more pronounced in succeeding presidential election years. In 1992 regular church attenders were ten percentage points more Republican than nonregular church attenders. The gap was a striking fourteen

Figure 6-4   Church Attendance and Party Identification: 1976–2000

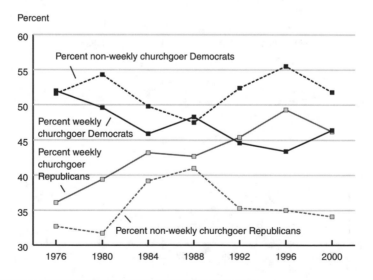

Source: American National Election Study, Cumulative File, 1948–2000.

points in 1996 and twelve points in 2000. The difference is even starker among whites. In 1976 white churchgoers and white nonchurchgoers shared basically the same party identification distribution. In 2000, however, white churchgoers were eighteen percentage points more Republican than white nonchurchgoers.

This cleavage is clearly an important feature of American politics today. Indeed, religious participation has a greater impact on party identification than such traditional factors as region and social class. Religion's new importance is due in part to the "family values" campaigns waged by Republican candidates over the last two decades and to the Republican party's pro-life position on abortion. Moreover, it also helps to explain the change in the voting behavior of Catholics, formerly a key element in the Democrats' coalition. White Catholics cast more votes for Bush than they did for Gore.[19] Religious denomination aside, the centrality of religion to a person significantly influences whether he is a Republican or a Democrat.

Evidence of the Growing Importance of Party

For the past twenty years, the conventional wisdom among political scientists was that party meant relatively little to American voters. The Michigan studies provided evidence that party identification in the electorate was very strong in the 1950s but declined after the political upheavals of the 1960s and 1970s. The political system became more media driven; and from the late 1960s through the early 1980s, there was ample evidence of party decline in the electorate. People identified less with parties, and they did not see them as effective problem solvers. Rather than viewing one party positively and the other negatively, as strong partisans do, people tended to view both parties in more neutral terms.[20] Parties were less able to structure voting behavior, particularly at the congressional level.[21] In an increasingly candidate-centered world, voters were becoming less and less likely to organize their thoughts about politics in party terms and images.

One development that resulted from Reagan's presidency is that ordinary people began to rely more on party—a trend that has continued into the new century. For example, the NES surveys ask people what they like and dislike about the major parties, allowing up to five likes and five dislikes about each party. Individuals who provide few responses obviously are not thinking about politics in terms of parties. Those who provide numerous likes and dislikes, however, reflect the fact that parties are doing more to inform their thinking. Figure 6-5 demonstrates that parties were much more salient in the 1990s than they were in the 1970s and 1980s.[22] In fact, the mean number of responses to the likes/dislikes questions in 1996 was higher than in any previous year except 1952 and 1968. The parties-in-decline thesis is applicable to the 1970s and early 1980s, but it is highly questionable today.[23]

This resurgence in party is somewhat puzzling, however, in today's media-driven and candidate-centered political world. Why has party made a comeback? Mass opinion does not change without cause. When it does shift, it usually does

Figure 6-5   Mean Total Number of Likes and Dislikes about the Parties: 1952–2000

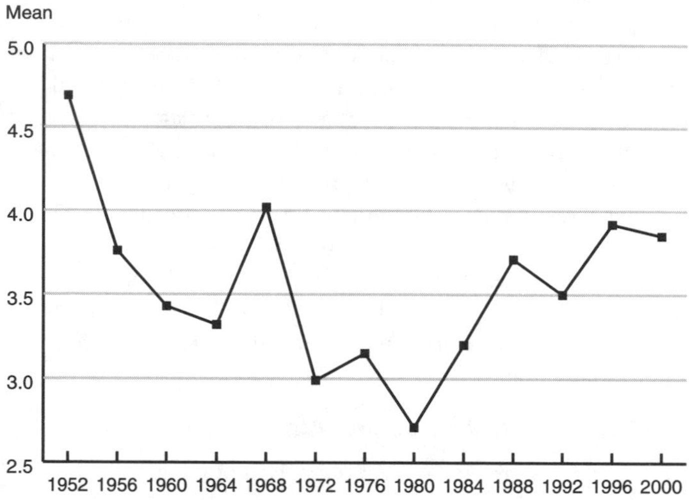

Source: American National Election Study, Cumulative File, 1948–2000.

so in response to changes in the information environment provided by political elites. V. O. Key Jr. put it this way: "[T]he voice of the people is but an echo chamber. The output of an echo chamber bears an inevitable and invariable relation to the input." [24] This means that, when politicians provide party-oriented cues, the public is likely to respond in a party-centric manner. They are unlikely to do so otherwise. [25]

The changes in Congress described in the last chapter are important for understanding the resurgence of party among ordinary Americans. The growing ideological divide between the congressional parties has had an impact on the public. Today, Americans are much better at placing the Democrats to the ideological left of Republicans than they were twenty years ago. In addition, they are much more likely to perceive important policy and ideological differences between them than they were a generation ago. [26] (See Figure 6-6.) Of greatest importance, Figure 6-6 shows that each increase in partisan thinking and behavior in the electorate was preceded by an increase in partisan behavior in Congress. As Congress became more partisan, the electorate followed suit.

Why should the parties' ideological polarization at the congressional level produce more partisan behavior among ordinary Americans? If the parties did not differ in basic respects, it would not matter who ran the government because policy outcomes would be roughly the same. But, in a political world characterized by significant cleavages between the parties, who wins and who loses matters a great deal. In short, greater partisan differences in Washington have created a more partisan public.

Figure 6-6 Decline and Resurgence of Party in the Electorate as a Function of Ideological Polarization in the U.S. House of Representatives: 1949–2000

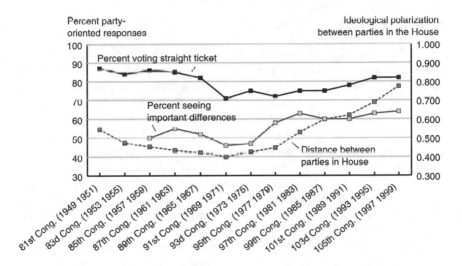

Sources: American National Election Study, Cumulative File, 1948–2000; and Keith Poole and Howard Rosenthal, DW-NOMINATE scores, 81st Congress–105th Congress.

Note: Measures of party in the electorate are taken in the year after the end of a congressional session.

Turnout: The Diminished Electorate

It is an unfortunate fact of American life that for a large proportion of the population politics carries no interest, registers no significance, and excites no demands. A vast array of evidence shows that the political role of the typical citizen is that of spectator, occasionally aroused by political events but more often inattentive to them. Whether greatly interested and active citizens are necessary in order to have strong and responsible political institutions is by no means clear. No neat or simple formula exists for assessing public support for political institutions. Does the presence of a large nonvoting population reflect substantial disillusionment with the political system and its processes, or does it reflect a general satisfaction with the state of things? The answer is elusive.

Whatever the consequences of low or modest turnouts for the vitality of a democratic political system, it is obvious that some American citizens use their political resources far more than others. Their political involvement is reflected not only in the fact that they vote regularly but also because they participate in politics in various other ways—perhaps by attempting to persuade other voters to support their candidates or party, by making campaign contributions, or by devoting time and energy to political campaigns. The net result of differential rates of participation is that some citizens gain access to political decision makers and can influence their decisions, whereas others are all but excluded from the political process.

Who Participates?

The act of voting is an appropriate point of departure for exploring the political involvement of American citizens, but it is not the only form of participation. A comprehensive survey of political participation in the United States by Sidney Verba and Norman H. Nie shows the range and dimensions of citizen activities in politics. (See Table 6-3.) Several findings should be emphasized. Perhaps of most importance, the only political activity in which a majority of American citizens participate is voting in presidential elections. Voting regularly in local elections follows as a rather distant second. The survey discloses that as political activity requires more time, initiative, and involvement of the citizen—working to solve a community problem, attempting to persuade others how to vote, working for a party or candidate, or contributing to political campaigns—participation levels drop even lower.

The impression that the data most deeply conveys is that a relatively small group of citizens performs most of the political activities of the nation. Yet, to some extent, the data underrepresent the political activity of citizens, because those citizens who perform one political act are not necessarily the same as those who perform another act. Verba and Nie indicate that less than one third of their sample reported engaging in no political activities (other than voting).[27] Even so, this is a fairly large lump of the citizenry.

The evidence indicates that people do not get involved randomly in politics. Instead, there is a hierarchy of political involvement. (See Figure 6-7.)[28] Individ-

Table 6-3 A Profile of the Political Activity of American Citizens

Form of activity	Percentage of citizens
Report regularly voting in presidential elections	72
Report always voting in local elections	47
Acting in at least one organization involved in community problems	32
Have worked with others in trying to solve some community problems	30
Have attempted to persuade others to vote as they were	28
Have ever actively worked for a party or candidates during an election	26
Have ever contacted a local government official about some issue or problem	20
Have attended at least one political meeting or rally in last three years	19
Have ever contacted a state or national government official about some issue or problem	18
Have ever formed a group or organization to attempt to solve some local community problem	14
Have ever given money to a party or candidate during an election campaign	13
Presently a member of a political club or organization	8

Source: Sidney Verba and Norman H. Nie, *Participation in America: Political Democracy and Social Equality* (New York: Harper and Row, 1972), 31.

Figure 6-7   Hierarchy of Political Involvement

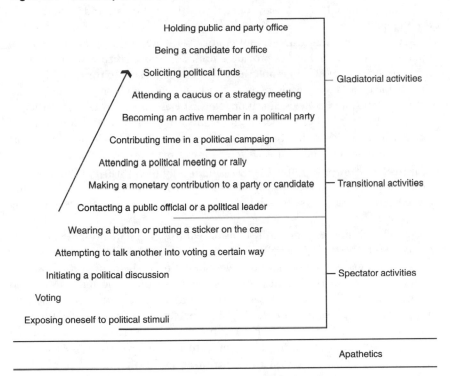

Holding public and party office

Being a candidate for office

Soliciting political funds   — Gladiatorial activities

Attending a caucus or a strategy meeting

Becoming an active member in a political party

Contributing time in a political campaign

Attending a political meeting or rally

Making a monetary contribution to a party or candidate   — Transitional activities

Contacting a public official or a political leader

Wearing a button or putting a sticker on the car

Attempting to talk another into voting a certain way

Initiating a political discussion   — Spectator activities

Voting

Exposing oneself to political stimuli

Apathetics

Source: Lester W. Milbrath, *Political Participation* (Chicago: Rand McNally, 1965), 18.

uals who are politically active engage in a wide variety of political acts. A major characteristic of their participation is that it tends to be cumulative. The active members of a political party, for example, are likely to be found soliciting political funds, contributing time and money to campaigns, attending meetings, and so on. Individuals who are minimally involved in politics typically take part only in limited activities such as those grouped near the base of the hierarchy. At the very bottom are those persons who stand on the outskirts of the political world, scarcely aware of the political forces that play on them or of the opportunities open to them to use their resources (including the vote) to gain political objectives.

Some portion of the explanation for the passivity of American citizens may lie with the parties and candidates themselves. They are not particularly active in clearing the way for popular participation. Traditionally, only a small proportion of citizens were contacted by party or candidate organization workers in an effort to win their vote, although there is some evidence that this is changing. During the 1992 election campaign, for instance, only 12 percent of the public reported that they had been contacted by someone from the Democratic party and only 10 percent by someone from the Republican party. In 2000, however, 22 percent reported having been contacted by the Democrats and 25 percent by the Republicans.[29]

Several social, demographic, and political variables are related to the act of voting. The data in Table 6-4 provide a profile of those citizens who are more likely to turn out at elections and those who are less likely to turn out. Some of the characteristics are closely related—for example, high income,[30] high occupational status, and college education. Nevertheless, the high rate of participation by citizens of higher socioeconomic status is not simply a function of status. The explanation lies in the civic orientations that are linked to upper-class status and environment. Upper-status citizens, for example, are more likely than citizens of lower status to belong to organizations and to participate in their activities, more likely to possess the resources and skills to be effective in politics, and more likely to be attentive to political problems and to feel efficacious in dealing with them.[31]

For all their interest, the distinctions drawn from the data presented in Table 6-4 cannot be taken at face value. The differences between voters and nonvoters are less apparent today than they were in the past. The participation rates of people who live in rural or urban areas are about the same today. Men and women now vote at about the same rate. Turnout in the South is on the rise, whereas it is decreasing in the North. A noticeable decline in voting by the middle-aged has occurred. What stands out most is that participation has declined along a broad demographic front. The lower turnout of Protestants is also deceptive—undoubtedly a result in part to the lower levels of participation of southern and rural voters, who happen to be largely Protestant. Finally, it should be

Table 6-4   A Profile of the More Active and Less Active Citizenry

More likely to vote	Less likely to vote
High income	Low income
High occupational status	Low occupational status
College education	Grade school or high school education
Middle-aged	Young and elderly
White	Black and Hispanic
Metropolitan area resident	Small-town resident
Northern state resident	Southern state resident
Resident in competitive party environment	Resident in noncompetitive party environment
Union member	Nonunion member
Homeowner	Renter
Married	Single, separated, divorced, widowed
Government employees	Private workers
Catholics and Jews	Protestants
Strong partisan	Independent

Sources: These findings were drawn from a large number of studies of the American electorate. For wide-ranging analyses, see Lester W. Milbrath, *Political Participation* (Chicago: Rand McNally, 1965); Raymond E. Wolfinger and Steven J. Rosenstone, *Who Votes?* (New Haven, Conn.: Yale University Press, 1980); and M. Margaret Conway, *Political Participation in the United States*, 2d ed. (Washington, D.C.: CQ Press, 1991).

stressed that the variables are not of equal importance. The best indicators of voting participation are those that reflect socioeconomic status: education, income, and occupation. And of these, education is the most important. (See Table 6-5.)[32]

Scholars who study electoral behavior contend that education is the predominant influence on turnout. The importance of education is said to derive from the fact that education inculcates a sense of civic duty, increases political efficacy, enhances political awareness, and makes registration easier. Although there is good evidence to support each of these explanations, Robert A. Jackson finds that education's impact on registration is especially important: "Advanced schooling cultivates skills and interests that make the hurdle of registration easier to overcome, which, in turn, elevates voting odds."[33]

Citizens who show enthusiasm for voting and who participate regularly in elections can be distinguished by their psychological makeup as well as by their social and economic backgrounds. The prospect that persons will vote is influenced by the intensity of their partisan preferences: the more substantial their commitments to a party, the stronger the probability that they will vote. Those who have a strong partisan preference and who perceive the election as close are virtually certain to vote.[34] Voters are also more likely than nonvoters to perceive major differences between the parties' positions on public policy questions such as Medicare, taxes, and the deficit.[35] Voters can also be distinguished by other indices of psychological involvement in political affairs. Survey research data show them to be more interested in campaigns and more concerned with election outcomes.[36] They are also more likely than nonvoters to possess a strong sense of political efficacy: that is, a disposition to see their own participation in politics as important and effective. Finally, in contrast to nonvoters, voters are more likely to accept the norm that voting is a civic obligation. In sum, the evidence suggests that psychological involvement—marked by interest in elections, concern over their outcome, a sense of political efficacy, and a sense of citizen duty—increases the probability that a person will pay the costs in time and energy that voting requires.

The most provocative question concerning participation is the one for which empirical evidence is in shortest supply: Does who votes matter? Does it affect public policy outcomes? How do parties play into this equation? When parties do

Table 6-5 Education and Voting Turnout in Presidential Elections

Educational level	Percentage voting				
	1980	1984	1988	1992	2000
Grade school	58.6	58.0	50.0	54.8	49.1
High school	65.4	66.3	59.2	65.4	62.9
College	82.6	85.5	85.1	88.1	84.8

Source: Adapted from M. Margaret Conway, *Political Participation in the United States,* 2d ed. (Washington, D.C.: CQ Press, 1991), 22 (updated). As Conway pointed out, individuals who are more highly educated are also more likely to overreport voting.

contact voters, the individuals most likely to be reached are those with high socio-economic status—in particular, those with a college education, a professional or business background, and a high income. That the better off are mobilized rather than the less well off will mean that office-seekers will be more inclined to confront the problems of the former rather than the latter group. Indeed, there is systematic evidence suggesting that the pattern of participation matters. Kim Quaile Hill and Jan E. Leighley found that where poor people have higher levels of turnout, welfare benefits are higher.[37] Steven Rosenstone and John Mark Hansen find a similar connection between African American participation and public policy designed to help this group.[38] It is not much of a reach to believe that economically advantaged elements in American society generally have a much stronger claim than inactive citizens on the attention and dispositions of their representatives. In short, who votes almost certainly matters profoundly.

Atrophy of the Electorate

Turnout was regularly high in presidential elections during the last quarter of the nineteenth century. In the election of 1876, for example, more than 85 percent of the eligible voters cast ballots. (See Figure 6-8.) Beginning around the turn of the century, however, a sharp decline in voting set in, reaching its nadir of 44 percent in 1920. A moderate increase in turnout occurred during the next several decades, with participation hovering around 60 percent during the 1950s

Figure 6-8   Percentage of Voting-Age Population Casting Votes for the Office of President: 1856–2000

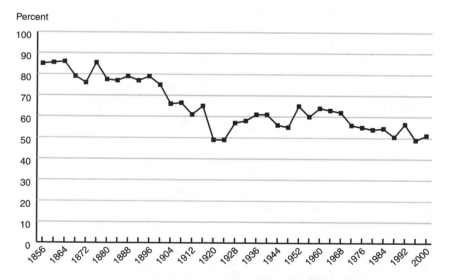

Percent

Source: Developed from data in Paul Allen Beck, "The Electoral Cycle and Patterns of American Politics," *British Journal of Political Science* 9 (April 1979): 134 (as updated).

and 1960s. But turnout has dropped with almost every election since 1960, falling to only 50 percent of the voting-age population in 1988. Although the three-way race in 1992 brought out significantly more voters than the previous five presidential elections had, turnout was lower in both 1996 and 2000 than in 1992.

Voter turnout is even lower in nonpresidential elections. In off-year congressional elections from 1950 to 1970, turnout percentages ranged between 41 and 45 percent of eligible voters, but a marked downturn occurred thereafter. In 1974 turnout dropped to 38.1 percent, and it has not reached the 40 percent mark since. Economic downturns like the 1982 recession and voter anger directed at Clinton's policies in 1994 can bring out a few more voters, but current off-year voting rates still do not approach those of the 1950s and 1960s. Even the great watershed victory by the Republicans in 1994 attracted only 38.8 percent of eligible voters.

Turnout in state and local elections is more of the same story of citizen indifference. An analysis of voting for the office of governor, for example, supports three main generalizations. First, the states differ sharply in their turnout patterns. As a rule, higher voter participation rates occur in the Midwest, the Great Plains and Rocky Mountain states, and New England. Many southern states and several far west states like Arizona, Nevada, and New Mexico usually vote at particularly low rates. Second, those states that elect governors in presidential years (about one fifth of the total) nearly always have higher turnouts than those in which gubernatorial elections occur in off years. Third, notwithstanding major variations among the states, overall citizen performance is disappointing. The average turnout in off-year gubernatorial elections hovers around 40 percent, and in some southern states it fails even to reach 30 percent.

The low point in participation is ordinarily plumbed in primary elections; a total primary vote of only 20 to 25 percent of the eligible electorate is not unusual. In certain southern states, however, participation in primary elections—often the decisive election in that region—is about as high as it is in general elections. Primary turnout is highest in states where primaries are open (and particularly high in blanket or nonpartisan primaries), where the parties are most competitive, where presidential primaries coincide with other primaries, and where higher educational levels are present among voters. There is some evidence that closeness of election stimulates turnout and that incumbency diminishes it. Each state has a different mix of these factors, thus contributing to variations in turnout rates.

What Caused the Turnout Decline?

It is a major and uncomfortable fact of American political life that a great many citizens—comprising half or more of the eligible electorate even in presidential years—are almost wholly detached from the political system and the processes through which its leadership is selected. Since this was not always the case, it is important to understand what caused the decline in voter participation. In answering this question, it is best to divide the decline into its two eras. The steepest took place in the early twentieth century, in the wake of the Progressive movement. The second, more gradual, decline took place after 1960.

Causes of the Early Twentieth-Century Decline

The most salient reason for turnout decline in the early twentieth century was that major changes were made in election rules. Before the Progressive movement took hold, voter registration was not widely used. People could simply show up to vote, receive a ballot from a party representative, and register their preferences at the ballot box. Indeed, there is strong evidence that the nearly 90 percent turnouts in the late 1800s were, at least in part, the result of fraud. In many counties, people voted "both early and often," which inflated turnout. Some counties recorded more people voting than there were residents of those counties. During the early twentieth century, registration laws became much more restrictive, making voting more difficult. Provisions were adopted, for example, requiring voters to register annually in person, purging voters' names from the registration rolls if they failed to vote within a particular period, and requiring that voters reside within a state at least a year (and sometimes two) before becoming eligible to register. As voting rules were tightened, fewer people voted, either legally or illegally.

In addition to registration laws, other election devices also caused turnout to drop. In the case of southern states, limitations placed on African American political participation shortly before the turn of the century drastically reduced turnout. A variety of legal abridgments and strategies, buttressed by social and economic sanctions of all kinds, effectively disfranchised all but the most persistent and resourceful African American citizens. The ingenuity of southern white politicians during this era can scarcely be exaggerated. Poll taxes, literacy tests, "understanding-the-Constitution" tests, white primaries,[39] stringent residence and registration requirements, and discriminatory registration administration were consciously employed by dominant elites to maintain a white electorate and thus to settle political questions exclusively among whites.

A counterintuitive explanation is that the sharp expansion of the franchise also contributed to lower turnout rates. Women were given the vote in 1920, but large numbers were indifferent to their new right and did not use it immediately. Although the size of the eligible electorate doubled with the inclusion of women, the turnout rate dropped because women voted at much lower rates than did men. The first two presidential years that women could first vote, 1920 and 1924, had among the lowest overall turnouts of the century. As women acquired political expertise—a strong predictor of voting—their participation increased.[40]

Another prime reason for the sharp contraction of the active electorate stems from the advent of one-party politics and the resultant drop in party competition throughout large sections of the country during the early twentieth century. Democratic domination of the South began shortly after the Civil War Reconstruction governments were terminated. The election of 1896, one of the most decisive in American history, culminated in the virtual disappearance of the Republican party in the South and in a precipitate drop in Democratic strength in the North.

The smothering effect of a noncompetitive environment on participation can be seen in election turnouts following the realignment of the 1890s. Between 1884 and 1904, for example, turnout in Virginia dropped 57 percent; in Mississippi, 51 percent; and in Louisiana, 50 percent. Part of the explanation for these drop-offs undoubtedly can be associated with the success of southern efforts to disfranchise African Americans, but one-party politics also had a decisive impact on the electorate. In the first place, the drop in participation was too large to be accounted for merely by the disappearance of African American votes. And in the second place, the impact of the new sectionalism was not confined exclusively to the South. Despite their growing populations, some fourteen northern states had smaller turnouts in 1904 than they had in 1896.[41] If the outcome of an election is predictable, voters have scant inducement to invest the time, energy, and other costs that voting requires.

Causes of the Contemporary Decline

The reasons for turnout decline after 1960 are both similar to those of the early twentieth century and also quite different. One analogous development is that a major expansion of the electorate occurred. After 1971, the number of potential voters increased when the voting age was lowered from twenty-one to eighteen. Although nearly half of eighteen-to-twenty year-olds voted in 1972, when the Vietnam War was still raging and a disproportionate number of young people were serving in the military, only 31 percent of this group voted in the 1996 presidential election.[42] Younger voters have, by far, the lowest participation rate of any group in American society. By adding another relatively unparticipatory group, the rate of voter turnout dropped.

In addition, the fact that there are fewer strong partisans today than there were when John F. Kennedy was elected president has contributed to turnout decline. Strong partisans vote at significantly higher rates than do lesser partisans. In 2000 the NES found that 74 percent of partisan leaners, the fastest growing group among the partisan categories, said that they voted, as contrasted with 88 percent of strong partisans. A loss of strong partisans translates into a loss of voters.

Steven Rosenstone and John Mark Hansen identify another party factor in explaining the more recent decline in voter turnout.[43] They demonstrate that more than half of the turnout decline that has occurred since 1960 is due to the diminished efforts of party organizations and social movements to mobilize voters. The parties were once labor-intensive organizations. At election time, party workers would go door to door, contacting other partisans to emphasize the importance of voting and sometimes even offering them rides to the polls (and maybe even a few dollars). The new capital-intensive parties put more stock in television advertising than voter mobilization. Hence they do less face-to-face work in turning out the vote. When parties do contact potential voters, moreover, they usually seek out those from middle- and upper-income brackets. Hence those with the fewest resources, which are also the same people who need party mobilization efforts the most, are least likely to be contacted. As a result, they are increasingly unlikely to vote.

Many people have also become more skeptical of the American political system. One measure of feeling toward the government is a sense of political efficacy. Those individuals who feel that they do not have a say in government are less likely to vote than those who feel that they do. In 1960 only 27 percent of Americans agreed with the statement, "People like me don't have any say about what the government does." By 2000, 45 percent of those providing an answer agreed with the statement.[44] Similarly, only 25 percent of Americans agreed that "public officials don't care about what people like me think" in 1960. By 2000, that percentage had more than doubled to 56 percent.[45]

A central explanation for nonvoting thus lies in the public's attitude toward politics and political institutions. Participation has declined because people believe that their votes will not make much difference and that public officials, not concerned about what they think, are unresponsive. The overall decline in the strength of voters' party identification has also played a role in the decline of electoral participation. Indifference, alienation, and declining party loyalty combine to cut the turnout rate in elections. Frequent elections also discourage turnout, particularly among the peripheral electorate—those people who easily lapse into nonvoting unless party and campaign organizations make a special effort to turn them out.

Recently, some scholars have argued that the decline in turnout since the 1960s is merely a result of the difficulties in measuring the size of the eligible electorate.[46] Although there is some merit to this argument, changes in the demographics of Americans should have brought a sizable increase in turnout. As noted earlier, no other factor is more closely associated with the turnout decision than education, and education levels have increased dramatically over the last forty years. In 1960 the average American had gone to school about nine years. By 2000, that average had increased to more than twelve years.[47] Other things being equal, turnout should have increased dramatically. It is apparent that several of the factors delineated above have offset the effect of increasing education.

The Nation's Response to Declining Voter Turnout

The United States' low voter turnout makes it an outlier among democracies. As Figure 6-9 shows, turnout in other democratic countries averages about 80 percent of the eligible electorate, compared with less than 50 percent in the two most recent American presidential elections. A study by G. Bingham Powell Jr. suggests that voter participation in the United States, as compared to the rest

Figure 6-9   Participation in Elections: Comparing the United States with Twenty-seven Other Nations; Highest Turnout, Any National Election: 1968–1986

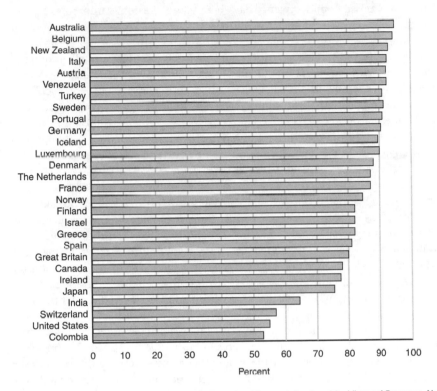

Source: Developed from data generated by the Congressional Research Service of the Library of Congress, November 1987.

of the democratic world, is largely the result of institutional factors such as voluntary registration (as opposed to automatic registration common in other nations), low levels of competition in many electoral districts, and weak linkages between parties and social groups (thus making the parties' task of voter mobilization more difficult). To approach the turnout levels of other democracies, Powell argues, the United States would need to adopt automatic registration laws and change the structure of party competition to mobilize lower-class voters.[48] Obviously, changing registration laws would be easier to accomplish than changing party character and party competition.[49]

However, turnout has continued to decline despite major changes that greatly relaxed registration laws. Poll taxes and literacy tests were eliminated by the Voting Rights Act of 1965. Periodic registration gave way virtually everywhere to permanent registration. As a result of an act passed by Congress in 1970, the residency requirement for federal elections is now limited to a maximum of thirty days before the election; moreover, for other elections, only a handful of states have closing dates earlier than thirty days. In about one third of the states, registration is possible up to twenty days before the election. Minnesota, Maine, Idaho, New Hampshire, and Wisconsin permit voters to register and vote on election day, and North Dakota and Wyoming have no registration laws at all. Although turnout rates in these states in the 2000 election were all among the top eleven with the exception of Idaho,[50] high turnout was generally the case in these states even before they liberalized their voting laws. Of course, such laws do not even ensure that turnout will remain uniformly high. Turnout dropped in Minnesota by five percentage points between 1996 and 2000, for example, even though the state continued to have same-day registration. Although less restrictive laws can enhance turnout, they are by no means magic bullets.

Another effort to expand the ranks of voters occurred in 1993, when Democratic majorities in Congress, with the help of a handful of moderate Republicans in the Senate, adopted the National Voter Registration Act, known popularly as the "motor voter" law. Effective in 1995, the law provides that states must permit citizens eighteen years or older to register to vote when they apply for or renew a driver's license. It also requires states to permit registration by mail and to make available registration forms at state and federal agencies that administer programs dealing with public assistance, disability benefits, and armed forces recruitment. Millions of new voters have been added to the rolls under this new federal statute.

Its effects on turnout and election outcomes, however, have been less than impressive. Most obviously, turnout rates in both 1996 and 2000—the first two elections after the adoption of the motor voter law—were significantly lower than in the election before its passage. In fact, one study shows that class differences in participation were even greater after passage of the law than before.[51] Of course, it is also true that the percentage of registered voters relative to the size of the eligible electorate also increased, so more people *could have* voted had they wished. Moreover, it is impossible to know how many people would have stayed home had it not been for the new law. Turnout might have been even lower than the 48 percent achieved in 1996. Still, it is clear that the motor voter law was not a panacea.[52]

Reforms to increase turnout typically fall short of expectations. While many point to the fact that federal elections occur on Tuesdays rather than on weekends or voting holidays as is the case of Europe, it is not clear that adoption of such rules would make a profound difference. For instance, Texas has lax registration laws by national standards and also allows early voting, where people can cast their ballots between seventeen and four days before election day. Moreover, polling stations are not housed in inconvenient locations. Instead, Texans can vote in places that they might otherwise visit as part of their workaday life, such as the grocery store. Despite the relative ease of voting, not to mention the fact that their governor was a presidential candidate, only 43.1 percent of Texans voted in 2000, ranking the state ahead of only Hawaii and Arizona in turnout.

In short, the liberalization of the country's voting laws has not much affected turnout. As Curtis Gans, director of the Committee for the Study of the American Electorate, notes, the best explanation for declining participation is declining motivation.[53] California may or may not be a special case, but a 1990 poll by the *Los Angeles Times* found that the main reason people in that state fail to vote is that they are too busy doing other things to bother. This reason was given by an extraordinary 35 percent of the respondents.[54] The next most frequent explanation, cited by 8 percent, was a lack of interest in politics. For many citizens, "voting simply isn't worth the effort."[55] Even as parties have increased their efforts at voter mobilization during the last few election cycles, turnout has remained flat. Absent a large crisis or other galvanizing event, it is hard to imagine what would cause American voters to go to the polls in numbers like in Great Britain or Germany.

NOTES

1. Angus Campbell, Philip Converse, Warren Miller, and Donald Stokes, *The American Voter* (New York: Wiley, 1960). The first large-scale academic survey work was done by scholars at Columbia University. These efforts produced *The People's Choice; How the Voter Makes Up His Mind in a Presidential Campaign*, by Paul F. Lazarsfeld, Bernard Berelson, and Hazel Gaudet (New York: Duell, Sloan and Pearce, 1944); and *Voting: A Study of Opinion Formation in a Presidential Campaign*, by Bernard Berelson, Paul F. Lazarsfeld, and William N. McPhee (Chicago: University of Chicago Press, 1954).

2. Berelson, Lazarsfeld, and McPhee, *Voting*.

3. For an excellent recent treatment of the importance of political events, see David O. Sears and Nicholas A. Valentino, "Politics Matters: Political Events as Catalysts for Preadult Socialization," *American Political Science Review* 91 (March 1997): 45–66.

4. M. Kent Jennings and Richard G. Niemi, "The Transmission of Political Values from Parent to Child," *American Political Science Review* 62 (March 1968): 169–184.

5. Charles H. Franklin and John E. Jackson, "The Dynamics of Party Identification," *American Political Science Review* 85 (December 1983): 957–973.

6. Campbell, Converse, Miller, and Stokes, *The American Voter*. Also see Jon Krosnick, "The Stability of Political Preferences: Comparisons of Symbolic and Nonsymbolic Attitudes," *American Journal of Political Science* 35 (August 1991): 547–576.

7. See, for example, Michael X. Delli Carpini and Scott Keeter, *What Americans Know About Politics and Why It Matters* (New Haven: Yale University Press, 1996); and Stephen Earl Bennet, "Americans' Knowledge of Ideology, 1980–1992," *American Politics Quarterly* 69 (September 1995): 476–490.

8. Howard Schuman, Charlotte Steeh, Lawrence Bobo, and Maria Krysan, *Racial Attitudes in America: Trends and Interpretations*, rev. ed. (Cambridge: Harvard University Press, 1997).

9. News release, Gallup Poll, December 6, 2000.

10. Martin P. Wattenberg, *The Decline of American Political Parties* (Cambridge: Harvard University Press, 1988).

11. Bruce Keith et al., *The Myth of the Independent Voter* (Berkeley, Calif.: University of California Press, 1992).

12. For an excellent discussion of the sources of partisan independence, see Steven Greene, "The Psychological Sources of Partisan-Leaning Independence," *American Politics Quarterly* 28 (October 2000): 511–537.

13. See, for instance, Gerald M. Pomper, *The Election of 2000: Reports and Interpretations* (New York: Chatham House Publishers, 2001).

14. VNS does not distinguish between leaning partisans and pure independents. If it did, data from the NES suggests that the Republicans' party loyalty advantage in 2000 would have been even starker. NES data show that 79 percent of leaning Republicans voted for Bush compared with only 72 percent of leaning Democrats voting for Gore.

15. Warren E. Miller, "Party Identification and the Electorate of the 1990s," in *The Parties Respond: Changes in American Parties and Campaigns*, 3d ed., ed. Sandy Maisel.

16. Karen M. Kaufmann and John R. Petrocik, "The Changing Politics of American Men: Understanding the Sources of the Gender Gap," *American Journal of Political Science* 43 (July 1999): 864–887.

17. Also see Warren E. Miller and J. Merrill Shanks, *The New American Voter* (Cambridge: Harvard University Press, 1996).

18. It is also worth noting that not all scholars agree with this explanation. For instance, Margaret C. Trevor argues that pre-adult socialization explains the gender differences. Specifically, she finds that women were much less inclined than men to shed their parents' party identification for the independent label when they were adolescents and young adults. Since most parents of this generation were Democrats, greater loyalty to their parents' party identification explains why women are more likely to be Democrats than men. See Margaret C. Trevor, "Political Socialization, Party Identification, and the Gender Gap," *Public Opinion Quarterly* 63 (spring 1999): 62–89.

19. See the Voter News Service exit poll.

20. See Martin P. Wattenberg, *The Decline of American Political Parties, 1952–1996* (Cambridge: Harvard University Press, 1998).

21. Morris P. Fiorina, *Retrospective Voting in American National Elections* (New Haven: Yale University Press, 1981).

22. This figure originally appeared in Marc J. Hetherington, "Resurgent Mass Partisanship: The Role of Elite Polarization," *American Political Science Review* 95 (September 2001): 619–631.

23. Also see Larry M. Bartels, "Partisanship and Voting Behavior, 1952–1996," *American Journal of Political Science* 44 (January 2000): 35–50.

24. V. O. Key Jr., *The Responsible Electorate: Rationality in Presidential Voting 1936–1960* (Cambridge: Harvard University Press, 1966).

25. See Benjamin I. Page and Robert Shapiro, *The Rational Public* (Chicago: University of Chicago Press, 1992); Richard A. Brody, *Assessing the President: The Media, Elite Opinion, and Public Support* (Stanford, Calif.: Stanford University Press, 1991); and John Zaller, *The Nature and Origins of Mass Opinion* (New York: Cambridge University Press, 1992).

26. See Hetherington, "Resurgent Mass Partisanship" for a detailed analysis.

27. The findings of these paragraphs are drawn from Sidney Verba and Norman H. Nie, *Participation in America: Political Democracy and Social Equality* (New York: Harper and Row, 1972), 25–43.

28. Lester W. Milbrath, *Political Participation* (Chicago: Rand McNally, 1965), 17–21. The holding that political participation involves a hierarchy of political acts—under which the citizen who performs a difficult political act, such as forming an organization to solve a local community problem, is virtually certain to perform less demanding acts—can be overstated. See Verba and Nie, *Participation in America*, especially chapters 2 and 3. Their general position is that "the citizenry is not divided simply into more or less active citizens. Rather there are many types of activists engaging in different acts, with different motives, and different consequences." Quotation on page 45.

29. Cumulative File, American National Election Study, 1948–2000.

30. Although the turnout of the highest-income group exceeds that of the lowest-income group by about twenty percentage points in the typical presidential election, there has been little change in socioeconomic class bias in the electorate since 1964. The only exception was in 1988 (Bush versus Dukakis), when class bias in turnout did increase. See Jan E. Leighley and Jonathan Nagler, "Socioeconomic Class Bias in Turnout, 1964–1988: The Voters Remain the Same," *American Political Science Review* 86 (September 1992): 725–736.

31. See Verba and Nie, *Participation in America*, 133–137.

32. See Jan E. Leighley and Jonathan Nagler, "Individual and Systemic Influences on Turnout: Who Votes? 1984," *Journal of Politics* 54 (August 1992): 718–740.

33. Robert A. Jackson, "Clarifying the Relationship between Education and Turnout," *American Politics Quarterly* 23 (July 1995): 279–299.

34. In information-poor environments, such as House elections, voters tend to rely on prior beliefs concerning the closeness of elections in making their decisions on whether to vote. Stephen P. Nicholson and Ross A. Miller, "Prior Beliefs and Voter Turnout in the 1986 and 1988 Congressional Elections," *Political Research Quarterly* 50 (March 1997): 199–213.

35. Mellman Group and Wirthlin Worldwide, *Analysis of a Survey on Nonvoting* (Washington, D.C.: League of Women Voters, 1996), 25.

36. See a study by David Moon that finds that voters with high levels of information are more likely to rely on issues in deciding how to vote than voters who have moderate or low levels of information. "What You Use Still Depends on What You Have: Information Effects in Presidential Elections, 1972–1988," *American Politics Quarterly* 20 (October 1992): 427–441.

37. Kim Quaile Hill and Jan E. Leighley, "The Policy Consequences of Class Bias in State Electorates," *American Journal of Political Science* 36 (May 1992): 351–365.

38. Steven Rosenstone and John Mark Hansen, *Mobilization, Participation, and Democracy in America* (New York: Macmillan, 1993).

39. The white primary in southern states resulted from the exclusion of African Americans from membership in the Democratic party, which was held to be a private organization. Because the real election at this time in most southern states occurred in the Democratic primaries, African Americans had little opportunity to make their influence felt. After many years of litigation, the Supreme Court in 1944 held that the white primary was in violation of the Fifteenth Amendment. The Court's position in *Smith v. Allwright* was that the primary is an integral part of the election process and that political parties are engaged in a public, not a private, function in holding primary elections. After the white primary was held unconstitutional, southern states turned to the development of literacy and understanding tests, along with discriminatory registration systems, to bar black access to the polls.

40. Michael X. Delli Carpini and Scott Keeter, *What Americans Know About Politics and Why It Matters* (New Haven: Yale University Press, 1996); Sidney Verba, Kay Lehman Schlozman, and Henry E. Brady, *Voice and Equality: Civic Voluntarism in American Politics* (Cambridge: Harvard University Press, 1995).

41. E. E. Schattschneider, *The Semisovereign People* (New York: Holt, Rinehart and Winston, 1975), 84.

42. The Federal Election Commission archives these turnout data. This information can be found on its website: www.fec.gov.

43. Rosenstone and Hansen, *Mobilization, Participation, and Democracy in America*.

44. These data are taken from the American National Election Study's Cumulative File, 1948–2000. The percentage was even higher in the mid-1990s.

45. Ibid.

46. Michael P. McDonald and Samuel L. Popkin, "The Myth of the Vanishing Voter," *American Political Science Review* 95 (December 2001): 963–975.

47. See Robert D. Putnam, *Bowling Alone, The Collapse and Revival of American Community* (New York: Simon and Schuster, 2000).

48. G. Bingham Powell Jr., "American Voter Turnout in Comparative Perspective," *American Political Science Review* 80 (March 1986): 17–43.

49. Why do close elections increase turnout? One explanation is that ordinary citizens are more likely to participate in close elections because they believe their vote will make a difference. A second possibility is that turnout increases because the closeness of any election prompts elites (candidates and their financial supporters) to focus on getting voters to the polls (thus stimulating campaign expenditures). A study by Gary W. Cox and Michael C. Munger finds that closeness of elections affects behavior at both mass and elite levels. "Closeness, Expenditures, and Turnout in the 1982 U.S. Elections," *American Political Science Review* 83 (March 1989): 217–231. Also see Kenneth D. Wald, "The Closeness-Turnout Hypothesis: A Reconsideration," *American Politics Quarterly* 13 (July 1985): 273–296. Along the same line, Priscilla L. Southwell finds that shifts in economic performance can have a mobilizing effect on turnout, particularly among less privileged individuals and groups, in "Economic Salience and Differential Abstention in Presidential Elections," *American Politics Quarterly* 24 (April 1996): 221–236.

50. Mark J. Fenster, "The Impact of Allowing Day of Registration Voting on Turnout in U.S. Elections from 1960 to 1992," *American Politics Quarterly* 22 (January 1994): 74–87. Fenster estimated that if all states permitted day-of-registration voting, turnout would increase by 5 percent.

51. Michael D. Martinez and David Hill, "Did Moter Voter Work?" *American Politics Quarterly* 27 (July 1999): 296–315.

52. Also see Benjamin Highton, "Easy Registration and Turnout," *Journal of Politics* 59 (May 1997): 565–575. Highton argues that motor voter will have a marginal effect on turnout.

53. Curtis B. Gans, "A Rejoinder to Piven and Cloward," *PS* 23 (June 1990): 176–178.

54. *Pittsburgh Press,* July 9, 1990.

55. Richard A. Brody, "The Puzzle of Political Participation in America," in *The New American Political System,* ed. Anthony King (Washington, D.C.: American Enterprise Institute for Public Policy Research, 1978), 306.

7 THE AMERICAN PARTY SYSTEM: PROBLEMS AND PERSPECTIVES

EXTOLLING THE VIRTUES OF THE AMERICAN PARTY system is something of an anomaly in popular commentary and scholarship. A few scholars have found merit in the party system, particularly in its contributions to unifying the nation, fostering political stability, reconciling social conflict, aggregating interests, and institutionalizing popular control of government. But the broad thrust in evaluations of this basic political institution has been heavily critical. American parties, various authors contend, are too much alike in their programs to afford voters a meaningful choice, are dominated by special interests, are unable to deal imaginatively with public problems, are beset by a confusion of purposes, are ineffective because of their internal divisions, are short on discipline and cohesion, are insufficiently responsive to popular claims and aspirations, and are deficient as instruments for assuming and achieving responsibility in government.

The Doctrine of Responsible Parties

The major ground for popular distress over the parties may be simply that most Americans are in some measure suspicious of politicians and their organizations. The criticism of scholars, meanwhile, has focused mainly on the lack of party responsibility in government. The most comprehensive statement on behalf of the doctrine of party responsibility is found in a report by the Committee on Political Parties of the American Political Science Association (APSA), *Toward a More Responsible Two-Party System*, published in 1950. This classic document in political science argues that what is required is a party system that is "democratic, responsible, and effective." In the words of the committee:

> Party responsibility means the responsibility of both parties to the general public, as enforced in elections. Party responsibility to the public, enforced in elections, implies that there be more than one party, for the public can hold a party responsible only if it has a choice. . . . When the parties lack the capacity to define their actions in terms of policies, they turn irresponsible because the electoral choice between the parties becomes devoid of meaning. . . . An effective party system requires, first, that the parties are able to bring forth programs to which they commit themselves and, second, that the parties possess sufficient internal cohesion to carry out these programs.[1]

Two major presumptions underlie the doctrine of responsible parties. The first is that the essence of democracy is to be found in popular control over government rather than in popular participation in the immediate tasks of government. A nation such as the United States is far too large and its government too complex for most citizens to become actively involved in its decision-making processes. But this fact does not rule out popular control over government. The direction of government can be controlled by the people only as long as they are consulted on public matters and possess the power to replace one set of rulers with another—the "opposition." The party, in this view, becomes the instrument through which the public—or, more precisely, a majority of the public—can decide who will run the government and for what purposes. Government by responsible parties is thus an expression of majority rule.

The second tenet in this theory holds that popular control over government requires that the public be given a choice between competing, unified parties capable of assuming collective responsibility to the public for the actions of government. A responsible party system would make three contributions. One, it "would enable the people to choose effectively a general program, a general direction for government to take, as embodied in a set of leaders committed to that program." Two, it would help to "energize and activate" public opinion. Three, it would increase the prospects for popular control by substituting the collective responsibility of an organized group, the party, for the individual responsibility assumed, more or less adequately, by individual officeholders.[2]

The responsible parties model proposed by the Committee on Political Parties is worth examining because it presents a sharp contrast to the contemporary party system. Disciplined and programmatic parties, offering clearer choices to voters, would replace the loose and inchoate institutions to which Americans have become accustomed. The committee's report deals with national party organizations, party platforms, congressional party organization, intraparty democracy, and nominations and elections.

National Party Organizations

The national party organizations envisioned by the committee would be very different from those existing today. The national convention, for example, would be composed of not more than five hundred or six hundred members, more than half of whom would be elected by party voters. Ex officio members drawn from the ranks of the national committee, state party chairs, and congressional leaders, along with certain prominent party leaders outside the party organizations, would make up the balance of the convention membership. Instead of meeting every four years, the convention would assemble regularly at least once every two years and perhaps in special meetings. Reduced in size, more representative of the actual strength of the party in individual states, and meeting more frequently and for longer periods, the new convention would gain effectiveness as a deliberative body for the development of party policy and as a more representative assembly for reconciling the interests of various elements within the party.

The most far reaching proposal for restructuring national party organization involves the creation of a party council of perhaps fifty members, composed of representatives from such units as the national committee, the congressional parties, the state committees, and the party's governors. Meeting regularly and often, the party council would examine problems of party management, prepare a preliminary draft of the party platform for submission to the national convention, interpret the platform adopted by the convention, screen and recommend candidates for congressional offices, consider possible presidential candidates, and advise such appropriate party organs as the national convention or national committee "with respect to conspicuous departures from general party decisions by state or local party organizations." Empowered in this fashion, the party council would represent a firm break with familiar and conventional arrangements that contribute to the dispersion of party authority and the elusiveness of party policy. The essence of the council's task would be to blend the interests of national, congressional, and state organizations to foster the development of an authentic national party, one capable of fashioning and implementing coherent strategies and policies.

Party Platforms

Party platforms, the report holds, are deficient on a number of counts. At times the platform "may be intentionally written in an ambiguous manner so as to attract voters of any persuasion and to offend as few voters as possible." State party platforms frequently espouse principles and policies in conflict with those of the national party. Congressional candidates and members of Congress may feel little obligation to support platform planks. No agency exists to interpret and apply the platform in the years between conventions. There is substantial confusion and difference of opinion over the binding quality of a platform—that is, whether party candidates are bound to observe the commitments presumably made in the adoption of the platform.

To put new life back into the party platform, the report recommends that it should be written every two years to take account of developing issues and to link it to congressional campaigns in off-year elections; that it should "emphasize general party principles and national issues" that "should be regarded as binding commitments on all candidates and officeholders of the party, national, state and local"; that state and local platforms "should be expected to conform to the national platform on matters of general party principle or on national policies"; and that the party council should take an active role in the platform-making process, both in preparing tentative drafts of the document in advance of the convention and in interpreting and applying the platform between conventions. In sum, the report argues that present party platforms and the processes through which they are formulated and implemented are inimical to the development of strong and responsible parties.

Congressional Party Organization

One of the most vexing problems in the effort to develop more responsible parties has been the performance of the congressional parties. The proliferation of leadership committees in Congress, the weakness of the caucus (or conference), the independence of congressional committees, and the seniority system have combined to limit possibilities for the parties to develop consistent and coherent legislative records. To tighten up congressional party organization would require a number of changes. First, each party in both the Senate and the House should consolidate its various leadership groups (for example, policy committees, committees on committees, and House Rules Committee) into a single leadership group; its functions would be to manage legislative party affairs, submit policy proposals to the membership, draw up slates of committee assignments, and assume responsibility for scheduling legislation.

Second, the party caucuses should hold more frequent meetings, their decisions to be binding on legislation involving the party's principles and programs. Moreover, members of Congress who ignore a caucus decision "should not expect to receive the same consideration in the assignment of committee posts or in the apportionment of patronage as those who have been loyal to party principles." In other words, leaders would routinely punish the rank and file for failing to support the party's program.

Third, the seniority system should be made to work in harmony with the party's responsibility for a legislative program. The report states:

> The problem is not one of abolishing seniority and then finding an alternative. It is one of mobilizing the power through which the party leadership can successfully use the seniority principle rather than have the seniority principle dominate Congress. . . . Advancement within a committee on the basis of seniority makes sense, other things being equal. But it is not playing the game fairly for party members who oppose the commitments in their party's platform to rely on seniority to carry them into committee chairmanships. Party leaders have compelling reason to prevent such a member from becoming chairman—and they are entirely free so to exert their influence.

Fourth, the assignment of members of Congress to committees should be a responsibility of the party leadership committees: "Personal competence and party loyalty should be valued more highly than seniority in assigning members to such major committees as those dealing with fiscal policy and foreign affairs." At the same time, the party caucus should review committee assignments at intervals of no more than two years. A greater measure of party control over committee assignments is essential if the party is to assume responsibility for a legislative program.

Fifth, party leaders should take over the function of scheduling legislation for floor consideration. In particular, the power of the House Rules Committee over legislative scheduling should be vested in the party leadership committee. If the party cannot control the flow of legislation to the floor and shape the agenda, there is little chance that it can control legislative output, which is the essence of responsible party performance in Congress.

Intraparty Democracy

The achievement of a system of responsible parties demands more than the good intentions of the public and of party leaders. It requires widespread and meaningful political participation by grassroots members of the party, democratic party processes, and an accountable leadership. According to the report:

> Capacity for internal agreement, democratically arrived at, is a critical test for a party. It is a critical test because when there is no such capacity, there is no capacity for positive action, and hence the party becomes a hollow pretense. It is a test which can be met only if the party machinery affords the membership an opportunity to set the course of the party and to control those who speak for it. The test can be met fully only where the membership accepts responsibility for creative participation in shaping the party's program.

The task of developing an active party membership capable of creative participation in the affairs of the party is not easy. Organizational changes at both the summit and the base of the party hierarchy are required: "A national convention, broadly and directly representative of the rank and file of the party and meeting at least biennially, is essential to promote a sense of identity with the party throughout the membership as well as to settle internal differences fairly, harmoniously, and democratically." Similarly, at the grassroots level, local party groups need to be developed that will meet frequently to generate and discuss ideas concerning national issues and the national party program. The emergence and development of local, issue-oriented party groups can be facilitated by national party agencies engaged in education and publicity and willing to undertake the function of disseminating information and research findings.

A new concept of party membership is required—one that emphasizes "allegiance to a common program" rather than mere support of party candidates in elections. In accordance with the concept of party advanced in the opening chapter, such an emphasis would track more closely with ideological rather than electoral definitions. Its development might take this form:

> The existence of a national program, drafted at frequent intervals by a party convention both broadly representative and enjoying prestige, should make a great dif-

ference. It would prompt those who identify themselves as Republicans and Democrats to think in terms of support of that program, rather than in terms of personalities, patronage, and local matters. . . . Once machinery is established which gives the party member and his representative a share in framing the party's objectives, once there are safeguards against internal dictation by a few in positions of influence, members and representatives will feel readier to assume an obligation to support the program. Membership defined in these terms does not ask for mindless discipline enforced from above. It generates the self-discipline which stems from free identification with aims one helps to define.

Nominations and Elections

The report's recommendations for changing nomination and election procedures fit comfortably within its overall political formula for strengthening the American party system. It endorses the direct primary—"a useful weapon in the arsenal of intraparty democracy"—while expressing preference for the closed rather than the open version. The open primary is incompatible with the idea of a responsible party system, because permitting voters to shift from one party to the other between primaries subverts the concept of membership as the foundation of party organization. Preprimary meetings of party committees should be held for the purpose of proposing and endorsing candidates in primary elections. Delegates to the national conventions should be selected by the direct vote of party members instead of by state conventions. Local party groups should meet prior to the convention to discuss potential candidates and platform planks.

Three major changes should be made in the election system. First, the electoral college should be changed to give "all sections of the country a real voice in electing the president and the vice-president" and to help develop a two-party system in areas now dominated by one party. Second, the term of members of the House of Representatives should be extended from two to four years, with coinciding election of House members and the president. If this constitutional change were made, prospects would be improved for harmonizing executive and legislative power through the party. Third, the report recommends a variety of changes in the regulation of campaign finance, the most important of which calls for a measure of public financing of election campaigns.

The Promise of Responsible Parties

In the broadest sense, the publication of *Toward a More Responsible Two-Party System* was an outgrowth of increased uneasiness among many political scientists over the performance of the nation's party system and the vitality of American government. Specifically, the report sought to deal with a problem that is central to the overall political system: the weakness of political parties as instruments for governing in a democratic and responsible fashion. The report is not a study in political feasibility. It does not offer a blueprint depicting where the best opportunities lie for making changes in the party system. What it does offer is a set of wide-ranging prescriptions consonant with a particular model of political organization. If the model sketched by the committee were to come into existence, the

American party system would bear only modest resemblance to that which has survived for well over a century. The key characteristics of the new parties would be the national quality of their organization, a much greater degree of centralization of party power, a tendency for party claims to assume primacy over individual constituency claims in public policy formation, heightened visibility of the congressional parties and their leadership and of the president as party leader, and a greater concern over party unity and discipline.

To its credit, the report was not accompanied by the usual somnolence that settles over prescriptive efforts of this kind. Nor, however, did queues of reformers form in the streets, in the universities, or elsewhere to push for its implementation. What occurred instead was that it gave substantial impetus to the study of American political parties and helped to foster a concern for reform that, in one respect or another, continues to the present.

The goal of advocates of party responsibility is to place the parties at the creative center of policy making in the United States. That is what party responsibility is all about. Voters would choose between two disciplined and cohesive parties, each distinguished by relatively clear and consistent programs and policy orientations. Responsibility would be enforced through elections. Parties would be retained or removed from power depending on their performance and the attractiveness of their programs. Collective responsibility for the conduct of government would displace the individual responsibility of officeholders. Such are the key characteristics of the model party system.

How well responsible parties would mesh with the American political system is another matter.[3] Critics have contended that disciplined parties might contribute to an erosion of consensus, to heightened conflict between social classes, to the formation of splinter parties (and perhaps to a full-blown multiple-party system), and to the breakdown of federalism. Moreover, the voting behavior and attitudes of the American people would have to change markedly to accommodate the model of centralized parties, because many voters are more oriented to candidates than they are to parties or issues. The indifference of the public to the idea of programmatic parties would appear to be a major obstacle to rationalizing the party system along the lines of the responsible parties model.

Responsible Parties and Party Reform

The reform wave of the past three decades has produced a number of organizational and procedural changes in the American party system and in Congress. Perhaps as much by accident as by design, a surprising number of these changes are largely or fully compatible with the recommendations of the APSA report.

Intraparty Democracy

Consider the steps that have been taken to foster intraparty democracy. No feature of the reform movement of the Democratic party, beginning with the guidelines of the Commission on Party Structure and Delegate Selection (the

McGovern-Fraser Commission), stands out more sharply than the commitment to make the party internally democratic and more responsive to its grassroots elements.

Commenting on the overall process by which delegates were selected to the 1968 convention, the McGovern-Fraser Commission[4] observed that "meaningful participation of Democratic voters in the choice of their presidential nominee was often difficult or costly, sometimes completely illusory, and, in not a few instances, impossible." For example, the commission found that:

1. in nearly half the states, rules governing the selection process were either nonexistent or inadequate, "leaving the entire process to the discretion of a handful of party leaders";
2. more than one third of the convention delegates had, in effect, been chosen prior to 1968—well before all the possible presidential candidates were known and before President Lyndon Johnson had withdrawn from the race;
3. "the imposition of the unit rule from the first to the final stage of the nominating process, the enforcement of binding instructions on delegates, and favorite-son candidacies were all devices used to force Democrats to vote against their stated presidential preferences";
4. in primary, convention, and committee delegate selection systems, "majorities used their numerical superiority to deny delegate representation to the supporters of minority presidential candidates";
5. procedural irregularities, such as secret caucuses, closed slate making, and proxy voting, were common in party conventions from the precinct to the state level;
6. the costs of participating in the delegate selection process, such as filing fees for entering primaries, were often excessive; and
7. certain population groups—in particular African Americans, women, and youth—were substantially underrepresented among the delegates.

To eliminate these practices and conditions, the commission adopted a series of guidelines to regulate the selection of delegates for future conventions. Designed to permit all Democratic voters a "full, meaningful, and timely" opportunity to take part in the presidential nominating process, the guidelines set forth an extensive array of reforms to be implemented by state parties.

The initial step required of state Democratic parties was the adoption of a comprehensive set of rules governing the delegate selection process to which all rank-and-file Democrats would have access. Not only were these rules to make clear how all party members could participate in the process but they were also to be designed to facilitate their "maximum participation." In addition, certain procedural safeguards were specified. Proxy voting and the use of the unit rule were outlawed. Party committee meetings held for the purpose of selecting convention delegates were required to establish a quorum of no fewer than 40 percent of the members. Mandatory assessments of convention delegates were prohibited. Adequate public notice of all party meetings called to consider delegate selection was required, as were rules to provide for uniform times and dates of meetings.

The commission enjoined state parties to seek a broad base of support. Standards eliminating all forms of discrimination against minority group members in the delegate selection process were required. To overcome the effects of past discrimination, moreover, each state was expected to include in its delegation African Americans, women, and young people in numbers roughly proportionate to their presence in the state population.

The commission adopted a number of specific requirements for delegate selection. For example, delegates must be selected in a "timely manner" (within the calendar year in which the convention is held), alternates must be selected in the same manner as delegates, delegates must be apportioned within the state on the basis of a formula that gives equal weight to population and to Democratic strength, and at least 75 percent of the delegates must be selected at the congressional district level or lower (in states using the convention system). The number of delegates to be selected by a party state committee was limited to 10 percent of the total delegation.

One of the most remarkable aspects of this unprecedented action by the national party was the response of the state parties. They accepted the guidelines, altered or abandoned a variety of age-old practices and state laws, and selected their delegations through procedures more open than anyone thought possible. And with "maximum participation" in mind, they produced a convention whose composition—with its emphasis on demographic representation—was vastly different from any previous one.[5] Whether for good or ill, the Democratic party had by 1972 accepted the main tenets of intraparty democracy.[6]

No evidence exists, however, that party democratization has contributed to the development of a more responsible party system. Indeed, the reverse is probably true: the greater the degree of intraparty democracy, the harder it is to develop a coherent program of party policy.[7]

Strengthening the Congressional Parties

Reform, like conflict, is contagious. Essentially the same forces that produced major changes in the electoral structure of the Democratic party have produced major changes in the Democratic congressional party, particularly in the House. The thrust of these changes is in line with the theory of responsible parties. Advocates of this theory have sought not so much to promote the formation of a new party structure in Congress as to breathe new life into existing party structures and procedures. The changes have been impressive. Long dormant, the Democratic caucus became a more influential force in the House, particularly in controlling committee assignments and in shaping rules and procedures. At the opening of the Ninety-fourth Congress (1975–1976), the caucus removed three committee chairs from their positions, increased party control over the committee assignment process, brought the Rules Committee more firmly under the leadership of the Speaker of the House, and established a requirement that the chairs of the appropriations subcommittees be ratified by the caucus. These were not stylized or marginal alterations. They should be seen for what they were: as systematically conceived efforts to reshape the power structure of Congress by diminishing the influence of senior leaders—who had often been out of step with a majority of the party—and augmenting the power of the party caucus and the leadership. There were other demonstrations of caucus power in the 1980s. At the outset of the Ninety-eighth Congress (1983–1984), the Democratic caucus voted to remove a southern party member from the Budget Committee because he had played a key role in fashioning President Ronald Reagan's budget strategy in the preceding Congress. Although party disciplinary action is not often taken, it can occur if the provocation is severe.

Similar developments have occurred in the Republican party. Supported by a cohesive party in the 104th Congress (1995–1996), Speaker Newt Gingrich ignored seniority in the selection of several committee chairs; named new members to the party's committee on committees, thus centralizing party control over assignments; directed an overhaul of the committee system that cut committee staffs and eliminated three standing committees; altered a variety of House procedures; and moved a "Contract with America" policy agenda through the House in the first one hundred days of the session. This interlude of responsible party government fell victim to the hubris of Republican leaders who shut down the government while trying to force President Bill Clinton to accept their 1995 budget. With much of the public blaming their party for the debacle, and made anxious by an approaching election, many House Republicans abandoned the Speaker, sought accommodation with the president on a variety of policy fronts, forgot about the "contract," and focused on constituency business. As inevitable as anything in American legislative politics, leader-centered party government gave way to individual member preferences, including self-preservation.

Organization, Platforms, Nominations, and Elections

The APSA report on responsible parties anticipated a potpourri of other recent reforms. Among them were the reassertion of the national convention's authority over the national committee, the selection of convention delegates by direct vote of the rank and file, the allocation of national committee members on the basis of the actual strength of the party within the areas they represent, the use of closed primaries for the selection of convention delegates, the public financing of presidential elections, and the provision for holding a national party conference between national conventions.[8]

In sum, many of the reforms that have been introduced in the party structure and in Congress are consistent with recommendations carried in *Toward a More Responsible Two-Party System*. They touch far more than the outer edges of the party and congressional systems. Nevertheless, there is no reason to suppose that responsible party government is around the corner—that these reforms will somehow result in the institutionalization of a durable, highly centralized, and disciplined party system. Traditional moorings throughout the political environment make change of this magnitude all but impossible. And the current trends in American politics have done more to disable the parties than to strengthen them.

Trends in American Politics

Office holding in the United States is dominated by the two major parties. The vast majority of aspirants for public office carry on their campaigns under the banner of either one or the other. So decisive is party affiliation for election outcomes, the most important fact to be known about the candidates in a great many electoral jurisdictions throughout the country is the party to which they belong. Virtually everywhere, save in nonpartisan environments, the trappings of party—symbols, sponsorship, slogans, buttons, and literature—are in evidence. The parties and their candidates collect money, spend money, and incur campaign deficits on a scale that dwarfs their budgets of a generation ago. Party bureaucracies are larger than in the past. More than two out of three citizens continue to see themselves as Democrats or Republicans, however imperfectly they may comprehend their party's program or the performance of its representatives. Party-based voting decisions are common in numerous jurisdictions.

Major problems nevertheless confront the party system. Moreover, many of the key trends over the last thirty years have put the parties on the defensive. And though the parties have responded well to many of these challenges, it is unlikely that they will regain the prominence that they enjoyed generations ago.

The Loss of Power by Electoral Party Organizations and Their Adjustments

At virtually every point in the recruitment and election of public officials, the party organizations have suffered an erosion of power. The reasons are many and varied. At the top of the list, perhaps, is the direct primary. "He who can make the nominations is the owner of the party," E. E. Schattschneider wrote some years ago, and there is no reason to doubt his observation.[9] Given that nonendorsed candidates may defeat party nominees in primaries, one may wonder whether, in some elections and in some jurisdictions, anyone except the candidates really owns the parties. The party label has lost significance as candidates of all political colorations, with all variety of relationships to the organization, earn the right to wear it by capturing primary elections. Most important, a party that cannot control its nominations finds it difficult to achieve unity once it has won office and is faced with the implementation of its platform. Candidates who defeat the organization may see little reason to subscribe to party tenets, defend party interests, or follow party leaders. Not only does the primary contribute to the fragmentation of party unity in office but it also divides the party at large.

> Primaries often pit party leaders against party leaders, party voters against party voters, often opening deep and unhealing party wounds. They also dissipate party

financial and personal resources. Party leadership usually finds that it has no choice but to take sides in a primary battle, the alternative being the possible triumph of the weaker candidate.[10]

An observer viewing the changes in the nomination process in the early 1980s would have noted that the situation was most dire for parties on the presidential level. Compared with the party boss system in place before the McGovern-Fraser reforms, the proliferation of primaries and the opening up of caucuses introduced a participatory system that undermined the role of party leaders and organizations in the presidential nominating process. The typical national convention became a party conclave in name only. As Byron Shafer observed, the Democratic reforms "restricted, and often removed, the regular party from the mechanics of presidential selection."[11] Worse yet, the Democratic party, which had done the most to democratize the nomination process, consistently chose sub-optimal candidates. Both George McGovern in 1972 and Walter Mondale in 1984 were swept away in landslides, and Jimmy Carter barely defeated Gerald Ford in 1976, despite Ford's extremely unpopular pardon of Richard Nixon. Of these three candidates, it is likely that only Mondale would have received the nomination under the traditional leader-dominated system.

With the perspective afforded by thirty years of experience with McGovern-Fraser, however, it is clear that the parties have adjusted well to their new environment, at least at the presidential level. Although bosses no longer meet in smoke-filled rooms to decide their party's nominee, the present system provides results that are close to those that the old system very likely would have produced. Today, once party leaders agree on the most electable candidate, they publicly endorse him in advance of the primary season. These endorsements, in turn, markedly increase public support for the candidate.[12] As pre-primary support increases, so too does the candidate's fund-raising power, which, in turn, makes him a more formidable candidate. Although party leadership support does not ensure a candidate's nomination, the track record since 1980 has been remarkable. McGovern's nomination in 1972 and Carter's in 1976 were generally unexpected, but there have been no such surprises since then. The front-runner for the nomination in the months leading up to the first caucuses and primaries has been a consistent winner over the last five presidential elections.[13] Even though both voters and the press may become enchanted with candidates during the primary season, as was the case with John McCain in 2000, ultimately the party's choice—George W. Bush—wins out.

This is not to suggest that parties today wield the same type of power that they did in the early part of the century. They do not. The great urban machines of generations past have practically disappeared. Employing an intricate system of rewards and incentives, the machines dominated the political process—controlling access to power, political careers, and, most important, votes. Their decline, for a number of reasons, has been accompanied by growing independence within the electorate and among politicians. Moreover, electoral party organization is not an integral part of the political lives of today's self-reliant candidates. Some members of Congress, for example, have created their own political action committees (PACs) for electoral purposes. Virtually all of them not only campaign continuously, using all the resources of their office, but they also have their own campaign operations, including staff aides assigned to the district, and reelection treasuries. John McCartney quotes a field representative of a California member of Congress:

> I'm never through campaigning—except for one evening every two years. Election night there's no campaign. We have a victory party, I drink a lot of champagne, and I go home and go to bed. Next morning I begin campaigning all over again.[14]

Candidate-centeredness is particularly evident below the presidential level. Ambitious, issue oriented, and media conscious, the "new model" members of Congress exploit their office resources to the hilt in gaining publicity, advertising their names, and strengthening their reelection base. Some years before he became Speaker, Thomas S. Foley (D-Wash.) commented on the new style of politician in Congress: "At worst, these guys say in effect, 'It doesn't matter. I am my own party,' [and] they emphasize their personal qualities."[15]

While the classic functions of party involve recruitment, nomination, and campaigning,[16] today's parties no longer dominate any of these activities. American politics in the media age is thoroughly candidate centered. For most offices, major and minor, candidates most of the time are on their own in making the decisions that count. No party organization or leadership tells them when to run, how to run, what to believe, what to say, or (once in office) how to vote.

Candidates may tolerate party nudging on some matters while they welcome party money, technical assistance, and services—resources that have become more available with the proliferation of soft money. But it is unmistakably the candidates who decide what to make of their party membership and party connections both in and out of government. And no one, including party leaders and party committees, can do much about it. In jurisdictions where American parties have more than ordinary importance, they are essentially facilitators, helping candidates who wear their label to do better what generally they would do in any case.

The Growing Importance of Professional Campaign Management Firms and the Media in Politics

American party organizations no longer dominate the process of winning political support for the candidates who run under their labels. The role of party organizations in campaigns has declined as professional management firms, pollsters, and media specialists—stirred by the prospects of new accounts and greater profits—have arrived on the political scene. To be sure, the parties continue to raise and spend money, to staff their headquarters with salaried personnel and volunteers, and to seek to turn out the vote on election day. And in a handful of targeted races each year, their presence can be quite strong. What they do matters, but much less so than it did in the past.

The center of major political campaigns now lies in the decisions and activities of individual candidates and in their use of consultants, campaign management firms, and the mass media—not in the party organizations or in the decisions of party leaders, except insofar as they recommend political consultants. Modern political campaigning calls for resources and skills that the parties can furnish only in part. Public opinion surveys are needed to pinpoint important issues, to locate sources of support and opposition, and to learn how voters appraise the qualities of the candidate. Electronic data processing is useful in the analysis of voting behavior and for the simulation of campaign decisions. For a fee, candidates with sufficient financial resources can avail themselves of specialists of all kinds: in public relations, advertising, fund-raising, communications, and financial counseling. They can hire experts in filmmaking, speechwriting, speech coaching, voter registration, direct-mail letter campaigning, computer information services, time buying (for radio and television), voter analysis, get-out-the-vote drives, campaign strategy, and "spinning" (interpreting) events and voter behavior. Fewer and fewer things are left to chance or to the vicissitudes of party administration. What a candidate hears, says, does, wears, and even thinks bears the heavy imprint of the specialist in campaign management.

Campaign consulting is a lucrative industry. Top guns can make upwards of $1 million a year in consulting fees alone. A recent American University study suggests that over 20 percent of consultants make more than $200,000 a year.[17] In addition, practitioners have become bona fide celebrities. James Carville and Paul Begala, the Democratic consultants who engineered Bill Clinton's 1992 victory, have both authored best-selling books, and they also appear regularly on national news programs. In fact, Carville and Begala serve as the liberal voice on CNN's political talk show *Crossfire*. In general, consultants whose candidates upset a favored opponent or win an overwhelming victory are celebrated by politicians and the media alike. They are hot commodities, and candidates vie to purchase their services. The right consultant often appears to be the key to victory.

The coming of age of the mass media, technocracy, and the techniques of mass persuasion has had a marked impact on the political system.[18] The new politics is dominated by image makers and technical experts—organizations and individuals who know what people want in their candidates and how to give it to them. Consider these views and prognoses for an issueless pseudopolitics:

> It is not surprising . . . that politicians and advertising men should have discovered one another. And, once they recognized that the citizen did not so much vote for a candidate as make a psychological purchase of him, not surprising that they began to work together. . . . Advertising agencies have tried openly to sell Presidents since 1952. When Dwight Eisenhower ran for reelection in 1956, the agency of Batton, Barton, Durstine and Osborn, which had been on a retainer throughout his first four years, accepted his campaign as a regular account. Leonard Hall, the national Republican chairman, said: "You sell your candidates and your programs the way a business sells its products."[19]

Day-by-day campaign reports spin on through regular newscasts and special reports. The candidates make their progress through engineered crowds, taking part in manufactured pseudo events, thrusting and parrying charges, projecting as much as they can, with the help of makeup and technology, the qualities of youth, experience, sincerity, popularity, alertness, wisdom, and vigor. And television follows them, hungry for material that is new and sensational. The new campaign strategists also generate films that are like syrupy documentaries: special profiles of candidates, homey, bathed in soft light, resonant with stirring music, creating personality images such as few mortals could emulate.[20]

In all countries the party system has folded like the organization chart. Policies and issues are useless for election purposes, since they are too specialized and hot. The shaping of a candidate's integral image has taken the place of discussing conflicting points of view.[21]

[Party] organizations find themselves increasingly dependent on management and consultant personnel, pollsters, and image-makers. The professional campaigners, instead of being the handmaidens of our major political parties, are independent factors in American elections. Parties turn to professional technicians for advice on how to restructure their organizations, for information about their clienteles, for fund-raising, and for recruiting new members. Candidates, winning nominations in primaries with the aid of professional campaigners rather than that of political parties, are increasingly independent of partisan controls. The old politics does not rest well beside the new technology.[22]

If we get the visual that we want, it doesn't matter as much what words the networks use in commenting on it.[23]

If you're not on television, you don't exist.[24]

No matter what happens, the national political parties of the future will no longer be the same as in the past. Television has made the voter's home the campaign amphitheater, and opinion surveys have made it his polling booth. From this perspective, he has little regard for or need of a political party, at least as we have known it, to show him how to release the lever on Election Day.[25]

The heightened importance of campaign professionals, and the partial eclipse of party, carries important normative implications. Voters can hold parties at least somewhat accountable for their actions in office. If a party adopts a policy that voters do not like, it can be punished in the next election. Consultants cannot be held similarly accountable. Once they help elect a candidate, their job is done. They do not become part of the government. Their calculations, therefore, are more likely to be based on electoral considerations than on those involving governance.

Rarely has this dichotomy been more evident than in September 2002, when Congress debated a war resolution that would allow President George W. Bush to use military force in Iraq. Working for Democratic members of Congress facing reelection in November, consultants advised the need to act swiftly on the war resolution in order to focus on domestic issues where Democrats had an advantage with voters. This advice seemed to be given with little regard for the profound consequences of war. For consultants, the focus was simply on the coming election and the best way to win it, irrespective of policy implications.

A Growing Effort to Professionalize and Strengthen Party Organization

Although the centrifugal force of candidate-centered, mass media–dominated politics eroded the role of party in the political process, its organizations have actually been strengthened in certain respects over the last twenty years. Evidence of professionalization and organizational strength is varied. It appears, for example, in the significant growth of permanent and professional party staffs at both national and state committee levels. The national committee's functions have been broadened and diversified, as the committee has shifted from an exclusive preoccupation with presidential matters. Both national party committees have become heavily involved in a range of party-building activities that include serious efforts to promote party fortunes in state and local election campaigns. The capacity of the national parties to raise funds, particularly in direct-mail campaigns and through soft money, has improved dramatically— in this respect, the Republican party again has led the way, but the Democrats have been gaining ground. On the Democratic side, national party authority has been substantially enlarged through the development of rules for state party participation in national nominating conventions. Although the Democratic party has increased the legal authority of its national organization, the new importance of the national Republican apparatus has stemmed from successful fund-raising that permits it to offer extensive services to state party organizations and candidates.[26]

The strength of state party organizations is partly a function of the party-building activities of the national party organization, leading to greater national-state party integration. The organizational strength of state parties appears in the form of services to candidates, staff size and complexity, newsletters and other communications, voter mobilization programs, public opinion polling, candidate recruitment, issue leadership, and money contributions to candidates. Many Republican state party organizations score high on these indicators. Virtually without exception, Democratic state organizations are substantially weaker than their Republican counterparts. Nonetheless, the weaker Democratic National Committee seems to have had more success than the stronger Republican National Committee in adding to the capabilities of its state party organizations, perhaps because any addition of resources renders a weak organization more effective. For the most part, national-state party integration (or influence) is a one-way street, because most state parties rank low in the degree to which they are involved in (and thus influence) national committee affairs.[27] Nonetheless, the new rules governing the regulation of soft money under the McCain-Feingold campaign finance reform plan, which was adopted in 2002, may strengthen state parties. Whereas national parties will no longer be able to raise soft money, state parties will be free to attract it.

The huge sums of soft money given to the parties over the last decade have enabled them to become more professional. At the national level, their financial strength never has been greater. Staff development has been impressive. Through their staffs, the parties have become sophisticated in the use of modern campaign technologies that involve computers, electronic mail, television, marketing, advertising, survey research, data processing, and direct-mail solicitations. And of considerable interest, influence generally flows from the national level downward, a distinctly different pattern from the state-dominated party structure of the past.[28]

Of interest is whether the structural changes and other developments have arrested the parties' downward slide and strengthened their capacity to function as parties. Are they better able to discharge the traditional party functions of recruitment, nomination, campaign, and control of government? Specifically, how strong is party performance today in grooming and recruiting candidates, controlling nominations, managing campaign resources (money, manpower, expertise), electing candidates and controlling a range of offices simultaneously, mobilizing voters, stimulating competition, maintaining effective coalitions, and inhibiting factional conflict? And how well does it perform the tasks of illuminating issues and fashioning policy alternatives, representing and integrating group interests, making public policy, enforcing discipline, providing public instruction, winning public acceptance and loyalty, and providing voters with a means for keeping government accountable? Exactly what a resurgence of the parties would consist of is hard to say, but it would seem to require them to conduct these activities, or at least most of them, reasonably well.

The record is a mixed bag. On the plus side, the parties' increased ability to raise money has made them more important players than they were a decade ago. With hundreds of millions of dollars in soft money available in each election cycle, the parties' opportunity to provide services to candidates has improved markedly. Moreover, party get-out-the-vote efforts have taken on an unprecedented scope, with 36 percent of Americans reporting that they were contacted by one of the major parties before the 2000 election—a much higher proportion than the 20 percent that reported being contacted in 1992, the last election before the soft money explosion. In addition, congressional parties have grown into disciplined organizations over the last two decades, maintaining party-line voting on most of the issues that traditionally divide the parties. The partisan polarization in Washington has also contributed to the fact that ordinary Americans now identify with parties more strongly than they have in generations.

In the old-fashioned sense of party organization as a network of individuals that does grassroots party work, however, the parties are in "precipitous decline."[29] Candidates and incumbents dominate the electoral system. Party coalitions, the quintessence of American parties, have atrophied. Control over nominations, the sine qua non of strong parties as E. E. Schattschneider and others have argued, is thin and insubstantial at all levels.[30] (In an ecumenical spirit, 5 to 4, the Supreme Court in 1986 opened the door for independents to vote in party primaries if the parties approve.)[31] Divided government is the norm in nation and state. Even though these outcomes stem more from the close partisan balance in the electorate than from weak parties, their immediate import is to make party control over government uneven and unpredictable. The influence of the media and interest groups in key phases of politics has probably never been greater. Indeed, in the presidential selection process, the media have simply supplanted the parties.[32]

Although American parties have made great strides, particularly in the last decade, their overall condition still leaves a great deal to be desired. All things considered, and despite their heightened professionalism and enhanced bureaucratization, the parties are only moderately more successful in some of the things they do today than they were in the weak-party era of the 1970s.

An Era of Party and Governmental Reform

Ordinarily, changes in American politics do not come easily. No democratic political system anywhere rivals the American system for the number of opportunities to prevent or delay the resolution of public problems or the adoption of new forms and practices. American politics is slow politics. Nonetheless, today many large-scale reforms have found their way into the party structure, into Congress, and into public policies that shape and regulate the political process. In the main, these changes took shape and were adopted during a time in which the political system was in substantial disarray. In the midst of an unpopular war, challenged on all sides, President Johnson withdrew from the presidential election campaign of 1968; Robert F. Kennedy was assassinated; the 1968 Democratic convention, meeting in Chicago, was an ordeal of rancor, tumult, and rioting. And then came the Watergate affair—an assault on the political process itself. Public alienation from the political system, which had been building for years, reached a high point. The stage was set for reform. Those who brought it about owed their success to their ability to seize on these unusual and transitory circumstances to develop new ways of carrying on political business.

From almost any perspective, the changes were remarkable. More reforms were adopted between 1968 and 1974 than at any time since the early nineteenth century.[33] The power of national party agencies to set standards for state party participation in national nominating conventions was established—and the Supreme Court added its imprimatur to this development. The first national party charter was adopted by the Democrats. At the state level, presidential primary laws were adopted to broaden political participation, and caucus-convention systems were opened up—thus contributing to the democratization of the nominating process. Nor was Congress immune to change. The seniority system was modified by providing for secret caucus ballots on nominees for committee chairs, thus increasing the responsiveness of these leaders to fellow party members. Committee power itself was dispersed as subcommittees and their chairs won new measures of authority. The filibuster rule was revised, making it easier for a Senate majority to assert itself. The party caucus took on new roles and new vigor. To reduce the influence of private money and big contributors in political campaigns, the Federal Election Campaign Act was adopted, with its provision for public financing of presidential campaigns. In sum, numerous new choices and opportunities were presented to politicians and public alike.

For the most part, the party reforms of the modern period were designed to democratize political institutions and processes. Concretely, reformers set out to reduce the power of elites (that is, party leaders or "bosses") and to augment the power of ordinary citizens. And they were successful, at least on the surface. But, as Nelson W. Polsby has shown, the reforms led to numerous other, unanticipated consequences, particularly on the Democratic side: state party organizations were weakened; party elites lost influence to media elites; candidate organizations came to dominate the presidential selection process; and the national convention fell under the sway of candidate enthusiasts and interest-group delegates as its role in the presidential nominating process shifted from candidate selection to candidate ratification.[34] These changes are truly momentous.

In evaluating the party reforms, it is easy to lose sight of their relationship to the strength of American parties. As David B. Truman observed, the McGovern-Fraser Commission reforms "could not have been accomplished over the opposition of alert and vigorous state parties. The commission staff exploited the limitations and weaknesses of the state parties; they did not cause them."[35] The reforms, in other words, weakened an institution already in more than a little trouble.

Party reform is thus not the same as party strengthening. A more open political process, for example, does not necessarily contribute to the increased participation of the general public or to popular acceptance of the parties. A demographically representative national convention, a central objective of the Democratic reforms, did not immediately lead to the selection of candidates who could best represent the party, unify it, or be elected. The public financing of presidential election campaigns has not by any means solved the problem of money in politics, as the spiraling costs of elections and the growing power of PACs show. Indeed, George W. Bush proved that candidates are often advantaged by eschewing public money, and the rules attached to it, in favor of personal fund-raising efforts. Certainly Bush raised more money and could spend it with greater flexibility than he would have had he accepted federal campaign funds.

Changes in party-committee relations in Congress have not altered congressional behavior in significant ways—Congress remains an institution whose members have an unusually low tolerance for hierarchy in any form. The adoption of a national party charter has not diminished the prevailing federalism of American politics or reduced the autonomy of state and local parties on most matters that count.[36] Parties are, in fact, more cohesive now than they have been in generations, but that owes more to the increasingly homogenous ideological preferences of the members within each caucus than to the effect of strong party leadership.

The reform of the party system must therefore be taken with a grain of salt—for a reason obvious to anyone who began reading this book in advance of this page. American parties are to an important extent the dependent variable in the scheme of politics, more the products of their environment than the architects of it. The only governmental system the parties have known is Madisonian, marked by division of power and made to order for weak parties. Federalism, the separation of powers, and all manner of structural arrangements and election laws (for example, the direct primary, candidate-oriented campaign regulations, nonconcurrent terms for executive and legislature, nonpartisan elections, and staggered elections) militate against the development of strong parties. Parties today are stronger by American standards, but the political environment will never allow them to match the strength of European parties. And by diminishing party control over the presidential nominating process, the reforms weakened the only national institution fully empowered to represent the party's constituent elements. The massive use of television for political campaigns; the increasing power of special-interest groups; and the arrival of public relations, media, survey, computer, and fund-raising experts also have contributed heavily to the current candidate-centered system that stresses personality over party and, frequently, style over substance. And for an American public that has never had much enthusiasm for parties, their current desuetude is not likely to be cause for popular concern.

The Escalation of Interest-Group Activity

The growth in the number and influence of interest groups is one of the key developments in American politics in recent years. Members of Congress have become acutely sensitive to the power of lobbies. To quote former senator Abraham Ribicoff (D-Conn.): "Lobbying has reached a new dimension and is more effective than ever in history. It has become a big computerized operation in which the Congress and the public are being bombarded by single-issue groups."[37]

The increasing influence of interest groups has contributed to the weakening of the parties. Interest groups and parties compete for the same political space. When legislators are more concerned with satisfying interest-group claims than with supporting party positions and leaders, the vitality of legislative party organizations is sapped. When party lines collapse, collective responsibility for decisions is diminished. Increasingly, individual members are on their own, crowded and pressured by groups intent on getting their way. Rep. David R. Obey (D-Wis.) said, "It's a lot more difficult to say no to anybody because so many people have well-oiled mimeograph machines."[38] Or, in the grimly blunt words of Sen. Edward M. Kennedy (D-Mass.): "We have the best Congress money can buy. Congress is awash in contributions from special interests that expect something in return."[39]

For the past three decades the main controversy over interest groups has centered on their gifts to candidates for office. Recent contributions, unquestionably, have been sizable. PAC gifts to House and Senate candidates in 1988, for example, totaled $148 million. In the midst of a substantial increase in spending by congressional candidates in 2000, PAC contributions reached $245 million. PAC money accounted for 32 percent of the receipts for all House candidates and 14 percent for all Senate candidates; as usual, incumbents claimed the lion's share (75 percent) of it.[40] Surveys find that a large portion of the public now perceives campaign financing to be a corrupt system—one in which legislators are "bought and sold" and forced to compromise their independence to satisfy interest-group claims. Although the evidence of such favoritism is skimpy, the issue remained sufficiently hot that Congress passed and President Bush signed campaign finance reform legislation in 2002. Even so, the reforms have been viewed skeptically by many observers, and the Federal Election Commission did much to water them down even before they had the opportunity to take effect.

Another dimension of the interest-group problem is that of single-issue groups.[41] Their issue is *the* issue; their position is the one on which legislators are to be judged. The compromises that occur naturally to practical politicians seldom carry much weight with the leaders of single-issue groups; members are either for or against gun control, abortion, tax reductions, equal rights, nuclear power, environmental safeguards, prayer in the public schools, or any of a number of other issues including certain foreign policies for which there are active domestic constituencies. Insistent groups gather on each side of each of these troublesome questions. Legislators do not find it easy to hide from such groups, especially because decision-making processes have opened up as a result of the reform wave of the 1970s.

Weakened parties provide slim protection for the harassed legislator in a free-for-all system. Middle-of-the-road politicians find themselves in trouble. Public service itself becomes increasingly frustrating in a politics of tiptoe and tightrope. Shortly before he was defeated for reelection in 1978, a northern Democratic senator observed:

> The single-interest constituencies have just about destroyed politics as I knew it. They've made it miserable to be in office—or to run for office—and left me feeling it's hardly worth the struggle to survive.[42]

The "special cause" quality of much of contemporary politics is also reflected in these comments by a leading official in Minnesota's Democratic-Farmer-Labor party:

> Frankly, there are very few of us in the party leadership now whose primary goal is the election of candidates committed to a broad liberal agenda. Most of the people in control are there to advance their own special causes. From the time we spend on it, you would think the most important problem in the world is whether there should be speedboats on six lakes in northern Minnesota.[43]

The arrival of narrow-issue politics has changed the American political landscape. Pragmatic politics has been diminished and compromise has declined as a way of doing business. In forming their positions on certain inflammatory, high-principle issues, members see a reduced margin for error. A wrong vote can cost them electoral support and produce new challenges to their reelection. And not in a few cases members believe they are faced with a no-win vote—where a vote on either side of a controversial, high-visibility issue appears likely to damage their electoral security.

The Increasing Nationalization of Politics

So unobtrusively has the change come about that a great many American citizens are unaware of the extent to which sectional political alignments have been replaced by a national political alignment. The Republican vote in the South in the 1952 presidential election was, it turns out, more than a straw in the wind. Eisenhower carried four southern states, narrowly lost several others, made the Republican party respectable for many southern voters, and, most important, laid the foundation for the development of a viable Republican party throughout the South.

From the latter part of the nineteenth century until recently, the main obstacle to the nationalization of politics was the strength of the Democratic party in the South. Presidential, congressional, state, and local offices were won, as a matter of course, by the Democrats. This is no longer the case. Republicans now dominate presidential elections in the South. In the three elections of the 1980s, for example, among southern states only Georgia—in 1980—voted for the Democratic presidential candidate, Jimmy Carter, the state's former governor. In 1992 the Republicans won eight southern states (Alabama, Florida, Mississippi, North Carolina, Oklahoma, South Carolina, Texas, and Virginia), even though the Democrats offered an all-southern ticket in Bill Clinton (Arkansas) and Al Gore (Tennessee). In 1996 Clinton and Gore won only five southern states (Arkansas, Florida, Kentucky, Louisiana, and Tennessee). And, in 2000, Gore and Joseph Lieberman won none.

Republican gains in southern congressional elections have been particularly impressive. (See Table 7-1.) The Republican statewide percentage of the vote for representative has grown more or less steadily since the 1950s. After the 2002 election, 59 percent of the southern delegation in both the House of Representatives and Senate was Republican. Vigorous two-party competition occurs even in the states of the Deep South (Alabama, Georgia, Louisiana, Mississippi, and South Carolina), and in some cases, the GOP has even begun to dominate these areas. In the 1950s, by contrast, the Republican party rarely even nominated candidates for the House of Representatives in the Deep South. In short, a strong breeze of Republicanism has been coursing through southern electorates.

The movement from parochial to national politics has not been limited to the South. No matter what its history of party allegiance and voting, no state is wholly secure from incursions by the minority party. Especially below the presidential level where the parties have developed strong regional bases, one-party political systems have dwindled: "It is probably safe to say that in national and state-wide politics we are in the time of the most intense, evenly-spaced, two-party competitiveness of the last 100 years,"[44] says Frank J. Sorauf.

Table 7-1 Republican Percentage of the Statewide Major-Party Vote for the U.S. House of Representatives, Selected Years, Southern States

State	Republican statewide percentage								
	1950	1952	1968	1978	1984	1988	1992	1996	2000
Alabama	0.7	5.4	30.8	42.9	27.3	37.4	38.5	54.3	64.0
Arkansas	0.0	14.3	53.0	60.1	21.0	41.7	40.4	56.3	53.7
Florida	9.6	25.9	42.8	41.7	48.9	44.4	52.7	52.8	59.1
Georgia	0.0	0.0	20.5	32.6	28.3	33.3	45.1	56.8	63.5
Louisiana	0.0	8.7	18.8	50.0	a	a	a	a	a
Mississippi	0.0	2.5	7.5	36.9	38.5	33.6	28.9	54.2	44.1
North Carolina	30.0	32.2	45.4	35.9	47.6	44.2	48.3	51.6	56.0
South Carolina	0.0	2.0	32.8	37.6	48.4	44.4	53.5	66.5	58.0
Tennessee	30.3	29.8	51.1	47.0	44.8	38.9	45.5	50.8	54.2
Texas	9.5	1.3	28.1	40.6	42.3	40.3	48.8	56.2	51.2
Virginia	24.9	31.0	46.4	50.2	55.8	57.3	49.8	48.1	54.7

Sources: Developed from data in *The 1968 Elections* (Washington, D.C.: Republican National Committee, 1969), 115–116; *Congressional Quarterly Weekly Report*, November 9, 1974, 3084–3091; November 11, 1978, 3283–3291; April 13, 1985, 689–695; November 8, 1986, 2864–2870; May 6, 1989, 1074–1080; April 17, 1993, 973–980; November 9, 1996, 3250–3257; and *Federal Elections 2000* (Washington, D.C.: Federal Election Commission, 2001).

[a] In Louisiana, House candidates run on a nonpartisan ballot in the September primary. If no candidate receives a majority in the district, the top two (irrespective of party) face each other in November. Candidates who receive a majority in the primary are considered to be elected.

Somewhat ironically, this increase in the national strength of both parties can serve as a challenge to party responsibility. State-level candidates often distance themselves from the positions of the national party to appeal to their state's particular constituency. In his efforts to win votes in rural southwestern Virginia in 2001, gubernatorial candidate Mark Warner (D-Va.) trumpeted his support for gun rights, a position that is in conflict with the gun control message advocated by the national Democratic party. Similarly, Sen. Max Baucus (D-Mont.) in his reelection campaign in 2002 stressed his agreement with Republican president George W. Bush on a range of issues of concern to his decidedly conservative state. Finally, Mark Pryor, a successful Arkansas senatorial candidate in 2002, provides the most explicit break from the national party to be competitive at home. He ran an advertisement that said, "Unlike some Democrats in Washington, I believe in strengthening the military," a winning position in his conservative southern state.[45] When party policy and constituency interest collide, constituency nearly always wins.

The sources for the growing nationalization of American politics are both numerous and varied. Social changes, rather than conscious party efforts to extend their spheres of influence, have provided the principal thrust for the new shape given to American party politics. Among the most important have been the emergence and extraordinary development of the mass media in political communications. Through the electronic media, national political figures can be created virtually overnight, national issues can be carried to the most remote and inaccessible community, and new styles and trends can become a matter of common knowledge in a matter of days or weeks. Insulation, old loyalties, and established patterns are difficult to maintain intact in the face of contemporary political communications.

For all their importance to the changes under way, the electronic media have not by themselves transformed the face of American politics. Changes in technology, the diversification of the economic bases of the states, the growth of an affluent society, the higher educational attainments of voters, the mobility of the population, the migration of African American citizens to the North, the enfranchisement of African American citizens in the South, the illumination of massive nationwide problems, the growth of vast urban conglomerations, and the assimilation of immigrant groups have all contributed to the erosion of internal barriers and parochialism and, consequently, to the strengthening of national political patterns. Whatever the complete explanation for this phenomenon, one thing is clear: the forces for the nationalization of politics are far more powerful than those for localism and sectionalism. A changing party system is the inevitable result.

A Continuation of Party Competition Based on Meaningful Policy Differences between the Parties

The American parties are often criticized for being Tweedledum and Tweedledee—for being so similar that even attentive voters can miss the alternatives they present. This criticism has limited merit. Consider, first of all, the ideology and policy attitudes of Democratic and Republican elites—in this case, delegates to the 2000 party conventions. (See Figure 7-1.) Fifty-seven percent of the Republican delegates described themselves as conservatives, as contrasted with a mere 4 percent of the Democratic delegates. At the other ideological pole, the differences are also striking: liberals made up 34 percent of the Democratic delegates but were virtually absent (1 percent) from the Republican delegation.[46]

Differences in ideological perception and in political philosophy translate into differences in public policy views and differences on the proper role of government. Democratic delegates to the 2000 party convention, for example, were much more likely than their Republican counterparts to agree with the following propositions: that affirmative action programs should be continued, that government should do more to regulate the environment and safety practices of business and do more to solve the nation's problems, that a nationwide ban on assault weapons should be instituted, and that laws to protect racial minorities are necessary. In addition, Democratic delegates were much more likely to be pro-choice than Republican delegates, whereas Republican delegates were much more likely to believe that organized prayer should be permitted in public schools. The differences between the activists of the two parties are important and unmistakable; one set is clearly liberal, the other clearly conservative.[47]

Figure 7-1   The Ideology of Democratic and Republican National Convention Delegates, 2000, Contrasted with the Ideology of Rank-and-File Democrats and Republicans

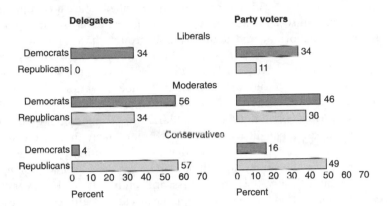

Source: Adapted from *New York Times*/CBS News poll, published in the *New York Times*, August 14, 2000.

Note: Ideological positions are based on self-classification. Party voters are self-identified Democrats and Republicans. Percentages may not add up to 100 because some respondents were unclassified.

Party conflict in Congress also occurs along liberal-conservative lines. Over the years most Democratic members have supported labor-endorsed legislation, measures to provide for government regulation of business, social welfare bills of great variety, civil rights legislation, federal aid to education, and limitations on defense expenditures. By contrast, Republican members have generally favored business over labor, social welfare programs of more modest proportions, private action rather than government involvement, state rather than federal responsibility for domestic programs, the interests of higher-income groups over those of lower-income groups, and a greater emphasis on national defense. When viewing the economy, party members typically focus on different problems: Republicans are more concerned about inflation, Democrats more concerned about unemployment.[48] Those who believe that there is not "a dime's worth of difference" between the parties have not paid much attention to the preferences of the parties' congressional members on contemporary issues involving labor, business, social welfare, civil rights, and a variety of contentious social issues such as abortion and the death penalty.

The important point is that the parties' weaknesses have not clouded the ideological differences between their leaders. Meaningful differences separate the parties in Congress (or at least majorities of the two parties). Even larger differences divide the parties' national convention delegates. Quite plainly, Democratic and Republican party elites do not evaluate public problems in the same light. Nor are they attracted to the same solutions.

Differences between the parties can also be examined from the perspective of the public. The survey data in Table 7-2 show the internal differences within the electoral parties as well as the broad differences between them. Obviously, neither party is monolithic, in the sense that its members share a common set of beliefs. On certain social issues, such as prayer in the public schools and abortions, certain Democratic and Republican subgroups share the same political space—one broadly defined in this Times Mirror study as intolerance for particular personal freedoms. Nevertheless, differences between the voters of the two parties appear to be more important. In their attitudes toward social justice, most Democratic partisans are easily distinguished from most Republican partisans. Democrats are aligned on the side of egalitarianism, social spending, the disadvantaged, and racial equality. They are much more likely than Republicans to favor increased spending on programs that assist minorities, the homeless, the unemployed, and the elderly. Republican voters tend to be dubious of big government, fiscally conservative, probusiness, anticommunist, and in favor of high defense spending. Divisions within Republican clusters are less serious than those found on the Democratic side. The profound point is that the policy views of the parties' adherents differ from one another in significant respects. Put another way, the parties do stand for something in the minds of many voters.

A survey by the *New York Times* prior to the 2002 congressional elections reinforces the Times Mirror study of popular perceptions of the two parties. Respondents found the Republican party much more likely than the Democratic party to make sure that the nation's military defenses are strong (62 to 20 percent) and to make the right decisions in combating terrorism (48 to 23 percent). Voters saw the Democratic party as the one most likely to make prescription drugs for the elderly more affordable (61 to 19 percent) and to make the right decisions about Social Security (48 to 30 percent). By a narrow margin (41 to 37 percent) voters said that Democrats would do a better job of dealing with gun control than Republicans and were evenly divided as to which party would do a better job of making the country prosperous. Overall, 54 percent of the respondents had a favorable opinion of the Republican party and 55 percent had a favorable opinion of the Democratic party—not a particularly high evaluation in either case.[49] That aside, in the public mind, the parties are surely not as similar as two peas in a pod.

The public's images of the parties are more sharply developed than commonly supposed. A comprehensive study of likely voters by Donald C. Baumer and Howard J. Gold, covering the period 1976 to 1992, finds that roughly two thirds of the electorate can articulate the dominant images of the parties. The Democratic party is viewed as "the party of inclusion and government spending" and the Republicans are viewed as "allies of the wealthy and opponents of government spending and intervention." Democrats are pictured by voters as "pro-common and working people," "pro-poor and needy people," "spenders," and "liberals." Republicans emerge as "pro–big business, rich, and upper-class" as well as "conservative."[50]

Table 7-2 Party in the Electorate: The Views of Democratic and Republican Voters on Major Social and Economic Issues

Position	Democratic groups				Republican groups	
	'60s Democrats	New Dealers	Passive poor	Partisan poor	Enterprisers	Moralists
Favor constitutional amendment to permit prayer in public schools	52%	83%	83%	81%	69%	88%
Favor mandatory drug testing for government employees	39	78	77	69	58	80
Favor changing laws to make it more difficult for a woman to get an abortion	26	54	47	38	40	60
Favor increased spending on programs that assist minorities	50	39	57	60	-2	21
Favor death penalty	53	79	78	66	78	85
Favor cutbacks in defense and military spending	69	49	58	57	31	31
Favor increased spending on:						
programs for the homeless	77	73	82	83	38	62
programs for the unemployed	40	49	62	68	11	30
improving the nation's health care	76	80	85	84	42	68
improving the nation's public schools	80	70	77	77	56	65
aid to farmers	62	69	72	70	29	60
Social Security	62	76	81	85	29	57
programs for the elderly	79	84	84	87	44	71

Source: Developed from data in *The People, the Press and Politics* (Los Angeles: Times Mirror, 1987), *passim.*

Note: '60s Democrats: well educated, upper-middle class, tolerant on personal freedom issues, mainstream Democrats, committed to social justice. New Dealers: aging, traditional Democrats, blue collar, union members, less tolerant on personal freedom issues, moderate income. Passive poor: aging, poor, less well educated, uncritical, disproportionately southern, committed to social justice. Partisan poor: firmly Democratic, very low income, poorly educated, urban, disproportionately black, concerned with social justice issues. Enterprisers: affluent, well educated, white, suburban, probusiness, antigovernment, tolerant or personal freedom issues. Moralists: middle-aged, middle income, white, disproportionately southern, suburban, small cities and rural areas, regular church-goers, anticommunist, prodefense.

Still other evidence points to the public's sensitivity concerning party differences. Survey data presented in Table 7-3 show the public's perceptions of the ideologies of the parties. Seventy-two percent of respondents correctly perceive the Democrats as left of center and 76 percent correctly perceive the Republicans as right of center. Whatever else may be said, the public is not "clueless." Some of the fine points doubtlessly are missed by the general public, but the fact is that most voters are essentially accurate in their appraisals of the Democratic party as liberal, the Republican party as conservative. This perception of liberal-conservative differences between the parties is a classic distinction in American politics.[51] It is salient for many voters, helping them to organize political information, interpret political conflict, and evaluate candidates.[52]

The Decline of Partisanship and Its Resurgence

For decades, strong party advocates lamented the decline in partisanship in the electorate. Absent strong parties and clear cues for voters, they contended ordinary people for whom politics is a minor concern would be unable to hold officeholders accountable for their actions. Indeed, evidence drawn from the period immediately following the party reform movement was clear. For many voters, party no longer carried much weight. A much greater percentage of Americans eschewed partisan labels in favor of political independence than in previous decades. As a result, third party or independent presidential candidates ran exceedingly well. Even among those who voted for major party candidates, split-ticket voting reached an apex. Droves of Democrats crossed party lines to create landslide winners of Republican presidential aspirants, such as Richard Nixon in 1972 and Ronald Reagan in 1980 and 1984, while at the same time maintaining a Democratic House of Representatives.

During this period, candidate considerations replaced the party. In the 1986 House elections, for example, a mere 8.4 percent of all voters said that the can-

Table 7-3   The Public's Perception of the Ideologies of the Parties during the 2000 Presidential Campaign

Question: We hear a lot of talk these days about liberals and conservatives. Here is a 7-point scale on which the political views that people might hold are arranged from extremely liberal to extremely conservative. Where would you place the Democratic party on this scale? The Republican party?

	Democratic	Republican
Extremely liberal	6%	1%
Liberal	44	6
Slightly liberal	22	5
Middle of road	14	11
Slightly conservative	5	20
Conservative	7	51
Extremely conservative	2	5

Source: National Election Study, Center for Political Studies, University of Michigan.

didate's party was the most important factor in influencing their voting choice. The most important consideration was the candidate's character and experience, according to 41 percent of the sample. For 23 percent, state and local issues loomed most important. And of unusual interest, in this *national* election, only 20 percent reported basing their decision on *national issues.*[53] An overwhelming majority of the public believes that "the best rule in voting is to pick the best candidate, regardless of party label."[54]

Candidate-centered voting has major ramifications for the control of government, as can be seen in an examination of the vote for presidential and congressional candidates within congressional districts. Table 7-4 includes data on the number and percentage of congressional districts with split election results—districts won by the presidential candidate of one party and by the congressional candidate of the other party—from 1920 to 2000. The data depict a significant

Table 7-4 Congressional Districts with Split Election Results: Districts Carried by a Presidential Candidate of One Major Party and by a House Candidate of Other Major Party: 1920–2000

Year and party of the winning presidential candidate	Number of districts	Number of districts with split results	Percentage
1920 R	344	11	3.2
1924 R	356	42	11.8
1928 R	359	68	18.9
1932 D	355	50	14.1
1936 D	361	51	14.1
1940 D	362	53	14.6
1944 D	367	41	11.2
1948 D	422	90	21.3
1952 R	435	84	19.3
1956 R	435	130	29.9
1960 D	437	114	26.1
1964 D	435	145	33.3
1968 R	435	141	32.4
1972 R	435	193	44.4
1976 D	435	124	28.5
1980 R	435	141	32.4
1984 R	435	191	43.9
1988 R	435	148	34.0
1992 D	435	101	23.2
1996 D	435	111	25.5
2000 R	435	87	20.0
Total	8,583	2,116	24.6

Source: Milton C. Cummings Jr., *Congressmen and the Electorate* (New York: Free Press, 1966), 32 (as updated).

Note: R = Republican; D = Democrat. Presidential returns for some congressional districts were not available between 1920 and 1948.

increase in split elections for these offices, followed by a stark reversal of this trend. A high point was reached in 1972, when 44 percent of all House districts split their results, due largely to the voters' rejection of George McGovern, the Democratic presidential nominee. The proportion of split results was almost as high in 1984 as voters everywhere voted for Ronald Reagan and Democratic House candidates. Especially from the late 1960s through the early 1980s, party provided less structure to voting than it had in the past.[55]

More recently, the trend toward politically independent behavior has reversed. In 2000 there were only 20 percent split-ticket results, the smallest proportion since 1952, when party voting was the order of the day. Of the 228 congressional districts carried by George W. Bush, only 40 were carried by Democratic House candidates. Similarly, Republican candidates only won 47 of the 207 congressional districts carried by Al Gore. Clearly, the 2000 election reflects a recent trend toward more partisan voting. Each of the last three presidential elections has featured fewer than 30 percent split-ticket results. One would have to return to the 1952 to 1960 period to find similar conclusions.

The incidence of landslide elections also provides clues as to the strength of partisanship in the electorate. Landslides occur because numerous partisans desert their party. In the sixteen presidential elections between 1836 and 1896, only one was of landslide dimensions (an election in which the winning candidate received 55 percent or more of the two-party vote). By contrast, three occurred between 1964 and 1984. In 1972 fully one third of Democrats voted for the Republican presidential nominee, Richard Nixon.

But no landslides have occurred since 1984. Party ties have come to shape voter decisions more and more in recent elections, thus diminishing the likelihood of one party winning an overwhelming victory. Overall, the present era resembles that of the Civil War period (1860–1892), which was distinguished by consistently competitive presidential elections. At the electoral level, as in Congress, it is clear that, overall, the parties are significantly stronger today than they were in the 1970s and early 1980s.

The Weakening of Group Attachments to the Democratic Party in Presidential Elections

Although partisanship in the electorate is now more noticeable, its expression in coalition formation has changed, much to the detriment of Democratic presidential candidates. Since Harry S. Truman's election in 1948 (the fifth consecutive win for the Democrats), the Democratic party has won only five of thirteen presidential elections—in 1960 (Kennedy), 1964 (Johnson), 1976 (Carter), 1992 (Clinton), and 1996 (Clinton). Among the explanations for the party's modest success, two stand out. One is that Democratic presidential candidates have been rejected by independents. Between 1952 and 1988, the Democratic presidential candidate gained a majority of the independent vote only in 1964, a landslide Democratic year. Two thirds of independents voted for Ronald Reagan in 1984.

In 2000 independents favored George W. Bush by a margin of forty-seven to forty-five, and their support proved decisive.

But a more important reason is that the Democratic coalition, which began to take shape during the presidency of Franklin D. Roosevelt, has lost much of its potency. During its heyday, Democratic candidates became accustomed to receiving strong support from Catholics, southerners, blue-collar (especially union) workers, ethnic minorities, big-city dwellers, African Americans, and young voters. The Reagan revolution in the 1980s altered the alignment of groups. The changes among Catholics, white southerners, and younger voters were particularly striking. In 1960 and 1964 about three out of four Catholics voted for John F. Kennedy and Lyndon Johnson. Support among Catholics for Jimmy Carter was also relatively high. But in all three elections of the 1980s, a majority of Catholic voters supported the Republican candidate. Younger voters also were drawn to the Republican candidates in the 1980s. Most decisive of all was the behavior of southern whites, once a mainstay of the Democratic coalition. They abandoned the Democratic party in droves, ultimately leading to George W. Bush's complete sweep of the region in 2000.

In fact, the groups that remained staunchly Democratic in the 1980s were few. Heading the list was the African American community. Even in two bad years for the Democratic presidential candidate (1984 and 1988), the African American vote for Mondale and Dukakis was about 90 percent. Also, about two out of three Jews, Hispanics, and unemployed persons voted for the Democratic candidates in 1984 and 1988.[56]

The erosion of the Democratic coalition in the 1970s and 1980s, however, did not presage an endless stream of Republican victories. Despite his foreign policy successes and the nation's dramatic victory in the Gulf War, George H. W. Bush's bid for reelection in 1992 was doomed by seemingly intractable problems of the domestic economy and the media's relentless dissemination of economic bad news.[57] Convinced of the need for change, nearly two out of three voters opted for Bill Clinton or Ross Perot in the election.

For purposes of this analysis, the most interesting feature of Clinton's 1992 vote is how minimally it reflected the classic Democratic coalition. His support among Catholics was no better than his national average. His support among whites (87 percent of the electorate) was well under his national average, and among southern whites (24 percent of the electorate) he fared poorly. Blue-collar workers gave Clinton a comfortable margin, but it was nothing like their support of Kennedy in 1960 (60 percent) or Johnson in 1964 (71 percent). Only among African Americans (8 percent of the electorate), Jews (4 percent), and Hispanics (3 percent) did Clinton receive unusually strong backing.[58] Joining these usually pro-Democratic groups, women voted for Clinton in convincing numbers, creating the largest gender gap to date.

In broad lines, voting patterns in 1996 resembled those of 1992. In defeating Bob Dole, Bill Clinton reconstructed, to some extent, the old Democratic coalition, but without the South, which is now among the most Republican sections of the country. As he had in 1992, Clinton ran well among African Americans, Jews, Hispanics, persons of low income, persons of both limited education and postgraduate education, and women. Among larger groups, his most impressive gains were reflected in the vote of unmarried women (53 percent in 1992, 62 percent in 1996), Hispanics (61 percent, 72 percent), union households (55 percent, 60 percent), Catholics (44 percent, 53 percent), voters aged eighteen to twenty-nine (43 percent, 52 percent), liberals (68 percent, 78 percent), and moderates (47 percent, 57 percent).[59]

Voting patterns in 2000 were closer to 1992 than to 1996. Al Gore had a strong appeal to some coalition members, such as African Americans, union members, Hispanics, and Jews, but he failed to dominate among Catholics (especially white Catholics, who cast a majority of their votes for Bush) and among younger voters. And, of course, he lost every state of the former Confederacy, the same region where FDR won every state in all of his four campaigns for the White House. While Democrats have picked up some support in other regions of the country, the loss of the formerly solid South means that Democratic candidates will not dominate national politics. They now have to be satisfied with less—that is, with simply "doing well," not "cleaning up," among traditional party followings.

The Growth of Racial Polarization in Voting

Historically, the great divide in racial voting occurred in the 1960s, beginning with a massive shift by African Americans in 1964 and continuing with a sizable shift by whites in 1968. In broad outline, this is what happened: Under the leadership of President Johnson, a bipartisan majority in Congress passed the Civil Rights Act of 1964, the most significant civil rights legislation since Reconstruction. The Republican National Convention shortly chose as its presidential nominee Barry Goldwater, a militant conservative, an exponent of states' rights, and one of the main opponents of the 1964 act. With the lines clearly drawn, African Americans voted overwhelmingly (94 percent) for Johnson in November. (See Table 7-5.) Of the six states carried by Goldwater, five were in the Deep South, where his states' rights/civil rights stance undoubtedly was attractive to white voters. Following Johnson's landslide victory, a top-heavy Democratic Congress passed an even more important civil rights bill: the Voting Rights Act of 1965. This landmark legislation paved the way for African Americans to enter fully into the nation's political life.

By 1968, as a result of movement by white voters, black-white voting divisions intensified; 85 percent of African Americans but only 38 percent of whites voted Democratic. With a southerner, Jimmy Carter, at the head of the ticket in 1976, more whites (but less than a majority) voted Democratic than in either of the previous two elections. But this election was merely a blip—a modest exception to a profound trend. Today there are no signs that racial cleavages are ebbing, and the current split is quite sharp. In a three-way race in 1992, more than eight out of ten African Americans voted for Bill Clinton, and six out of ten whites voted for George H. W. Bush or Ross Perot. It was the same story in 1996,

Table 7-5 Growing Racial Polarization in Voting in Presidential Elections

	1956	1960	1964	1968	1972	1976	1980	1984	1988	1992	1996	2000
Percentage of electorate voting Democratic	42	50	61	43	38	50	41	41	46	43	49	49
Percentage of whites voting Democratic	41	49	59	38	32	46	36	34	41	40	43	43
Percentage of blacks voting Democratic	61	68	94	85	87	85	86	87	82	82	84	90
Racial differential: percentage-point difference between black and white Democratic vote	20	19	35	47	55	39	50	53	41	42	41	47

Sources: Developed from data in *Gallup Report*, November 1988, 6–7; *Gallup Poll Monthly*, November 1992, 9; 1996, 2000 national exit poll of Voter News Service.

when more than eight out of ten African Americans voted for Clinton, and 55 percent of whites chose Bob Dole or Ross Perot. In 2000, African Americans increased their support for Al Gore to fully 90 percent, compared with 8 percent for Bush. Whites, on the other hand voted 54–42 for Bush. The division of the races along party lines, grounded in economic and social policies as well as civil rights, is one of the outstanding facts of contemporary American politics.[60]

The Public's Declining Confidence in Political Institutions

The confidence of the American public in its political institutions is substantially lower today than it was in the 1960s, a change that has important consequences. Although the public's feelings about government have often largely been ignored, the surge in public spiritedness following the September 11 terrorist attacks placed a spotlight on these attitudes.

It is important to note that popular disillusionment concerning politics and political institutions did not emerge as a result of Watergate. The trend began in the mid to late 1960s. (See Table 7-6.) The disclosures of criminal activities by White House officials, and Nixon's role in the cover-up, merely accentuated it.

No simple explanation exists for the decline of trust in government. Many factors have been at work, probably the most important of which center on public dissatisfaction with policy outcomes—including urban unrest and riots in the 1960s, the Vietnam War, and the government's inability to solve certain social and economic problems.[61] In addition, the media's steady preoccupation with negative news, such as policies that go awry, and with skewering politicians, especially the president, have played a crucial, if unintended, role in maintaining the public's negative feelings about Washington and politics in general.[62]

At least for a short while, all this changed after Towers 1 and 2 of the World Trade Center were destroyed on September 11, 2001. Trust in political institutions surged to a level not seen since the mid-1960s. Some commentators suggested that this was a watershed time for government revitalization. The surge, however, proved short-lived. (See Figure 7-2.) Within three months, the percentage of people saying that they trusted the government in Washington to do

Table 7-6   Popular Trust in Government: 1972– 2000

Question: How much of the time do you think you can trust the government in Washington to do what is right—just about always, most of the time, or only some of the time?

Response	1972	1974	1978	1980	1984	1988	1992	1996	2000
Always	5%	3%	3%	2%	4%	4%	3%	3%	4%
Most of the time	48	34	27	23	40	37	26	26	40
Some or none of the time	45	62	68	73	54	58	70	69	55
Don't know	2	1	2	2	2	1	1	2	1

Source: National Election Studies, Center for Political Studies, University of Michigan.

Figure 7-2   Changes in Trust in Government, 2000–2002

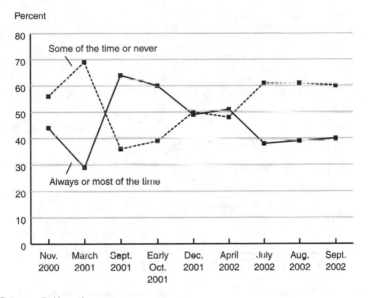

Percent

Source: Data compiled by authors.

what was right all or most of the time had dropped by fifteen percentage points. By July 2002, less than a year after the terrorist attacks, trust in government had dropped below the level it had been when Bill Clinton left office. In a word, people began to think about the political system in terms of a prolonged slump in the stock market, a softening economy, and a rash of corporate scandals, which caused their evaluations of government to sour.

These negative feelings about government are pervasive. For the last three decades, more than 60 percent of people have said, for example, that "government is pretty much run by a few big interests looking out for themselves." More than half of those surveyed contend that "public officials don't care much what people like me think" (Figure 7-3). Since the mid-1970s, at least 60 percent of the public has thought that the government wastes "a lot" of money.

The consequences of the public's negative feelings toward government are hard to measure in a precise way. Interestingly, there is almost no difference between voters and nonvoters in the level of their distrust of government, hence distrust does not bear on turnout.[63] Nevertheless, there is considerable evidence that those who distrust the government are much less likely to vote for an incumbent president and more likely to support a third party candidate than those who trust the government. As a consequence, the incumbent party's presidential candidate lost five of the nine elections between 1968 and 2000, the worst record for the incumbents since the early to mid-1800s, and Ross Perot

Figure 7-3   Evidence of Public Alienation from Government

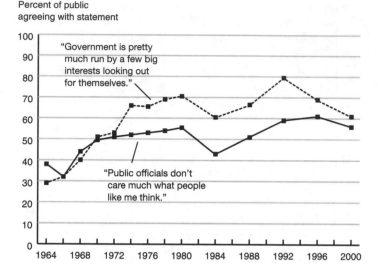

Percent of public
agreeing with statement

"Government is pretty
much run by a few big
interests looking out
for themselves."

"Public officials don't
care much what people
like me think."

1964   1968   1972   1976   1980   1984   1988   1992   1996   2000

Source: Data drawn from National Election Studies, Center for Political Studies, University of Michigan.

secured historically large percentages of the vote in 1992 and 1996. Presidential approval ratings are, generally speaking, no longer as high today as they were in the 1950s and 1960s, and declining political trust helps account for that fact. In addition, political distrust has a major impact on how much the public wants the government to do. Those who are distrustful are much less supportive of government programs, especially those directed toward African Americans and the poor, than those who trust the government.[64] Indeed, the demise of the Clinton administration's efforts to provide universal health insurance was largely the result of people's negative feelings about government. Americans looked askance at the prospect of an incompetent government, as they saw it, administering a large new bureaucracy.[65]

In addition, declining trust in government has undoubtedly affected the relative success of the parties over the last political generation. The Democratic party has traditionally favored using the government to level the economic playing field, while the Republican party has generally opposed this notion. Given popular suspicions of government, it is not surprising that the Republicans have dominated national politics since 1968, winning the presidency in six of nine elections. The party's small government philosophy obviously is attractive to a public distrustful of government.

Nothing about this condition of declining trust is immutable. Changes in political leadership, reorientations in governmental policies leading to amelioration or resolution of nagging problems, successful new policy ventures, and the more complete fulfillment of popular expectations could strengthen trust in government.[66] That political trust increased markedly since 1994 suggests that sustained economic growth and public satisfaction with political leadership can effect positive change. The quick drop in trust after its post–September 11 high, however, shows that such increases can prove fleeting in a political environment in which cynicism is never much below the surface and where a mood of disenchantment and disconnection is commonly present.

The Prospects

The American party system has been shaped more by custom and environment than by intent. Indeed, in broad contour, the parties of today resemble closely those of previous generations. For as long as can be remembered, the major parties have been loose and disorderly coalitions, heavily decentralized, lacking in unity and discipline, preoccupied with winning office, and no more than erratically responsible for the conduct of government and the formation of public policy. There is, of course, another side to them. They have performed at least as well as the parties of other democratic nations—and perhaps far better. Democratic politics requires the maintenance of a predictable legal system; institutionalized arrangements for popular control of government and the mobilization of majorities; methods and arenas for the illumination, crystallization, and reconciliation of conflict; and means for endowing both leaders and policies with legitimacy. To each of these requirements the parties have contributed steadily and often in major ways.[67]

A truism of American politics is that it is invariably difficult to cut free from familiar institutions. Old practices die hard. Conventional arrangements hang on and on. Change arrives incrementally and unnoticed. Most Americans are habituated to weak parties, and the parties themselves are accustomed to the environment in which they function. It would seem that prospects for the development of a system of responsible parties are thin at best. But the matter deserves a closer look.

On many counts the parties have lost ground since the era of reform in the late 1960s and early 1970s. The electoral party organizations have been weakened. Their control over the nominating process, once a virtual monopoly, has gradually slipped away. Primary battles for major offices occur frequently. Increasingly, candidates use the party label "in the same spirit that ships sail under Liberian registry—a flag of convenience, and no more."[68] While the parties have responded favorably to some of these challenges, they have nowhere near the same control that they enjoyed generations ago. The power of local party leaders probably never has been weaker than it is today. The media, public relations consultants, campaign management firms, and political action committees are now as much a part of campaigns as the party organizations—at least when important offices are at stake. So-called "independent candidates" can be very successful. Popular dissatisfaction with the parties was so widespread in

1992 that Texas billionaire Ross Perot, running as an independent, won nearly one fifth of the presidential vote in a folksy and quirky campaign reduced essentially to peppery sound bites on the nation's ills. If nothing else, the Perot vote was a wake-up call for both major parties.

The sum of these developments is that American parties compete within the political process but do not dominate it. In some jurisdictions they are all but invisible. A great deal of contemporary politics lies outside the parties and beyond their control. Most troubling of all is that many voters profess deep skepticism of parties, politicians, and government. Even though the parties have made certain gains in the last decade, the prospects remain dim for the development of a full-blown responsible party system. Too many obstacles—constitutional, political, and otherwise—stand in the way. But this is not to say that responsible party performance in government is unattainable. The way in which parties govern is not dependent on the strength and vitality of the electoral party organizations or on the way in which individuals are elected to office. The party-in-the-government, it is worth remembering, is both different from the party-in-the-electorate and largely independent of it.

The essence of a responsible party system is not to be found in party councils, closed primaries, demographically representative national conventions, off-year party conventions, government financing of elections, or intraparty democracy. Instead, the key idea is party responsibility for a program of public policy. Such responsibility requires, in the first place, a strong measure of internal cohesion within the party-in-the-government in order to adopt its program and, in the second place, an electorate sufficiently sensitive to party accomplishments and failures that it can hold the parties accountable for their records, particularly in the case of the party in power. At times, neither requirement can be met to any degree. Nevertheless, occasionally American political institutions function in a manner largely consonant with the party responsibility model.

A responsible party system at the national level demands a particular kind of Congress—one in which power is centralized rather than dispersed. Over long stretches of time, Congress has not been organized to permit the parties, *qua* parties, to govern. The seniority system, the independence of committees and their chairs, the filibuster, the weaknesses present in elected party positions and agencies, and the unrepresentativeness of Congress itself have made it difficult for party majorities to assert themselves and to act in the name of the party. These barriers to party majority building have been notably diminished in recent years.

Every so often the congressional party comes fully alive. Consider the first session of the Eighty-ninth Congress (1965)—"the most dramatic illustration in a generation of the capacity of the president and the Congress to work together on important issues of public policy":

> In part a mopping up operation on an agenda fashioned at least in spirit by the New Deal, the work of the 89th Congress cut new paths through the frontier of qualita-

tive issues: a beautification bill, a bill to create federal support for the arts and humanities, vast increases in federal aid to education. . . . [The] policy leadership and the legislative skill of President Johnson found a ready and supportive response from a strengthened partisan leadership and a substantial, presidentially oriented Democratic majority in both houses. A decade of incremental structural changes in the locus of power in both houses eased the President's task of consent-building and of legislative implementation. Yet Congress was far from being just a rubber stamp. On some issues the President met resounding defeat. On many issues, presidential recommendations were modified by excisions or additions—reflecting the power of particular committee chairmen, group interests, and bureaucratic pressures at odds with presidential perspectives.

[The lessons of the Eighty-ninth Congress] proved that vigorous presidential leadership and sizable partisan majorities in both houses of the same partisan persuasion as the President could act in reasonable consonance, and with dispatch, in fashioning creative answers to major problems. The nation's voters could pin responsibility upon a national party for the legislative output. If that partisan majority erred in judgment, it could at least be held accountable in ensuing congressional and presidential elections.[69]

Party responsibility came to the fore again in the Ninety-seventh Congress (1981–1982). President Reagan was the beneficiary of the highest party support scores received by any president in the preceding three decades. His legislative proposals received unusually strong support in Congress. During the first session of the Ninety-seventh Congress, Senate Republicans voted in agreement with the president 80 percent of the time and House Republicans 68 percent of the time.[70] At session end, Republicans could reasonably claim that their party had moved the nation in a new direction. The major elements of their program consisted of major budget cuts, sizable reductions in individual and business taxes, the largest peacetime defense appropriation in the nation's history, a significant cutback in federal regulations, and a moderate reordering of federal-state relations that gave the states greater discretion in the use of funds provided through federal aid. Consonant with the party responsibility model, the performance of the Reagan administration was the overriding issue in the off-year election of 1982, in which Republicans lost twenty-six seats in the House while holding Democrats to a standoff in Senate races. In sum, presidential leadership, in concert with Republican congressional leaders and bolstered by party imagination and discipline, characterized the Ninety-seventh Congress (especially the first session) almost as much as it had the Eighty-ninth. From the perspective of the president, these were halcyon days, but they passed by quickly. Conflict between the branches intensified, the president's legislative successes declined, and legislative assertiveness during the latter stages of the Reagan administration, and particularly during the One-hundredth Congress (1987–1988), became manifest.

Government by party was conspicuously absent during the succeeding Bush administration. For one thing, the president's domestic agenda was limited. And second, the Democrats controlled both houses of Congress. Conflict between the parties increased in both houses over the course of Bush's term, reaching a near record level during his last year in office; the president's success rate in Congress in 1992 was the lowest of any president in forty years. Few administration bills were passed, confrontations were frequent, and the president vetoed a number of major Democratic bills involving taxes, family planning, crime, campaign finance, fetal tissue research, cable television, and trade with China. Low public opinion ratings further undermined the president's position. Toward the end of the Bush administration, "gridlock" vied with "morass" to become the most fashionable term to describe the state of Washington politics.

Control of the presidency and both houses of Congress by the Democrats in 1993 provided the first opportunity for authentic majority-party policy leadership in more than a decade. But getting the Democratic party to hang together did not come easily. President Clinton's major initiatives in his first year, including his deficit-reduction plan, were threatened by liberal-conservative conflict within his own party as well as by the concerted opposition of Republicans in both houses. One after another Clinton administration bill became a hostage to intraparty bargaining and deal-cutting for member, local, bloc, and regional advantages. Conflict between the parties was also at unusually high levels during the first three years of the Clinton administration, particularly in 1995, following the Republicans' off-year capture of both houses of Congress. More than 70 percent of all recorded floor votes were *party votes*—votes in which a majority of one party voted against a majority of the other party.[71] With the Democrats holding the presidency and the Republicans in control of Congress, little was accomplished. The government itself was shut down on two occasions, and the Republicans got most of the blame for the debacles. As the 1996 election approached and apprehension increased, both parties muted their partisanship, adopted more centrist positions, and cooperated to pass a number of major bills ranging from welfare to the minimum wage. The response of the voters to the bipartisan mood was to reelect Clinton by a comfortable margin (but short of a majority) and to return a (narrowed) Republican majority to Congress. (Many citizens simply stayed home, and turnout fell below 50 percent of the voting-age population.)

The 2000 election offered another opportunity for responsible party government when the Republicans captured both the presidency and Congress. With razor thin majorities in both houses, Republicans were able to pass the large tax cut promised by George W. Bush in his campaign for president. Republican control was short-lived, however. Democrats gained control of the Senate when Sen. James Jeffords of Vermont, elected as a Republican, became an independent and began voting with the Democrats, providing them with a majority. Although bipartisan cooperation increased somewhat following the September 11 terrorist attacks, most initiatives prior to the 2002 off-year election fell victim to partisan maneuvering and conflict. The reality is that when parties cannot bridge the gap between the branches, Washington politics becomes particularly unpredictable.

The conditions must be right for responsible party government to move forward: a partisan majority in general ideological agreement (or an effective majority, such as the Republican-led conservative coalition in the House during the Ninety-seventh Congress) and a vigorous president are essential. The experience of the 107th Congress (2001–2003) also suggests that the majority must be larger than a single seat. A long or innovative policy agenda may also be required. In any case, the essential point is that, under the right circumstances, the deadlocks in American politics can be broken and the political system can function vigorously and with a high degree of cooperation between the branches of government. Party responsibility can thrive even if unrecognized and unlabeled. The evidence of these Congresses suggests that the first requirement for government by responsible parties—a fairly high degree of internal party agreement on policy—can, at least occasionally, be met.

Indeed, the election of Republican majorities in the House and Senate in 2002 makes party rule a livelier prospect than it was at any time since the early 1990s. As has been shown repeatedly throughout this book, the parties at the beginning of the twenty-first century are very distinct ideologically. Party-line voting in Congress is at a historic high point, and Republicans today have a well-defined agenda, which includes an interventionist foreign policy, significant changes to the tax code, and aggressive changes in social policy. In all these areas, Democrats have a different vision.

However, the second requirement of responsible party government—an electorate attuned to party performance in government—is a different matter. This is the point at which the system of responsible parties tends to break down:

> What the public knows about the legislative records of the parties and of individual congressional candidates is a principal reason for the departure of American practice from an idealized conception of party government. . . . The electorate sees very little altogether of what goes on in the national legislature. Few judgments of legislative performance are associated with the parties, and much of the public is unaware even of which party has control of Congress. . . . Many of those who have commented on the lack of party discipline in Congress have assumed that the Congressman votes against his party because he is forced to by the demands of one of several hundred constituencies of a superlatively heterogeneous nation. In some cases, the Representative may subvert the proposals of his party because his constituency demands it. But a more reasonable interpretation over a broader range of issues is that the Congressman fails to see these proposals as part of a program on which the party—and he himself—will be judged at the polls, because he knows the constituency isn't looking.[72]

Although the public today is better at seeing differences between the parties than they were a generation ago, Americans are far from experts about politics. The first requirement of voters in a responsible party model is for them to know which party holds a majority of seats in Congress, so they can hold the appropriate side responsible for successes and failures. According to data from the 2000 National Election Study, however, barely one half (55 percent) of Americans knew that the Republicans held the majority in the House before the election, a percentage comparable with decades past.[73] Moreover, this percentage is likely inflated by a fair number of people who guess the right party without really knowing the answer.

Experiments with forms of party responsibility, like fashion, will perhaps always possess a probationary quality—tried, neglected, forgotten, and rediscovered. The tone and mood of such a system will appear on occasion, but without the public's either anticipating it or recognizing it when it arrives. More generally, however, the party system is likely to resemble, at least in broad lines, the model to which Americans are adjusted and inured: the parties situated precariously atop the political process, threatened and thwarted by a variety of competitors, unable to control their own nominations or to elect "their" nominees, active in fits and starts and often in hiding, beset by factional rifts, shunned or dismissed by countless voters (including many new ones), frustrated by the growing independence of voters, and moderately irresponsible. From the vantage point of both outsiders and insiders, the party system ordinarily will appear, to the extent that it registers at all, in disarray. And indeed it is in disarray, but not to a point that either promises or ensures its enfeeblement and disintegration.

NOTES

1. *Congressional Quarterly Weekly Report,* December 21, 1996, 3432.

2. Donald E. Stokes and Warren E. Miller, "Party Government and the Saliency of Congress," in *Elections and the Political Order,* ed. Angus Campbell (New York: Wiley, 1966), 209–211.

3. There are a number of excellent analyses of party responsibility. See Austin Ranney, "Toward a More Responsible Two-Party System: A Commentary," *American Political Science Review* 45 (June 1951): 488–499; T. William Goodman, "How Much Political Party Centralization Do We Want?" *Journal of Politics* 13 (November 1951): 536–561; Evron M. Kirkpatrick, "Toward a More Responsible Two-Party System: Political Science, Policy Science, or Pseudo-Science?" *American Political Science Review* 65 (December 1971): 965–990; Gerald M. Pomper, "From Confusion to Clarity: Issues and American Voters, 1956–1968," *American Political Science Review* 66 (June 1972): 415–428; Michael Margolis, "From Confusion to Confusion: Issues and the American Voter (1956–1972)," *American Political Science Review* 71 (March 1977): 31–43; and David S. Broder, "The Case for Responsible Party Government," in *Parties and Elections in an Anti-Party Age,* ed. Jeff Fishel (Bloomington: Indiana University Press, 1978), 22–32.

4. The recommendations of the commission are found in *Mandate for Reform* (Washington, D.C.: Commission on Party Structure and Delegate Selection, Democratic National Committee, 1970).

5. The price of these reforms was high. Delegates of the new-enthusiast variety were far more numerous than party professionals. Moreover, the ideological cast of the delegates was markedly different—that is, much more liberal—from that of the general run of Democrats. And fewer delegates belonging to labor unions were present than is ordinarily the case. In some respects the new rules produced a most unrepresentative convention. The candidate it nominated, George McGovern, was overwhelmingly defeated in the election—a result in part to the defection of party moderates and conservatives. Ironically, though it was expected that the quota sys-

tem for African Americans, women, and youth would increase support among these groups in the election, nothing of the sort occurred. African Americans and youths supported the 1972 Democratic presidential candidate in about the same proportion as they did the 1968 candidate. Support among women voters declined notably. See Austin Ranney, *Curing the Mischiefs of Faction: Party Reform in America* (Berkeley: University of California Press, 1975), 153–156, 206–208.

6. To achieve a system of responsible parties, according to *Toward a More Responsible Two-Party System,* "The internal processes of the parties must be democratic, the party members must have an opportunity to participate in intraparty business, and the leaders must be accountable to the party." Committee on Political Parties of the American Political Science Association, *Toward a More Responsible Two-Party System,* 23.

7. See the analysis by Kenneth Janda, "Primrose Paths to Political Reform: 'Reforming' versus Strengthening American Parties," in *Paths to Political Reform,* ed. William J. Crotty (Lexington, Mass.: Heath, 1980), especially 319–327.

8. In addition, though tangential to this account, certain major recommendations of the report have been met through action by the federal government. A number of barriers to voting were eliminated as a result of the passage of the Voting Rights Act of 1965 and the adoption of the Twenty-sixth Amendment to the Constitution in 1971.

9. E. E. Schattschneider, *Party Government* (New York: Holt, Rinehart and Winston, 1942), 64.

10. Frank J. Sorauf, *Political Parties in the American System* (Boston: Little, Brown, 1964), 102.

11. Byron E. Shafer, *Quiet Revolution: The Struggle for the Democratic Party and the Shaping of Post-Reform Politics* (New York: Russell Sage Foundation, 1983), 529.

12. See an outstanding paper by Marty Cohen, David Darol, Hans Noel, and John Zaller, "Beating Reform: The Resurgence of Parties in Presidential Nominations, 1980 to 2000" (Paper delivered at the annual meeting of the American Political Science Association, Boston, 2002).

13. The only possible exception is Gary Hart in 1988, who was the Democratic front-runner after his stronger than expected showing in 1984. Hart all but disqualified himself after an extramarital affair came to light in 1987.

14. This quotation appears in Burdett A. Loomis, *The New American Politician: Ambition, Entrepreneurship, and the Changing Face of Political Life* (New York: Basic Books, 1988), 187.

15. Ibid., 10.

16. David B. Truman, "Party Reform, Party Atrophy, and Constitutional Change: Some Reflections," *Political Science Quarterly* 99 (winter 1984–1985): 167.

17. Susan B. Glasser, "Hired Guns Fuel Fundraising Race," *Washington Post,* April 30, 2000.

18. See an analysis by Benjamin Ginsberg, "Money and Power: The New Political Economy of American Elections," in *The Political Economy,* ed. Thomas Ferguson and Joel Rogers (Armonk, N.Y.: M. E. Sharpe, 1984), 163–179.

19. Joe McGinniss, *The Selling of the President* (New York: Trident Press/Simon and Schuster, 1968), 27.

20. Robert MacNeil, *The People Machine: The Influence of Television on American Politics* (New York: Harper and Row, 1968), xvii.

21. Marshall McLuhan, as quoted by McGinniss, *The Selling of the President,* 28.

22. Dan Nimmo, *The Political Persuaders: The Techniques of Modern Election Campaigns* (Englewood Cliffs, N.J.: Prentice Hall, 1970), 197.

23. Comment by a Bush adviser quoted in *Time,* November 14, 1988, 66.

24. An unnamed gubernatorial candidate quoted by Barbara G. Salmore and Stephen A. Salmore, *Candidates, Parties, and Campaigns* (Washington, D.C.: CQ Press, 1989), 139.

25. Harold Mendelsohn and Irving Crespi, *Polls, Television, and the New Politics* (Scranton, Pa.: Chandler, 1970), 310–311.

26. Cornelius P. Cotter and John F. Bibby, "Institutional Development of Parties and the Thesis of Party Decline," *Political Science Quarterly* 95 (spring 1980): 1–27. For a close analysis of the services made available to congressional candidates by national party committees, especially those of the Republican party, see Paul S. Herrnson, "Do Parties Make a Difference? The Role of Party Organizations in Congressional Elections," *Journal of Politics* 48 (August 1986): 589–615.

27. Robert J. Huckshorn, James L. Gibson, Cornelius P. Cotter, and John F. Bibby, "Party Integration and Party Organizational Strength," *Journal of Politics* 48 (November 1986): 976–991.

28. For the development of these and cognate themes that point to a political rebirth of the American party system, see Xandra Kayden and Eddie Mahe Jr., *The Party Goes On: The Persistence of the Two-Party System in the United States* (New York: Basic Books, 1985). Also see Xandra Kayden, "The New Professionalism of the Oldest Party," *Public Opinion* 8 (June/July 1985): 42–44, 49.

29. Byron E. Shafer, "The Democratic Party Salvation Industry," *Public Opinion* 8 (June/July 1985): 47. Also see the analysis of Michael Margolis and Raymond E. Owen, "From Organization to Personalism: A Note on the Transmogrification of the Local Political Party," *Polity* 18 (winter 1985): 313–328. For a finding that local parties have not become less active and less organized in the current era, see James L. Gibson, Cornelius P. Cotter, John F. Bibby, and Robert J. Huckshorn, "Whither the Local Parties? A Cross-Sectional and Longitudinal Analysis of the Strength of Party Organizations," *American Journal of Political Science* 29 (February 1985): 139–160. In addition, see Barbara C. Burrell, "Local Political Party Committees, Task Performance and Organizational Vitality," *Western Political Quarterly* 39 (March 1986): 48–66.

30. Schattschneider, *Party Government*, 64ff.

31. *Tashjian v. Republican Party of Connecticut*, 479 U.S. 208 (1986). Political scientists are divided on the *Tashjian* case. See an analysis by Leon D. Epstein, "Will American Political Parties Be Privatized?" *Journal of Law & Politics* 5 (winter 1989): 239–274.

32. Thomas Patterson, *Out of Order* (New York, Knopf, 1994).

33. Ranney, *Curing the Mischiefs of Faction*, 3.

34. For an elaboration of these themes, see Nelson W. Polsby, *Consequences of Party Reform* (Oxford: Oxford University Press, 1983), especially chapter 2.

35. Truman, "Party Reform, Party Atrophy, and Constitutional Change," 169.

36. Apart from its provisions concerning intraparty democracy, the Democratic party charter boasts very little that is new. The midterm party convention that adopted the charter in 1974 rejected numerous provisions designed to centralize the party and to alter its federal character, including a dues-paying membership, a mandatory national party conference every other year, an independent national chairman elected for a four-year term (to reduce the presidential nominee's influence over the chairman), an elaborate regional party organization, and a strong national party executive committee. Few changes were made in the major organs of the party: the national convention, the national committee, and the office of the national chair. The vast majority of the compromises reached both prior to and during the convention were struck on the side of those who wanted to preserve a party system notable for its decentralization. See an interesting account of the convention's issues involving centralization versus decentralization by David S. Broder, *Washington Post*, December 1, 1974.

37. *Time*, August 7, 1978, 15.

38. *Time*, January 29, 1979, 12.

39. *U.S. News and World Report*, January 29, 1979, 24.

40. Press release, Federal Election Commission, May 15, 2001.

41. See a discussion of single-issue and ideological PACs in William J. Crotty and Gary C. Jacobson, *American Parties in Decline* (Boston: Little, Brown, 1980), 117–155.

42. *Washington Post,* September 13, 1978. The comment was made by Sen. Wendell R. Anderson (D-Minn.) to columnist David S. Broder.

43. *Washington Post,* September 13, 1978.

44. Frank J. Sorauf, *Party Politics in America* (Boston: Little, Brown, 1980), 48.

45. "Hutchinson Struggling to Keep Arkansas Senate Seat for GOP," *Washington Post,* October 28, 2002. "

46. These data on the 2000 national convention delegates are drawn from the *New York Times* August 14, 2000, edition. The data were obtained from interviews or written questionnaires with 1,042 delegates to the Democratic National Convention and with 1,055 delegates to the Republican National Convention.

47. See a study of party-switching among county-level activists in the 1988 presidential campaign by John A. Clark, John M. Bruce, John H. Kessel, and William G. Jacoby, "I'd Rather Switch Than Fight: Lifelong Democrats and Converts to Republicanism among Campaign Activists," *American Journal of Political Science* 35 (August 1991): 577–597. This study of elite realignment found that one third of the Republican leaders and one tenth of the Democratic leaders once considered themselves as members of the opposite party. Sharp policy differences distinguished the two groups of leaders. For interesting evidence that party leaders at the county level, in presidential elections, tend to be "true believers" (firmly committed to the enactment of certain policies), see John M. Bruce, John A. Clark, and John H. Kessel, "Advocacy Politics in Presidential Parties," *American Political Science Review* 85 (December 1991): 1089–1105.

48. Concerning this point, see Edward R. Tufte, *Political Control of the Economy* (Princeton, N.J.: Princeton University Press, 1978), especially chapter 4. See a study of presidential elections from 1948 through 1984 that finds that the *state of the economy* is an even better predictor of election outcomes than the *candidates' popularity* (or the voters' relative liking of them). Robert S. Erickson, "Economic Conditions and the Presidential Vote," *American Political Science Review* 83 (June 1989): 567–573.

49. *New York Times,* November 3, 2002.

50. Donald C. Baumer and Howard J. Gold, "Party Images and the American Electorate," *American Politics Quarterly* 23 (January 1995): 33–61.

51. For good evidence that Republican party activists in the South are substantially more conservative than their Democratic counterparts, see Harold D. Clarke, Frank B. Feigert, and Marianne C. Stewart, "Different Contents, Similar Packages: The Domestic Political Beliefs of Southern Local Party Activists," *Political Research Quarterly* 48 (March 1995): 151–167.

52. Ronald B. Rapoport finds that popular and unpopular presidential candidates have a significant impact on voters' assessments of the parties. Parties find it hard to recover from the mistake of nominating an unpopular candidate. "Partisan Change in a Candidate-Centered Era," *Journal of Politics* 59 (February 1997): 185–199.

53. These data are derived from a *New York Times/CBS* News poll, as reported in the *New York Times,* October 7, 1986.

54. See Jack Dennis, "Public Support for the Party System, 1964–1984" (Paper delivered at the annual meeting of the American Political Science Association, Washington, D.C., August 28–31, 1986), 19; and Martin Wattenberg, *The Decline of American Political Parties* (Cambridge, Mass.: Harvard University Press, 1986), 22.

55. See an analysis that finds ideology supplanting party as the primary structuring agent in presidential elections: George Rabinowitz, Paul-Henri Gurian, and Stuart Elaine Macdonald, "The Structure of Presidential Elections and the Process of Realignment, 1944 to 1980," *American Journal of Political Science* 28 (November 1984): 611–635.

56. See the exit interview data assembled by the *New York Times*/CBS News poll, as reported in the *New York Times*, November 10, 1988; and the ABC exit poll, as reported in the *Washington Post*, November 9, 1988.

57. Patterson, *Out of Order.*

58. *New York Times*, November 5, 1992.

59. See the Voter News Service 1996 exit poll.

60. For analysis of the voting patterns of African Americans and whites, as well as other groups, see Harold W. Stanley and Richard G. Niemi, "Partisanship and Group Support, 1952–1988," *American Politics Quarterly* 19 (April 1991): 189–210; Harold W. Stanley, William T. Bianco, and Richard G. Niemi, "Partisanship and Group Support over Time: A Multivariate Analysis," *American Political Science Review* 80 (September 1986): 970–976; and Edward G. Carmines and James A. Stimson, "Racial Issues and the Structure of Mass Belief Systems," *Journal of Politics* 44 (February 1982): 2–20.

61. See, for example, Arthur H. Miller, "Political Issues and Trust in Government, 1964–70," *American Political Science Review* 68 (September 1974): 989–1001; Jack Citrin, "Comment: The Political Relevance of Trust in Government," *American Political Science Review* 68 (September 1974), 973–988; Marc J. Hetherington, "The Political Relevance of Political Trust," *American Political Science Review* 92 (December 1998): 791–808.

62. See, for example, Joseph A. Cappella and Kathleen Hall Jamieson, *The Spiral of Cynicism: The Press and the Public Good* (New York: Oxford University Press, 1997).

63. See Citrin, "Comment."

64. Marc J. Hetherington, *Declining Political Trust and the Demise of American Liberalism* (Princeton: Princeton University Press, forthcoming).

65. Haynes Johnson and David S. Broder, *The System: The American Way of Politics at the Breaking Point* (Boston: Little, Brown, 1996); Theda Skocpol, *Boomerang: Clinton's Health Security Effort and the Turn Against Government in U.S. Politics* (New York: W. W. Norton, 1996).

66. See Jack Citrin and Donald Philip Green, "Presidential Leadership and the Resurgence of Trust in Government," *British Journal of Political Science* 16 (October 1986): 431–453.

67. To explore the literature that defends the American party system, see in particular Herbert Agar, *The Price of Union* (Boston: Houghton Mifflin, 1950); Pendleton Herring, *The Politics of Democracy* (New York: Norton, 1940); Arthur N. Holcombe, *Our More Perfect Union* (Cambridge: Harvard University Press, 1950); and Edward C. Banfield, "In Defense of the American Party System," in *Political Parties, U.S.A.*, ed. Robert A. Goldwin (Chicago: Rand McNally, 1964), 21–39.

68. *Time*, November 20, 1978, 42.

69. Stephen K. Bailey, *Congress in the Seventies* (New York: St. Martin's Press, 1970), 102–103. Among the other major accomplishments of the first session of the Eighty-ninth Congress were the passage of bills to provide for medical care for the aged under Social Security, aid to depressed areas, the protection of voting rights, federal scholarships, the Teacher Corps, immigration reform, and a variety of programs to launch the "war on poverty."

70. *Congressional Quarterly Weekly Report*, January 2, 1982, 20–21.

71. *Congressional Quarterly Weekly Report*, December 21, 1996, 3432.

72. Donald E. Stokes and Warren E. Miller, "Party Government and the Saliency of Congress," in *Elections and the Political Order*, ed. Angus Campbell (New York: Wiley, 1966), 209–211.

73. Data taken from the 2000 American National Election Study.

INDEX

Page references followed by *t*, *f*, or *n* indicate
tables, figures, or notes, respectively.

close elections and, 196n49
for direct primaries, 67
distrust of government and, 231
education level and, 185, 185t
election frequency and, 91n26, 190
international comparison, 190–191, 191f
parties' influence on, 4
patterns of decline, 181–182, 186–187, 186f
personal contact and, 189–190
in presidential primaries, 70–71, 71t, 91n28, 187
prior election closeness and, 195n34
profile, voter versus nonvoter, 184–186, 184t
registration laws and, 118, 191–192
Republican advantage, 176
runoff primaries and, 65
skepticism and, 190
socioeconomic status and, 176, 184, 195n30
in state and local elections, 187
women, after suffrage gained, 188
by young voters, 189
Voting age, 189
Voting behavior. See also Ticket-splitting
analysis of, as RNC service for national and state candidates, 18
candidates' qualities and, 92n44
direct primaries and, 65–66
issues, and information level, 195n36
party-based, 207
political party coalitions and, 33–35
racial polarization, 228–230, 229t
Voting rights, 239n8
Voting Rights Act (1965), 153, 191, 228

W

Wald, Kenneth D., 196n49
Waldman, Paul, 94n63
Wallace, George C., 34, 41, 49, 52, 52t
Warner, Mark, 219
Washington State, 44, 46, 63, 64
Watergate, 107, 230
Wattenberg, Martin P., 193n10, 194n20, 241n54
Watts, Meredith W., 90n8
Wayman, Frank M., 55n4
Wayne, Stephen J., 91n27, 92n29, 94n63
Weaver, James B., 52t
Weber, Ronald E., 92n43
Weinberg, Lee S., 28n50
Weisberg, Herbert F., 162n2
Wekkins, Gary D., 62–63, 90n6
Welch, Susan, 163n9
Welfare state, 22
West Virginia, 42, 74
Whigs, 51
Whip organization in Congress, 143
White, Theodore, H., 100, 126n20
White primaries, 195n39
Wilde, Linda, 3
Winger, Richard, 57n25
Wink, Kenneth A., 93n52
Winner-take-all plan, 72, 73
Winner-take-more plan, 72
Winograd Commission, 71–72
Wirt, William, 52t
Wisconsin, 42, 60, 63, 69
Wofford, Harris, 100
Women. See also Gender
delegates to national conventions, 80, 81
Democratic party delegate selection and, 71
Ferraro vice-presidential nomination, 85